Vegetarian

Vegetarian

bay books

Contents

Introduction

Protein

Protein provides the basic structure for the human body—it is the main source of building material for our cells, tissues, muscles, nails, hair, skin, bones, blood and internal organs. We need protein to make and repair cells and tissues, and to create hormones, enzymes, antibodies and other immune-system molecules. It is also needed for the regulation of the body's internal environment, including acid and alkaline balance, water balance, and the proper elimination of wastes.

AND WHAT IS IT?

Protein is made up of small compounds known as amino acids, which are arranged in chains of varying combinations. There are approximately 22 amino acids, most of which are termed 'non-essential' as they can be made in the body.

But not all amino acids can be manufactured in the body—some must be derived from the diet, and these are termed the 'essential' amino acids. There are eight essential amino acids for adults—isoleucine, leucine, lysine, phenylalanine, methionine, threonine, tryptophan, valine—and an extra one, histidine, for infants.

Sources of these essential amino acids are animal products: meat, poultry, fish and dairy foods. There are also good vegetarian and vegan sources of protein: nuts and legumes (beans, peas, lentils, soya beans and products such as soy flour, soy milk, tofu and tempeh), but they don't have all the essential amino acids in the one food source like animal proteins do.

BEST LEGUMES FOR PROTEIN
Black beans
Black-eyed beans
Broad (fava) beans
Chickpeas
Kidney beans
Lentils
Mung beans
Navy beans
Peas
Soya beans

Plant proteins do have an advantage over animal proteins, as they contain fibre and carbohydrates, which makes them easy to digest as well as being high in vitamins and minerals and low in saturated fats and kilojoules.

IS PROTEIN COMBINING NECESSARY?

In the past it was thought that because the vegetarian sources of protein don't have all the essential amino acids, it was necessary to carefully combine them with other foods, such as wholegrains, to provide all the essential amino acids in their correct proportions.

However, recent research suggests that as long as there is a healthy mix of legumes, nuts, seeds, wholegrains and vegetables in the diet, the body will obtain enough protein for its needs. So, once again, the basic message is to have a balanced diet.

DAILY INTAKE

Our daily requirement of protein is approximately 12–20% of our total kilojoule intake, varying according to an individual's size, weight, levels of stress and activity, and health. Extra protein is needed during periods of growth: childhood, adolescence, pregnancy and lactation.

PROTEIN DEFICIENCY

Insufficient protein in the diet may result in such symptoms as anaemia, lethargy, muscle weakness and wasting, dry and dull hair, dry skin, poor wound healing, weak nails, outbursts of temper, decreased immunity to infection, bloating, digestive complaints and, in severe cases, amenorrhoea. Children with protein deficiency may not reach their full growth potential, while extreme cases of protein deficiency in children will result in the often fatal disease, kwashiorkor. However, Western vegetarians have very little chance of suffering from a protein deficiency.

PROTEIN IN EXCESS

In fact, in most Western diets, there is a much greater chance of consuming an excess of protein than there is of not consuming enough. Excess protein consumption can result in fluid imbalance, with symptoms such as diarrhoea, tissue swelling and frequent urination, which can lead to dehydration. It may also set up highly acidic conditions, which can lead to strong body odour, allergies, arthritis and gout. The extra burden on the digestive system may eventually cause liver and kidney damage.

SAMPLE MEAL IDEAS
BREAKFAST
- Muesli with soy milk (top with ground nuts/seeds and banana)
- Porridge with soy milk
- Baked beans on wholemeal (whole-wheat) toast
- Boiled egg with wholemeal (whole-wheat) toast
- Nut butter (e.g. almond, Brazil, cashew or peanut) on toast

LUNCH
- Lentil/bean/pea curry with rice
- Pumpkin and red lentil soup (page 76)
- Hummus (page 59) and salad in wholemeal (whole-wheat) pitta bread
- Felafel with tomato salsa (page 57)
- Bean nachos (page 44) with avocado
- Miso soup with tofu, rice and vegetables
- Soya bean/tofu burger

DINNER
- Dhal and rice
- Tofu with rice and vegetables
- Mushroom risotto (page 162)
- Vegetable and tofu kebabs (page 166) with tomato sauce
- Mushroom nut roast with tomato sauce (page 228)

SNACKS
- Seeds (e.g. sesame or sunflower)
- Tahini/hummus on wholewheat/ rye/rice crackers

EXCELLENT PROTEIN SOURCE
Eggs, Cheddar, tempeh, lentils, ricotta (and other cheeses), sesame seeds, split green peas, peanuts, kidney beans, tofu.

VERY GOOD PROTEIN SOURCE
Bagels, English spinach, barley, bulgur, sunflower seeds, silverbeet (Swiss chard), chickpeas, cashew nuts, lima beans, cottage cheese, peas.

GOOD PROTEIN SOURCE
Bread, milk, fruit, vegetables, rice (brown and white), pasta, yoghurt.

Bread, honey, muesli, dried fruit, flour (wholemeal/whole wheat and white), Lebanese bread, fruit loaf, polenta (cornmeal), couscous.

EXCELLENT CARBOHYDRATE SOURCE

Pasta, baked beans, berries, breakfast wheat biscuits, bananas, pumpkin, potatoes, rice, noodles.

VERY GOOD CARBOHYDRATE SOURCE

Tofu, vegetables, milk, fruit, oats, lentils, nuts, yoghurt.

GOOD CARBOHYDRATE SOURCE

Carbohydrates

The principal energy source in the diet is carbohydrate. The vital role carbohydrates play cannot be underestimated as they provide fuel for both the muscles and the brain. Carbohydrates occur in the form of starches and sugars from grains and their products (e.g. flour, bread, pasta) as well as potatoes, legumes, fruits and, to a lesser degree, nuts.

WHAT DO THEY DO?

Carbohydrates break down in the body into glucose and glycogen, both of which are used for energy. The body uses up glucose first and if there is a shortage (for example, during exercise) it converts glycogen, which is stored in the liver, to glucose.

Carbohydrates are generally divided into two categories: simple and complex. A simple carbohydrate is consumed in a form closest to sugar, which takes little breaking down by the body, giving a quick rush of energy, then usually a drop which makes you feel tired or down.

Complex carbohydrates take longer to break down in the body, giving a slower release of sugar and more sustained energy. You probably recognise this phenomenon—you may need a boost, and grab a snack bar or soft drink. Initially you feel better, but soon you will feel worse than you did to start with. Snacking on a complex carbohydrate, such as bread, will give you longer-lasting energy.

FAT OR FICTION?

Carbohydrates have had a bad rap in the past and have been labelled fattening, mainly because of their bulk. But we now know that this is why they are so valuable—they are filling yet usually contain little or no fat. All carbohydrates have less than half the amount of kilojoules per gram than dietary fat and the body converts dietary fat into body fat more efficiently than it does carbohydrates. When you eat carbohydrates your chance of storing their calories as fat is 20% lower than if you eat fat.

Some people argue that fresh or dried fruits are sweet and are therefore high in sugar. This may be so, but fruit also contains valuable nutrients and fibre that the body needs. It is processed cane sugar—found in so many snack foods—that should be avoided. It provides no nutritional value and is often accompanied by lots of fat.

DAILY INTAKE

It is recommended that about 60% of your daily kilojoules should come from carbohydrates. (See the table below for further information.)

VALUE FOR VEGETARIANS

In a vegetarian diet, complex carbohydrates give substance to a meal by filling you up and giving a feeling of satisfaction and repleteness. However, take care what you eat with your carbohydrates. Often a jacket potato is loaded with butter or sour cream, or a pasta dish may have a rich creamy sauce. It is the toppings that make carbohydrates fatty, not the carbohydrates themselves.

Wherever possible, choose carbohydrates that are the least refined. For instance, use brown rice rather than white, go for wholemeal (whole-wheat) instead of white bread, and rolled oats in the form of porridge or muesli at breakfast rather than processed (and often high in added sugar) cereals. These wholegrain products are broken down slowly by the body and therefore give a more sustained release of energy.

Complex carbohydrates are particularly important at breakfast to keep you alert and productive throughout the day, which is why breakfast is traditionally cereal and/or toast. Research has shown that by skipping breakfast, students are less attentive and workers less productive. A major danger in missing breakfast is that sugary snacks will be eaten later on in the day.

SAMPLE MEAL IDEAS

BREAKFAST
- Puffed corn cereal (page 24)
- Porridge
- Mixed berry couscous (page 20)

LUNCH
- Pumpkin and red lentil soup (page 76)
- Sushi
- Wholegrain muffin with tomato

DINNER
- Udon noodle stir-fry (page 140)
- Couscous vegetable loaf (page 224)
- Chunky chickpea and herb soup (page 67)

SNACKS
- Vietnamese spring rolls (page 103)
- Nuts and dried fruit

HOW MUCH CARBOHYDRATE DO I NEED?

The amount of carbohydrate that you need depends on your weight and the amount and level of activity you do. Use this chart as a guide.

Activity level	Continuous exercise	Carbohydrate/kg body weight per day
Light	< 1 hour/day	4.0–4.5 g
Light-moderate	1 hour/day	4.5–5.5 g
Moderate	1–2 hours/day	5.5–6.5 g
Moderate-heavy	2–4 hours/day	6.5–7.5 g
Heavy	4–5 hours/day	7.5–8.5 g

Example: A man who weighs 90 kg and does less than 1 hour continuous light exercise each day needs 360–405 grams of carbohydrate per day.
Note: To convert grams to ounces, multiply by 0.035. To convert kilograms to pounds, multiply by 2.2046.

Dietary fibre

Dietary fibre consists of the cellulose and gums found in fruits, vegetables, grains and legumes—there is no fibre at all in any animal products. Fibre is not a nutrient, but rather a substance that ensures proper digestive functioning. It is a group of food components that pass through the stomach and small intestine largely undigested and reach the large intestine virtually unchanged.

SOLUBLE AND INSOLUBLE

Dietary fibre may be classified as soluble or insoluble. Soluble fibre is abundant in legumes, oats, barley and most fruits and vegetables. It has the consistency of a gel and tends to slow digestion time, which has the effect of regulating blood sugar—this is particularly important for diabetics.

Insoluble fibre is found in fruit and vegetable skins and the bran coating around grain kernels. Wholegrains (especially wheat, rice and maize), vegetables and nuts are good sources of insoluble fibre. Insoluble fibre passes through the digestive tract largely unchanged and speeds up the passage of material through it.

Foods that provide both types of soluble and insoluble fibre are apples, dried fruits and wholegrains. It is important to have a variety of soluble and insoluble fibre in the diet because each type has a different function.

GETTING ENOUGH FIBRE
- Where possible, leave the skin on fruit and vegetables, such as apples and potatoes.
- Eat whole pieces of fruit and vegetables rather than consuming them as juices.
- Choose wholegrain products such as breads, breakfast cereals, wholemeal (whole-wheat) pasta and brown rice.
- Drink plenty of water during the day to help digest fibre (6–8 glasses is recommended).
- Snack on fresh or dried fruit rather than biscuits or cakes.

SOLUBLE AND INSOLUBLE FIBRE FOODS

Good sources of insoluble fibre
- Cellulose — plant foods, wholegrains, bran, dried fruit, cabbage family
- Lignin — grains, vegetables, fruit
- Hemicellulose — wheat bran, bran cereal

Good sources of soluble fibre
- Pectins — slippery elm, agar, okra, psyllium
- Gums/mucilages — apples, citrus fruit, sugar beet

BENEFITS

There are many benefits to a high-fibre diet. Both soluble and insoluble fibre readily absorb water, increasing stool bulk and making it softer and easier to expel. However, dietary fibre is not just important for efficient bodily functions and for comfort; it can also help in the prevention of colon cancer, reduce the risk of diabetes, lower cholesterol (which helps prevent heart disease), reduce the incidence of constipation and haemorrhoids, and help prevent bowel cancer and other bowel disorders. And, the more unrefined the source of fibre, the more effective it is for improved gastrointestinal health.

FIBRE DEFICIENCY

Diets that lack fresh, whole high-fibre foods and instead contain an abundance of refined foods together with animal products (which contain no fibre) have a much higher incidence of diabetes, cardiovascular disease, diverticulitis and bowel and rectal cancer.

FIBRE IS NOT BORING!

There are many misconceptions surrounding the consumption and benefits of fibre. As people turned to 'health foods' in the last few decades, it was thought that large amounts of so-called roughage, such as bran, were needed in the diet. Some of the roughage that was consumed was fairly unpalatable, and this is probably where health foods and vegetarian diets earned a reputation for being wholesome but boring and unappetizing.

With the greater knowledge of the last few years, we now realise just how wrong this perception is. Fibre is present in different forms and in many different foods that we probably already consume on a daily basis, so the addition of 'roughage', such as bran, to other foods is not really necessary, and in fact can be detrimental as it can inhibit the metabolism of other nutrients (for example, iron). Eating a variety of sources of fibre is essential as excessive fibre from a single rather than varied source can inhibit the absorption of other nutrients

BONUS FOR VEGETARIANS

Vegetarians have the edge over meat eaters when it comes to fibre intake, as the bulk of a vegetarian diet, such as cereals and beans, along with fruit and vegetables, are generally rich in fibre. The main thing to remember is to eat a wide variety of foods, thereby ensuring that a range of dietary fibre is consumed—both soluble and insoluble.

DAILY INTAKE

Nutritionists recommend an intake of 30 grams of fibre per day. A typical serving of grains, fruits or vegetables contains between 1–3 grams of dietary fibre. To get the recommended levels of dietary fibre, you need to consume at least 10 or more servings of fibre-containing foods daily. This should be an easy task for most vegetarians.

EXCELLENT DIETARY FIBRE SOURCE
Split peas, kidney beans, fruit (e.g. kiwi fruit), vegetables (e.g. pumpkin), wholemeal (whole-wheat) pasta, haricot beans, garlic, wheat bran.

VERY GOOD DIETARY FIBRE SOURCE
Wholemeal (whole-wheat) bread, dried fruit, peanuts (and other nuts), baked beans, pasta, chickpeas, lentils, raspberries, corn.

GOOD DIETARY FIBRE SOURCE
Apples, tempeh, Brussels sprouts, mushrooms, carrots, wholegrain bread, tomatoes, bananas, brown rice, strawberries.

Vitamins

VITAMINS	FUNCTIONS	DEFICIENCY SIGNS	VEGETARIAN SOURCES
Vitamin A	Promotes healthy eyes, skin and hair and also maintains the mucous membranes of the lungs and intestines. Improves immunity.	Eye, skin and hair problems, poor night vision, impaired bone growth and increased susceptibility to infections.	Eggs, dairy foods, butter, margarine, apricots and mint.
Beta Carotene (can be converted by the body to Vitamin A)	One of the carotenoids— antioxidants that provide the yellow and orange colours in fresh produce. It improves immunity and protects against the effects of ageing and some cancers.	Increased susceptibility to infections.	Yellow, green, orange and red vegetables and fruit.
Vitamin B group	Provides energy. Important for normal function of the nervous and circulatory system. Needed for healthy skin, hair, nails and eyes.	Anaemia, fatigue, nerve problems, decreased ability to cope with stress, depression, skin problems and greying hair.	Yeast, wholegrain breads and cereals, seeds, nuts, legumes, eggs, milk and leafy green vegetables.
Vitamin B9 (Folate)	Essential for protein synthesis and red blood cell production. Needed to make DNA.	Irritability, insomnia, anaemia. Most common vitamin deficiency.	Brewer's yeast, soy flour, wheat germ, bran, green vegetables, avocados, peanuts, peas, grains.
Vitamin B12	Essential for the functioning of all cells, red blood cell production, bone marrow maintenance, and protein, fat and carbohydrate metabolism.	Anaemia, numbness, unsteady gait, impaired memory, concentration and learning ability, confusion, depression, mental disorders.	Dairy products, microbes (not often found in foods anymore). Vegans may need to take a supplement.
Vitamin C	Produces collagen, which is needed for healthy skin, bones, cartilage and teeth. Improves stress response and helps the body to absorb iron.	Tissue breakdown, easy bleeding and bruising, fatigue, loss of appetite and depression.	Fruit and vegetables (especially citrus fruits, berries, broccoli, pineapple and cabbage).
Vitamin D	Needed to absorb calcium and phosphorus for healthy bones and teeth.	Muscle and bone weakness.	Egg yolk, cheese, margarine, milk, vegetable oils and sprouted seeds.
Vitamin E	Antioxidant. Needed for healthy circulation and healthy muscles, including the heart. Heals scar tissue.	Deficiency is rare. Prevents normal growth.	Egg yolks, corn, nuts, seeds, wholegrain cereals, wheat germ, vegetable oils and margarine.
Vitamin K	Helps to form blood clots. Essential for the formation of protein substances in the bones and kidneys.	Nose bleeds, excessive bleeding.	Broccoli, lettuce, cabbage, spinach, mushrooms, soya beans, potatoes, carrots.

Minerals

MINERALS	FUNCTIONS	DEFICIENCY SIGNS	VEGETARIAN SOURCES
Calcium	Maintains healthy bones and teeth. Regulates nerve and muscle function. Also needed for blood clotting.	Rickets, osteoporosis, osteomalacia, cramps, muscle problems, high blood pressure and heart arrhythmias.	Dairy products, almonds, brazil nuts, egg yolk, soya beans, brewer's yeast, carob, kelp, tofu and dried figs.
Iron	Carries oxygen to the body cells via the blood.	Fatigue, poor circulation, anaemia, dizziness, sore tongue and mouth ulcers.	Legumes, nuts, wholegrain breads and cereals, eggs, molasses, leafy green vegetables, apricots, sunflower seeds, pumpkin seeds and kelp.
Magnesium	Transmits nerve impulses. Helps muscle contraction and relaxation. It also catalyses many essential enzymes and their reactions.	Apathy, weakness, fatigue, anxiety, agitation, confusion, anger, insomnia, muscle tremors, cramps, convulsions and heart rhythm disturbances.	Wholegrain cereals, wheat germ, brewer's yeast, almonds, molasses, kelp, soya beans and leafy green vegetables.
Phosphorus	Essential for the growth of bones and teeth. Helps nutrient absorption, energy production, nerve transmission, metabolism and muscle contraction.	Deficiency is rare. Anxiety, fatigue, muscle weakness, bone pains, osteoporosis, rickets and osteomalacia.	Dairy, eggs, wholegrains, legumes, garlic, nuts and seeds.
Potassium	Maintains nerves, cells and muscles and promotes normal blood pressure and heartbeat.	Apathy, extreme thirst and fatigue.	Vegetables, fruit, avocados, wholegrain cereals, seeds, dates, raisins, nuts, potatoes and pulses.
Selenium	Prevents dry skin and the oxidization of vitamin E.	Premature ageing, muscle degeneration, liver disease.	Butter, wheat germ, barley, wholemeal (whole-wheat) bread, garlic, brazil nuts, cider vinegar.
Silicon	Required for formation of new bones. Essential for the synthesis of collagen and elastin and for wound healing and hair and nail growth.	Poor joint formation, gout, stunted growth, brittle nails, bone fractures.	Alfalfa, wholegrain cereals, soya bean meal.
Sodium	Needed for nerves and muscles and regulating the balance of fluid in the body.	Deficiency is rare. Apathy, dehydration, vomiting and cramps.	Salt, yeast extract, bread, cheese, margarine, some take-away foods, olives, celery and peas.
Zinc	Needed for healthy eyes and skin and improves immunity. Essential for taste, smell and appetite. Maintains normal reproduction.	Decreased fertility and libido, poor sense of taste and smell, lack of appetite, poor wound healing, growth retardation and mental lethargy.	Eggs, ginger, yeast, milk, legumes and wholegrain cereals.

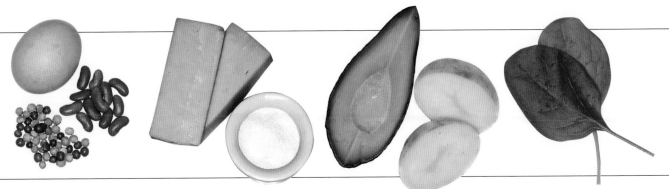

Fat

Fats are our most concentrated dietary energy source. At 37 kilojoules per gram, there are more than double the kilojoules of carbohydrates and protein. This is probably what gives this nutrient group its bad reputation, but, in fact, fat is a vital part of our diet.

THE GOOD NEWS

Everyone needs a certain amount of fat in their body to help with growth and development. Fats supply and help absorb the fat-soluble vitamins A, D, E, K, and they are involved in the conversion of beta-carotene to vitamin A. It is not fat itself that is the problem, rather the quantity and type of fat that we eat.

BAD FATS

The fats most commonly linked to health problems are saturated fats. They are usually solid at room temperature and are derived primarily from animal sources—meat and dairy foods—but they are also found in coconut and palm oils.

The body uses saturated fats mainly for storage, insulation and body heat or energy. An excess consumption of saturated fats in the diet tends to raise blood cholesterol levels and cause fatty deposits in the arteries and blood vessels. This can lead to hardening of the arteries, elevated blood pressure and the formation of blood clots—greatly increasing the risk of heart disease and stroke.

GOOD FATS

The best fats are unsaturated fats, which are usually liquid at room temperature and are derived from vegetable, nut or seed sources. There are two different types of unsaturated fats—monounsaturated fats and polyunsaturated fats.

Monounsaturated fats are generally considered to be good fats, as they do not increase cholesterol levels. They are found in significant amounts in most nuts, olives and olive oil. Other

TIPS FOR REDUCING FAT INTAKE

- Make your meals as filling as possible by choosing foods which take longer to chew and swallow (e.g. whole fruit not fruit juice, whole potatoes, not mashed).
- Don't skip meals or you'll snack later.
- Spread your food intake over the day to keep you calm and full of energy.
- Become aware of times when you are likely to overeat (stressed, bored, free food around) and check your real hunger level before eating.
- Use low-fat plain or skim-milk yoghurt in sauces instead of cream.
- Be careful of hidden fats in snack and processed foods—cakes, biscuits, french fries, potato chips, corn chips, crackers and fast foods. The vegetable oils used in processed foods are the saturated coconut and palm oils.
- Choose polyunsaturated or monunsaturated oil and margarine, which may help lower cholesterol levels.
- Snack on fruits and raw vegetables so you won't feel hungry.

good vegetarian sources are avocados, chickpeas, eggs and sesame seeds.

Polyunsaturated fats are also considered to be good fats. They are found in nuts, grains and seeds and are usually soft or liquid at room temperature. These fats are the most important group of fats as they are the only source of the two essential fatty acids—omega-3 and omega-6 fats.

It is very important to get an adequate intake of omega-3 and omega-6 because they protect against cardiovascular disease, promote healthy skin and are necessary for normal functioning of the nervous and immune systems. Good vegetarian sources of omega-3 are walnuts and some vegetable oils such as soya, canola, mustard seed and linseed. Omega-6 can also be found in vegetable oils such as safflower, sunflower, sesame and soya bean, as well as in evening primrose oil.

CHOLESTEROL

Cholesterol is yet another type of fat. It is a wax-like substance present in all animals but not in plants. It is an essential element for good health and is part of every living cell of the human body. It is not necessary to obtain cholesterol from dietary sources as it is manufactured by the liver and adrenal glands to make stress and sex hormones. It is also required for the nervous system, and it is essential for the breakdown and elimination of fats. Vegetarian foods that are high in

cholesterol include egg yolks and dairy foods. Cholesterol intake should be monitored, but research has shown that it is more important to reduce saturated fat intake, which raises cholesterol, than it is to reduce dietary cholesterol itself.

DAILY INTAKE

It is recommended that you try to have no more than about 30–40 g of fat per day (30 g for women and small men, 40 g for men and taller women). Nutritionists estimate that most people living on a Western diet consume twice the amount of fat that they actually need. And vegetarians cannot assume that all vegetarian meals are low in fat, particularly if dairy foods are eaten.

DON'T GO HUNGRY
SNACK IDEAS

- Fresh fruit and vegetables (but go easy on the avocado)
- Fresh fruit and vegetable juices
- Skim milk and low-fat milk drinks; low-fat yoghurt
- Pasta with tomato-based sauces
- Steamed rice with vegetables
- Baked jacket potato with low-fat yoghurt and cheese
- Wholegrain bread and bread rolls
- Rice cakes

HIGH FAT SOURCE

UNSATURATED cashews, pine nuts, olive oil, almonds, walnuts.

SATURATED butter, milk, coconut milk and cream, mayonnaise, (palm oil is another culprit).

MODERATE FAT SOURCE

UNSATURATED soy linseed (flax seed) bread, oats, soya beans, avocados, tofu puffs.

SATURATED eggs, puff pastry, cream, sour cream, cheese.

LOW FAT SOURCE

UNSATURATED bread, tomato paste (purée), fruit, tofu, tempeh, pasta, rice, vegetables.

SATURATED low-fat milk, cottage cheese, yoghurt, filo pastry (without butter).

Breakfasts & brunches

MIXED BERRY COUSCOUS

Preparation time: 15 minutes
Total cooking time: 5 minutes
Serves 4

185 g (6½ oz/1 cup) instant
   couscous
500 ml (17 fl oz/2 cups) apple
   and cranberry juice
1 cinnamon stick
2 teaspoons orange zest

250 g (9 oz/2 cups) raspberries
250 g (9 oz/1⅔ cups) blueberries
250 g (9 oz/1⅔ cups)
   strawberries, halved
200 g (7 oz) Greek-style plain
   yoghurt
2 tablespoons golden syrup or
   honey
fresh mint leaves, to garnish

1 Place the couscous in a bowl. Pour the apple and cranberry juice into a saucepan and add the cinnamon stick. Cover and bring to the boil, then remove from the heat and pour over the couscous. Cover the couscous and leave for about 5 minutes, or until all the liquid has been absorbed. Remove the cinnamon stick.

2 Separate the grains of couscous with a fork, then gently fold in the zest and most of the berries. Spoon the couscous mixture into four serving bowls and sprinkle with the remaining berries. Serve with a dollop of the yoghurt, then drizzle with the golden syrup or honey. Garnish with mint leaves and serve.

Pour the hot apple and cranberry juice over the couscous.

Separate the grains of couscous with a fork.

Gently fold in the raspberries, blueberries and strawberries.

POACHED EGGS WITH GARLIC YOGHURT DRESSING AND SPINACH

Preparation time: 10 minutes
Total cooking time: 15 minutes
Serves 4

125 g (4½ oz/½ cup) sheep's
　milk yoghurt
1 small clove garlic, crushed
1 tablespoon snipped fresh
　chives

300 g (10½ oz) baby English
　spinach leaves, washed
30 g (1 oz) butter, chopped
herbed salt (see Note)
4 tomatoes, halved
1 tablespoon white vinegar
8 eggs
1 round loaf light rye bread,
　cut into eight thick slices

1 To make the dressing, mix together the yoghurt, garlic and chives.
2 Wash the spinach and place it in a large saucepan with a little water clinging to the leaves. Cook, covered, over low heat for 3–4 minutes, or until wilted. Add the butter. Season with herbed salt. Set aside and keep warm. Cook the tomatoes under a hot grill (broiler) for 3–5 minutes.
3 Fill a frying pan three-quarters full with cold water and add the vinegar and some salt to stop the egg whites spreading. Bring to a gentle simmer. Gently break the eggs one by one into a small bowl, carefully slide each one into the water, then reduce the heat so that the water barely moves. Cook for 1–2 minutes, or until the eggs are just set. Remove with an egg flip. Drain.
4 Toast the bread. Top each slice of toast with spinach, an egg and some dressing. Serve with tomato halves.

COOK'S FILE

Note: Herbed salt is available at the supermarket.

Cook the spinach leaves until they are wilted, then stir in the butter.

Cook the eggs until they are just set, then remove with an egg flip.

RICOTTA PANCAKES WITH GOAT'S MILK YOGHURT AND PEARS

Preparation time: 15 minutes
Total cooking time: 50 minutes
Serves 4

185 g (6½ oz/1½ cups) plain
   (all-purpose) flour
2 teaspoons baking powder
2 teaspoons ground ginger
2 tablespoons caster (superfine)
   sugar
4 eggs, separated
350 g (12 oz) low-fat ricotta
1 pear, peeled, cored and grated
315 ml (11 fl oz/1¼ cups) milk
40 g (1½ oz) butter
3 beurre bosc pears, unpeeled
40 g (1½ oz) butter, extra
1 tablespoon soft brown sugar
1 teaspoon ground cinnamon
200 g (7 oz) goat's milk yoghurt

1 Sift the flour, baking powder, ginger and sugar into a bowl and make a well in the centre. Pour the combined egg yolks, ricotta, grated pear and milk into the well and mix until smooth.
2 Beat the egg whites until soft peaks form, then fold into the mixture.
3 Melt butter in a frying pan over medium heat. Pour 60 ml (2 fl oz/¼ cup) of the batter into the pan and swirl to create an even pancake. Cook for 1–1½ minutes, or until bubbles form, then turn and cook the other side for 1 minute, or until golden. Repeat with the remaining butter and mixture to make 11 more pancakes. Keep warm.
4 Cut the pears lengthways into thick slices. Melt the extra butter in a frying pan and stir in the sugar and cinnamon until the sugar dissolves. Cook the pears in batches, turning once, until tender. Serve stacks of pancakes with the pears and yoghurt.

Stir the combined egg yolks, ricotta, grated pear and milk into the flour.

Cook the pancakes until bubbles form on the surface, then turn.

Cook the pears in batches in the buttery sauce, turning to coat in the mixture.

FRUIT SALAD IN VANILLA, GINGER AND LEMON GRASS SYRUP

Preparation time: 20 minutes + chilling time
Total cooking time: 15 minutes
Serves 4

500 g (1 lb 2 oz) watermelon, cut into large cubes
260 g (9 oz) honeydew melon, cut into large cubes
½ small pineapple, cut into large pieces
1 mango, cut into 2 cm (¾ inch) cubes
250 g (9 oz 1⅔ cups) strawberries, halved
3 tablespoons small mint sprigs

Lemon grass syrup
125 ml (4 fl oz/½ cup) lime juice
3 tablespoons soft brown sugar
1 stem lemon grass, finely sliced
2 tablespoons grated fresh ginger
1 vanilla bean, split

1 Mix together the fruit and mint.
2 To make the syrup, place the lime juice, sugar and 125 ml (4 fl oz/½ cup) water in a small saucepan and stir over low heat until the sugar dissolves. Add the lemon grass, ginger and vanilla bean, bring to the boil, then reduce the heat and simmer for 10 minutes, or until reduced. Remove the vanilla bean, pour the syrup over the fruit and chill.

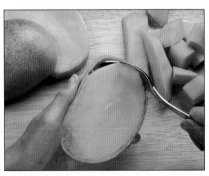

Remove the skin from the mango and cut the flesh into cubes.

Simmer the lemon grass syrup until it is reduced and slightly thick.

PUFFED CORN CEREAL

Preparation time: 10 minutes
Total cooking time: 15 minutes
Serves 20

85 g (3 oz) puffed corn
85 g (3 oz) puffed millet
2 x 200 g (7 oz) packets
  dried fruit and nut mix
180 g (6 oz) unprocessed
  natural bran

60 g (2¼ oz/1 cup) flaked
  coconut
60 g (2¼ oz) pepitas
185 ml (6 fl oz/¾ cup) maple
  syrup
70 g (2½ oz) processed bran
  cereal
400 g (14 oz) dried fruit
  salad mix, cut into small
  pieces

1 Preheat the oven to moderate 180°C
(350°F/Gas 4). Spread out the corn,
millet, fruit and nut mix, bran, coconut
and pepitas in a large roasting tin.
2 Pour the maple syrup over the
mixture and stir until well coated.
3 Stir in the bran cereal and fruit
salad mix and bake for 15 minutes, or
until golden, turning the cereal several
times during cooking. Cool completely.

*Using scissors, cut the dried fruit salad
mixture into small pieces.*

*Spread out the puffed corn mixture in a
large roasting tin.*

*Pour the maple syrup evenly over the dry
ingredients.*

BAKED RICOTTA WITH PRESERVED LEMON AND SEMI-DRIED TOMATOES

Preparation time: 15 minutes
+ 10 minutes standing
Total cooking time: 30 minutes
Serves 8–10

2 kg (4 lb 8 oz) wheel ricotta
olive oil spray
2 cloves garlic, crushed
1 preserved lemon, rinsed, pith and flesh removed, cut into thin strips
150 g (5½ oz) semi-dried (sun-blushed) tomatoes, roughly chopped
30 g (1 oz/1 cup) finely chopped fresh flat-leaf (Italian) parsley
50 g (1¾ oz/1 cup) chopped fresh coriander (cilantro) leaves
4 tablespoons extra virgin olive oil
3 tablespoons lemon juice

1 Preheat the oven to very hot 250°C (500°F/Gas 10). Place the ricotta on a baking tray lined with baking paper, spray lightly with the oil spray and bake for 20–30 minutes, or until golden brown. Stand for 10 minutes then, using egg flips, transfer to a large platter. (If possible, have someone help you move the ricotta.)
2 Meanwhile, place the garlic, preserved lemon, semi-dried tomato, parsley, coriander, oil and lemon juice in a bowl and mix together well.
3 Spoon the dressing over the baked ricotta, and serve with crusty bread.

Remove the flesh from the lemon and cut the rind into thin strips.

Mix all the dressing ingredients together in a bowl.

Spoon the dressing evenly over the baked ricotta.

MIXED MUSHROOMS IN BRIOCHE

Preparation time: 15 minutes
Total cooking time: 20 minutes
Serves 6

750 g (1 lb 10 oz) mixed
    mushrooms (Swiss brown,
    shiitake, button, field, oyster)
75 g (2½ oz) butter
4 spring onions (scallions),
    chopped
2 cloves garlic, crushed
125 ml (4 fl oz/½ cup) dry white
    wine
300 ml (10½ fl oz) cream
2 tablespoons chopped fresh
    thyme
6 small brioche

1 Preheat the oven to moderate 180°C
(350°F/Gas 4). Wipe the mushrooms
with a clean damp cloth to remove any
dirt. Cut the larger mushrooms into
thick slices but leave the smaller ones
whole.
2 Heat the butter in a large frying
pan over medium heat. Add the spring
onion and garlic and cook for
2 minutes. Increase the heat, add the
mushrooms and cook, stirring
frequently, for 5 minutes, or until the
mushrooms are soft and all the liquid
has evaporated. Pour in the wine and
boil for 2 minutes to reduce slightly.
3 Stir in the cream and boil for a
further 5 minutes to reduce and
slightly thicken the sauce. Season to
taste with salt and cracked black
pepper. Stir in the thyme and set aside
for 5 minutes.
4 Slice the tops off the brioche and,
using your fingers, pull out a quarter
of the bread. Place the brioche and
their tops on a baking tray and warm
in the oven for 5 minutes.
5 Place each brioche onto individual
serving plates. Spoon the mushroom
sauce into each brioche, allowing it to
spill over one side. Replace the top and
serve warm.

COOK'S FILE

Note: Brioche are available from
patisseries. You can use bread rolls
instead, but the flavour isn't as good.

*Cut the large mushrooms into thick slices,
but leave the smaller ones whole.*

*Cook the mushrooms, stirring frequently,
until they are soft.*

*Add the cream and cook until the sauce
thickens slightly.*

*Pull a quarter of the bread out of the
centre of the brioche.*

WARM ASPARAGUS AND EGG SALAD WITH HOLLANDAISE

Preparation time: 5 minutes
Total cooking time: 15 minutes
Serves 4

Hollandaise
175 g (6 oz) butter
4 egg yolks
1 tablespoon lemon juice
4 eggs, at room temperature
310 g (10½ oz) asparagus
  spears
Parmesan shavings, to serve

1 To make the hollandaise, melt the butter in a small saucepan and skim off any froth. Remove from the heat and cool. Mix the egg yolks and 2 tablespoons water in another small saucepan for 30 seconds, or until pale and foamy. Place the saucepan over very low heat and whisk for 2–3 minutes, or until thick and foamy—do not overheat or it will scramble. Remove from the heat. Gradually add the butter, whisking well after each addition (avoid using the whey at the bottom). Stir in the lemon juice and season. If the sauce is runny, return to the heat and whisk until thick—do not scramble.

2 Place the eggs in a saucepan half filled with water. Bring to the boil and then cook for 6–7 minutes, stirring occasionally to centre the yolks. Drain and cover with cold water until the eggs can be handled, then peel off the shell.

3 Plunge the asparagus into a large saucepan of boiling water and cook for 3 minutes, or until just tender. Drain and pat dry. Divide among four plates. Spoon on the hollandaise. Cut the eggs in half, arrange two halves on each plate and top with Parmesan.

Whisk the yolks over very low heat until thick, foamy and the whisk leaves a trail.

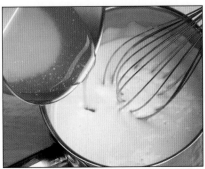

Gradually add the cooled butter, whisking well between each addition.

Cook the asparagus in a large saucepan of boiling water until just tender.

27

THAI CORN PANCAKES WITH CORIANDER MAYONNAISE

Preparation time: 15 minutes
Total cooking time: 5 minutes each
  batch
Serves 6

2 garlic cloves
1 small red chilli
2 cm (¾ inch) piece fresh ginger
440 g (15½ oz) can sweet corn
  kernels, drained
2 eggs
3 tablespoons cornflour
  (cornstarch)
2 tablespoons fresh coriander
  (cilantro) leaves
1 tablespoon sweet chilli sauce
1 tablespoon peanut oil

Coriander mayonnaise
160 g (5½ oz/⅔ cup) whole egg
  mayonnaise
3 tablespoons lime juice
4 tablespoons coriander
  (cilantro) leaves, chopped
8 spring onions (scallions),
  finely chopped

1 Roughly chop the garlic; chop the chilli and ginger. Place half the sweet corn, eggs, cornflour, coriander, garlic, chilli, ginger and chilli sauce in a food processor. Season with pepper. Using the pulse action, process for 30 seconds, or until smooth. Transfer to a bowl and fold in the remaining corn.

2 Heat the oil in a large frying pan. Spoon 2 tablespoons of corn mixture into the pan and cook over a medium heat for 2–3 minutes, or until golden.

Turn over and cook the other side for 1–2 minutes, or until cooked through. Repeat process until all mixture is used. Drain pancakes on paper towels.

3 To make the coriander mayonnaise, combine the mayonnaise, lime juice, coriander and spring onions in bowl. Mix well. Add pepper to taste. Serve pancakes hot or cool with a dollop of coriander mayonnaise.

COOK'S FILE

Storage time: Coriander mayonnaise can be made up to one day in advance. Store, covered, in refrigerator. Corn pancakes can be made several hours in advance. Reheat gently just before serving.

Variation: Frozen corn kernels can be used in place of canned corn.

VEGETABLE, FETA AND PESTO PARCELS

Preparation time: 40 minutes
Total cooking time: 30 minutes
Serves 4

25 g (1 oz) butter
2 cloves garlic, crushed
155 g (5½ oz) asparagus spears,
    trimmed and cut into
    2 cm (¾ inch) pieces
1 carrot, cut into julienne strips
1 zucchini (courgette), cut into
    julienne strips
1 red capsicum (pepper), cut
    into julienne strips
6 spring onions (scallions),
    thinly sliced on the diagonal
80 g (3 oz) mild feta cheese,
    crumbled
8 sheets filo pastry
60 g (2¼ oz) butter, melted
4 tablespoons good-quality
    ready-made pesto
2 teaspoons sesame seeds

1 Preheat the oven to moderately hot
200°C (400°F/Gas 6). Heat the butter in
a large frying pan, then add the garlic
and vegetables. Cook over medium
heat for 3–4 minutes, or until just
tender. Cool completely and fold in the
feta. Divide the vegetable mixture into
four equal portions.
2 Work with four sheets of pastry at
a time, keeping the rest covered with a
damp tea towel. Brush each sheet with
melted butter and lay them on top of
one another. Cut in half widthways
and spread 1 tablespoon of the pesto
in the centre of each half, leaving a
2 cm (¾ inch) border lengthways.
Place one portion of the filling on top
of the pesto. Repeat with the
remaining pastry, pesto and filling.
3 Brush the edges of filo with a little
butter, tuck in the sides and fold over
the ends to make four parcels. Place on
a greased baking tray, seam-side-
down, brush with the remaining butter
and sprinkle with sesame seeds. Bake
for 20–25 minutes, or until golden. Cut
in half diagonally and serve hot with
tomato chutney.

*Cut the carrot and zucchini into julienne
strips (the size and shape of matchsticks).*

*Cook the garlic and vegetables over medium
heat until just tender.*

*Cover the pesto with one portion of the
vegetable feta mixture.*

*Tuck in the sides and roll up the parcel
until it sits on the unsecured end.*

CARROT TIMBALES WITH CREAMY SAFFRON AND LEEK SAUCE

Preparation time: 25 minutes
Total cooking time: 1 hour
Serves 6

60 g (2¼ oz) butter
2 leeks, sliced
2 cloves garlic, crushed
1 kg (2 lb 4 oz) carrots, sliced
375 ml (13 fl oz/1½ cups)
    vegetable stock
1½ tablespoons finely chopped
    fresh sage
3 tablespoons cream
4 eggs, lightly beaten

Creamy saffron and leek sauce
40 g (1½ oz) butter
1 small leek, finely sliced
1 large clove garlic, crushed
3 tablespoons white wine
pinch saffron threads
4 tablespoons crème fraîche

1 Preheat the oven to warm 170°C (325°F/Gas 3). Lightly grease six 185 ml (6 fl oz/¾ cup) timbale moulds. Heat the butter in a saucepan over medium heat, add the leek and cook for 3–4 minutes, or until soft. Add the garlic and carrot and cook for a further 2–3 minutes. Pour in the stock and 500 ml (17 fl oz/2 cups) water, bring to the boil, then reduce the heat and simmer, covered, for 5 minutes, or until the carrot is tender. Strain, reserving 185 ml (6 fl oz/¾ cup) of the liquid.
2 Blend the carrot mixture, 125 ml (4 fl oz/½ cup) of the reserved liquid and the sage in a food processor or blender until smooth. Cool the mixture

slightly and stir in the cream and egg. Season and pour into the prepared moulds. Place the moulds in a roasting tin filled with enough hot water to come halfway up their sides. Bake for 30–40 minutes, or until just set.
3 Meanwhile, to make the sauce, melt the butter in a saucepan and cook the leek over medium heat for 3–4 minutes

without browning. Add the garlic and cook for 30 seconds. Add the wine, remaining reserved liquid and saffron and bring to the boil. Reduce the heat and simmer for 5 minutes, or until reduced. Stir in the crème fraîche.
4 Invert the timbales onto serving plates and serve with the sauce.

Pour the mixture into the prepared moulds and place in a roasting tin.

Cook the leek, garlic, wine, reserved liquid and saffron on low heat until reduced.

Gently invert the carrot timbales onto serving plates.

Quarter the capsicums, then remove the seeds and membranes.

Chargrill the eggplant, sweet potato and zucchini in batches until well browned.

Remove the soft bread from inside the loaf, leaving a shell.

Layer the sweet potato and eggplant inside the loaf over the other ingredients.

MEDITERRANEAN LAYERED COB

Preparation time: 45 minutes +
  30 minutes standing + overnight
  refrigeration
Total cooking time: 30 minutes
Serves 6

2 eggplants (aubergines)
2 large red capsicums (peppers)
500 g (1 lb 2 oz) orange sweet
    potato, cut into thin slices
4 zucchini (courgettes), cut into
    1 cm (½ inch) slices
    lengthways
4 tablespoons olive oil
23 cm (9 inch) round cob loaf
165 g (6 oz) good-quality
    ready-made pesto
200 g (7 oz) ricotta
4 tablespoons grated Parmesan

1 Cut the eggplants lengthways into 1 cm (½ inch) slices and put in a colander. Sprinkle with salt and leave for 30 minutes, then rinse well and pat dry with paper towels.

2 Quarter the capsicums and remove the seeds and membranes. Cook under a hot grill (broiler), skin-side-up, until the skin blisters and blackens. Cool in a plastic bag, then peel. Brush the eggplant, sweet potato and zucchini with oil and chargrill or barbecue in batches until well browned.

3 Cut the lid from the top of the loaf. Remove the soft bread from inside, leaving a 1 cm (½ inch) shell. Brush the inside and the lid with pesto. Layer the zucchini and capsicum inside the loaf, then spread with the combined ricotta and Parmesan. Layer the sweet potato and eggplant, lightly pressing down. Replace the lid.

4 Cover the loaf with plastic wrap and place on a baking tray. Put a tray on top of the loaf and weigh down with food cans. Refrigerate overnight.

5 Preheat the oven to very hot 250°C (500°F/Gas 10). Remove the plastic wrap, then bake for 10 minutes, or until crispy. Cut into wedges to serve.

FRIED TOMATOES WITH MARINATED HALOUMI

Preparation time: 15 minutes +
    overnight marinating
Total cooking time: 10 minutes
Serves 4

400 g (14 oz) haloumi cheese,
    cut into eight 1 cm (½ inch)
    slices
250 g (9 oz) cherry tomatoes,
    halved
250 g (9 oz) teardrop (pear)
    tomatoes, halved

1 clove garlic, crushed
2 tablespoons lemon juice
1 tablespoon balsamic vinegar
2 teaspoons fresh lemon thyme
3 tablespoons extra virgin
    olive oil
2 tablespoons olive oil
1 small loaf good-quality
    wholegrain bread, cut into
    eight thick slices

1 Place the haloumi and tomatoes in a non-metallic dish. Whisk together the garlic, lemon juice, vinegar, thyme and extra virgin olive oil and pour over the haloumi and tomatoes.

Cover and marinate for 3 hours or overnight. Drain well, reserving the marinade.
2 Heat the olive oil in a large frying pan. Cook the haloumi in batches over medium heat for 1 minute each side, or until golden. Remove and keep warm. Add the tomatoes and cook over medium heat for 5 minutes, or until their skins begin to burst. Remove and keep warm.
3 Toast the bread until golden. Serve the haloumi on top of the toasted bread, piled high with the tomatoes and drizzled with the reserved marinade. Serve immediately.

Pour the marinade over the haloumi and mixed tomatoes.

Cook the haloumi until golden brown on both sides.

Cook the tomatoes until their skins start to burst.

CORN AND POLENTA PANCAKES WITH TOMATO SALSA

Preparation time: 15 minutes
Total cooking time: 10 minutes
Serves 4

Tomato salsa
2 ripe tomatoes
150 g (5½ oz/1 cup) frozen broad (fava) beans
2 tablespoons chopped fresh basil
1 small Lebanese (short) cucumber, diced
2 small cloves garlic, crushed
1½ tablespoons balsamic vinegar
1 tablespoon extra virgin olive oil

Corn and polenta pancakes
90 g (3¼ oz/¾ cup) self-raising flour
110 g (3¾ oz/¾ cup) fine polenta (cornmeal)
250 ml (9 fl oz/1 cup) milk
310 g (10½ oz) can corn kernels, drained
olive oil, for pan-frying

1 Score a cross in the base of each tomato, then place in boiling water for 30 seconds. Plunge into cold water and peel the skin away from the cross. Dice. Pour boiling water over the broad beans and leave for 2–3 minutes. Drain and rinse. Remove the skins. Combine the beans, tomato, basil, cucumber, garlic, vinegar and oil.

2 To make the pancakes, sift the flour into a bowl and stir in the polenta. Add the milk and corn and stir until just combined, adding more milk if the mixture is too dry. Season.

3 Heat the oil in a frying pan and spoon half the mixture into the frying pan, making four 9 cm (3½ inch) pancakes. Cook for 2 minutes each side, or until golden and cooked through. Repeat with the remaining mixture, adding more oil if necessary. Drain. Serve with the salsa.

After blanching, peel the skin off the broad beans.

Stir the milk and corn kernels into the flour and polenta mixture.

Cook the pancakes for 2 minutes each side, or until golden brown.

SWEET POTATO MUFFINS

Preparation time: 15 minutes
Total cooking time: 25 minutes +
    10 minutes cooling
Makes 12

175 g (6 oz) sweet potato
250 g (9 oz/2 cups) self-raising
    flour
125 g (4½ oz/1 cup) finely
    grated Cheddar cheese

90 g (3¼ oz) butter, melted and
    cooled
1 egg, lightly beaten
185 ml (6 fl oz/¾ cup)
    buttermilk

1 Preheat oven to 180°C (350°F/
Gas 4). Brush melted butter or oil into
12 deep muffin tins. Finely grate sweet
potato. Sift flour into large mixing
bowl. Add sweet potato and cheese,
stir to combine. Make a well in
the centre.
2 Add butter, egg and buttermilk all
at once to dry ingredients. Using a
wooden spoon, stir until ingredients
are just combined; do not overbeat.
3 Spoon mixture into prepared muffin
tins. Bake for 25 minutes, until puffed
and lightly golden. Turn onto a wire
rack to cool for 10 minutes before
serving. Serve warm with butter.

SAVOURY TARTS

Preparation time: 40 minutes
Total cooking time: 15–20 minutes
Makes 20

50 g (1¾ oz) butter, melted
1 garlic clove, crushed
20 slices white bread

Filling
1 large carrot
1 large zucchini (courgette)
1 tablespoon oil
1 teaspoon grated fresh ginger
2 spring onions (scallions),
    finely sliced
90 g (3¼ oz) cauliflower, cut in
    small florets
1 tablespoon wholegrain mustard

½ teaspoon dried basil
2 tablespoons chopped fresh
    chives

1 Preheat oven to 180°C (350°F/
Gas 4). Grease two 12-cup shallow
patty tins. Cut carrot and zucchini into
short thin strips.
2 Combine the butter and garlic in
small bowl. Remove crusts from bread
with a sharp knife. Using a rolling pin,
flatten each slice of bread. Cut bread
slices into rounds, using a 5 cm (2 inch)
plain or fluted cutter. Brush bread
with butter mixture. Place bread
rounds into the prepared tins, press
firmly. Bake for 10 minutes, or until
golden and crisp. Transfer to wire rack
to cool.
3 To make filling, heat oil in medium
heavy-based frying pan. Add ginger
and spring onions, cook over medium
heat 1 minute. Add carrot, zucchini
and cauliflower. Cook a further
5 minutes, or until vegetables are
tender. Add mustard, basil and
chives, season to taste and stir until
combined. Remove from heat. Spoon
one tablespoon of the vegetable
filling into each tart case. Sprinkle
with extra chopped chives. Serve
warm or cold.

COOK'S FILE

Storage time: Tart cases can be
prepared and cooked a day in advance.
Store in an airtight container. Prepare
the filling and fill the bread cases just
before serving.
Variation: Use wholemeal (whole-
wheat) or whole-grain bread in place
of white.

*Sweet Potato Muffins (top) and
Savoury Tarts.*

Dips & snacks

GUACAMOLE

Preparation time: 30 minutes
Total cooking time: Nil
Serves 6

3 ripe avocados
1 tablespoon lime or lemon juice
1 tomato
1–2 red chillies, finely chopped
1 small red onion, finely
    chopped
1 tablespoon finely chopped
    coriander (cilantro) leaves
2 tablespoons sour cream
1–2 drops Tabasco or habanero
    sauce

1 Roughly chop the avocado flesh and place in a bowl. Mash lightly with a fork and sprinkle with the lime or lemon juice to prevent the avocado discolouring.

2 Cut the tomato in half horizontally and use a teaspoon to scoop out the seeds. Finely dice the flesh and add to the avocado.

3 Stir in the chilli, onion, coriander, sour cream and Tabasco or habanero sauce. Season with freshly cracked black pepper.

4 Serve immediately or cover the surface of the dip with plastic wrap and refrigerate for 1–2 hours. If refrigerated, leave at room temperature for 15 minutes before serving.

COOK'S FILE

Hint: You will need 1–2 limes to produce 1 tablespoon of juice, depending on the lime. A heavier lime will probably be more juicy. To get more juice from a citrus fruit, prick it all over with a fork and then heat on High (100%) in the microwave for 1 minute. Don't forget to prick it or the fruit may burst.

Use disposable gloves when chopping chilli to avoid skin irritation.

Remove the avocado stone by chopping into it with a sharp knife and lifting up.

Cut the tomato in half horizontally and scoop out the seeds with a teaspoon.

You will only need a couple of drops of Tabasco or habanero—they are very hot.

WHITE BEAN, CHICKPEA AND HERB DIP

Preparation time: 20 minutes +
  overnight soaking
Total cooking time: 1 hour
Serves 10–12

180 g (6 oz) dried cannellini
  beans
100 g (3½ oz) dried chickpeas
3 slices white bread
3 tablespoons milk

2 spring onions (scallions),
  finely chopped
4 tablespoons thick plain
  yoghurt
1 tablespoon lemon juice
2 teaspoons finely grated lemon
  rind
1 tablespoon chopped parsley
2 teaspoons chopped oregano
2 tablespoons olive oil

1 Soak the beans and chickpeas in cold water overnight. Rinse well and transfer to a pan. Cover with cold water and bring to the boil. Reduce the heat and simmer for 1 hour, or until very tender, adding more water if needed. Skim any froth from the surface. Drain well, cool and mash.

2 Remove the crusts from the bread, place in a bowl and drizzle with the milk. Leave for 2 minutes, then mash with your fingertips until very soft. Mix together with the beans.

3 Add the spring onion, yoghurt, lemon juice, rind, fresh herbs and oil and season well. Mix together well and serve at room temperature.

Simmer the beans and chickpeas for an hour, skimming froth from the surface.

Soak the bread in the milk for 2 minutes, then mash up with your fingertips.

Add the spring onion, yoghurt, herbs, oil, lemon juice, rind and seasoning.

39

MARINATED ROASTED VEGETABLE DIP

Preparation time: 55 minutes +
4 hours marinating
Total cooking time: 50 minutes
Serves 8

1 small eggplant (aubergine),
    sliced
2 zucchinis (courgettes), sliced
1–2 tablespoons salt
3 red capsicums (peppers)
125 ml (4 fl oz/½ cup) extra
    virgin olive oil
2 cloves garlic, sliced
2 Roma (plum) tomatoes
200 g (6½ oz) canned, drained
    artichoke hearts
3 tablespoons oregano leaves
250 g (8 oz/1 cup) ricotta cheese
3 tablespoons sliced black olives

1 Place the eggplant and zucchini in a colander over a bowl and sprinkle with the salt, then stand for 15–20 minutes. Meanwhile, cut the capsicums into large flat pieces, removing the seeds and membrane. Brush with a little of the olive oil and place, skin-side-up, under a hot grill (broiler) until the skin blackens and blisters. Leave to cool under a tea towel or in a plastic bag, then peel away the skin. Reserve about a quarter of the capsicum to garnish and place the rest in a large non-metallic bowl.

2 Place half of the olive oil in a bowl, add 1 of the garlic cloves and a pinch of salt and mix together well. Rinse the eggplant and zucchini and pat dry with paper towels. Place the eggplant on a non-stick or foil-lined tray and brush with the garlic oil. Cook under a very hot grill for 4–6 minutes each side, or until golden brown, brushing both sides with the oil during cooking. The eggplant will burn easily, so keep a close watch. Allow to cool while cooking the zucchini in the same way. Add the eggplant and zucchini to the capsicum in the bowl.

3 Slice the tomatoes lengthwise, place on a non-stick or foil-lined baking tray and brush with the garlic oil. Reduce the temperature slightly and grill (broil) for 10–15 minutes, or until soft. Add to the bowl with the other vegetables.

4 Cut the artichokes into quarters and add to the bowl. Mix in any remaining garlic oil along with the remaining olive oil. Stir in the oregano and remaining garlic. Cover with plastic wrap and refrigerate for at least 2 hours.

5 Drain the vegetables and place them in a food processor. Add the ricotta and process for 20 seconds, or until smooth. Reserve 1 tablespoon of olives to garnish and add the remainder to the food processor. Mix together in a couple of short bursts, then transfer to a non-metallic bowl and cover with plastic wrap. Chill for at least 2 hours.

6 Slice the reserved roasted red capsicum into fine strips and arrange over the top of the dip with the reserved olives.

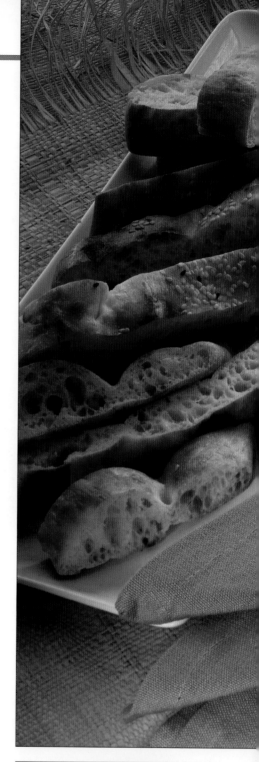

Slice the eggplant and zucchini, then place in a colander and sprinkle with salt.

Leave the capsicum to cool under a tea towel and the skin will peel away easily.

Add the grilled eggplant and zucchini to the roasted capsicum.

Slice the tomatoes lengthways, brush with the garlic oil and grill (broil) until soft.

Add the fresh oregano leaves and the other clove of garlic to the vegetables.

Add the ricotta to the food processor and mix until the dip is smooth.

41

BABA GANOUJ (EGGPLANT DIP)

Preparation time: 15 minutes +
20 minutes standing
Total cooking time: 35 minutes
Serves 6–8

2 medium eggplants
   (aubergines)
3–4 cloves garlic, crushed
2 tablespoons lemon juice
2 tablespoons tahini
1 tablespoon olive oil
sprinkle of paprika, to garnish

1 Halve the eggplants lengthways, sprinkle with salt and leave to stand for 15–20 minutes. Rinse and pat dry with paper towels. Preheat the oven to moderate 180°C (350°F/Gas 4).

2 Bake the eggplants for 35 minutes, or until soft. Peel away the skin and discard. Place the flesh in a food processor with the garlic, lemon juice, tahini and olive oil and season to taste with salt and pepper. Process for 20–30 seconds. Sprinkle with paprika and serve with Lebanese bread.

COOK'S FILE

Note: We sprinkle eggplants with salt and leave them before using because they can have a bitter taste. The salt draws the bitter liquid from the eggplant. Slender eggplants do not need to be treated before use. Tahini is a paste made from crushed sesame seeds.

Sprinkle the eggplant with salt to remove any bitterness.

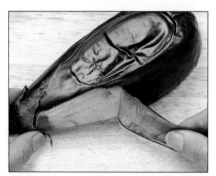

Once the eggplant has been roasted, the skin will peel away easily.

Process the eggplant with the garlic, lemon juice, tahini and olive oil.

CRISP POTATO SKINS WITH CHILLI CHEESE DIP

Preparation time: 30 minutes
Total cooking time: 1 hour 15 minutes
Serves 4–6

6 medium potatoes
oil, for shallow-frying

Chilli cheese dip
1 tablespoon oil
1 small onion, finely chopped
1 garlic clove, crushed
1 teaspoon mild chilli powder
185 g (6½ oz/¾ cup) sour cream
250 g (9 oz/2 cups) grated
    Cheddar cheese

1 Preheat oven to 210°C (415°F/ Gas 6–7). Scrub potatoes and dry thoroughly; do not peel. Prick each potato twice with a fork. Bake for 1 hour, until skins are crisp and flesh is soft when pierced with a knife. Turn once during cooking. Remove from oven and cool.
2 Cut the potatoes in half and scoop out flesh, leaving about 5 mm (¼ inch) of potato in the shell. Set aside flesh for another use. Cut each half into three wedges.
3 Heat oil in a medium heavy-based pan. Gently place batches of potato skins into moderately hot oil. Cook for 1–2 minutes, or until golden and crispy. Drain on paper towels. Serve immediately with chilli cheese dip.
4 To make the chilli cheese dip, heat oil in a small pan. Add onion and cook over a medium heat 2 minutes, or until soft. Add garlic and chilli powder, cook 1 minute, stirring. Add sour cream and stir until it is warm and thinned down slightly; add cheese and stir until melted and mixture is almost smooth. Serve hot.

COOK'S FILE

Storage time: Potatoes may be baked and prepared for frying up to eight hours in advance. Fry just before serving. Prepare chilli cheese dip just before serving.
Variation: Cut the whole baked potatoes into wedges, fry and serve as described above.

BEAN NACHOS

Preparation time: 20 minutes
Total cooking time: 10 minutes
Serves 4

4 large ripe tomatoes
2 ripe avocados, mashed
1 tablespoon lime juice
1 tablespoon sweet chilli sauce
1 tablespoon oil
2 small red onions, diced
1 small red chilli, chopped
2 teaspoons ground oregano
2 teaspoons ground cumin
¼ teaspoon chilli powder
1 tablespoon tomato paste
  (concentrated purée)
250 ml (9 fl oz/1 cup) white wine
880 g (2 lb) can red kidney
  beans, rinsed and drained
3 tablespoons chopped fresh
  coriander (cilantro) leaves
200 g (7 oz) natural corn chips
85 g (3 oz/⅔ cup) grated
  Cheddar
sour cream, to serve

1 Score a cross in the base of each tomato. Place in a bowl of boiling water for 30 seconds, then plunge into cold water and peel the skin away from the cross. Cut in half and scoop out the seeds with a teaspoon. Chop.
2 Place the avocado, lime juice and sweet chilli sauce in a bowl and mix.
3 Heat the oil in a large frying pan. Cook the onion, chilli, oregano and spices over medium heat for 2 minutes. Add the tomato, paste and wine and cook for 5 minutes, or until the liquid reduces. Add the beans and coriander.
4 Divide the corn chips into four on an oven tray. Top with the beans and sprinkle with cheese. Cook under a hot grill (broiler) until the cheese melts. Serve with avocado and sour cream.

Scoop out the seeds of the tomatoes and roughly chop the flesh.

Cook the onion, chilli, oregano and spices in a large frying pan.

Cook the mixture until the liquid is reduced and the tomato is soft.

Put the dried chickpeas in a bowl, cover with water and leave to rehydrate.

Simmer the chickpeas for 45 minutes, skimming any scum from the surface.

Make sure the carrots are coated in the spices, then drizzle with honey.

Mash the carrot and spice mixture in the pan, to keep all the pan juices.

MOROCCAN SWEET CARROT AND HONEY DIP

Preparation time: 20 minutes + soaking overnight
Total cooking time: 1 hour
Serves 6

150 g (5 oz) dried chickpeas
50 g (1¾ oz) butter
½ teaspoon ground cumin
½ teaspoon ground coriander
½ teaspoon ground cinnamon
¼ teaspoon chilli powder
200 g (6½ oz) carrots, chopped
1 tablespoon honey
4 tablespoons thick natural yoghurt
2 tablespoons chopped parsley
2 tablespoons olive oil
1 tablespoon olive oil, extra

1 Place the chickpeas in a bowl, cover with water and soak overnight. Drain and rinse well, then place in a saucepan and cover with cold water. Bring to the boil, reduce the heat and simmer for 45 minutes or until tender. Skim off any scum that rises to the surface. Drain, rinse and mash well.

2 Melt the butter in a heavy-based frying pan; add the cumin, coriander, cinnamon, chilli and carrots. Cook, covered, over low heat for 5 minutes, turning the carrots to coat them in the spices. Drizzle with honey. If the carrots start to stick add 1 tablespoon water. Cover and cook for 20 minutes until the carrots are very tender and a caramel brown colour. Cool slightly and mash in the frying pan to include all the bits on the base of the pan.

3 Combine the mashed chickpea and carrot, with the yoghurt, parsley and olive oil, and season well with salt and pepper. Spoon into a serving bowl and drizzle with extra oil. Serve with celery sticks or blanched green beans.

COOK'S FILE

Note: If you use canned chickpeas, the cooking time will be much shorter but the flavour not quite as good.

To thoroughly clean a leek, split with a knife and hold under running water.

Cook the leek for 15 minutes, adding the garlic for the last 5 minutes.

Add the shredded sorrel leaves and the cumin and cook for another minute.

Blend in a food processor with the ricotta, sour cream and lemon juice.

LEEK AND SORREL DIP

Preparation time: 35 minutes
Total cooking time: 20 minutes
Serves 8

50 g (1¾ oz) butter
2 leeks, chopped
3 cloves garlic, crushed
60 g (2 oz/1 cup) shredded
    sorrel leaves
1 teaspoon ground cumin
125 g (4 oz/½ cup) ricotta
125 g (4 oz/½ cup) sour cream
1 tablespoon lemon juice
1 tablespoon sesame seeds,
    toasted

1 Melt the butter in a large frying pan that has a lid. Add the leek and stir well. Cover and cook over low heat for 15 minutes, or until very soft. Make sure that the leek does not burn. During the last 5 minutes of cooking, add the garlic and stir well.

2 Add the sorrel and cumin and cook for another minute. Remove from the heat and allow to cool.

3 Place in a food processor with the ricotta, sour cream and lemon juice and process for 15 seconds, or until smooth. Season with salt and pepper and scatter with the toasted sesame seeds to serve.

COOK'S FILE

Hint: Always wash leeks very well before cooking as the compact layers can harbour a lot of grit.

AVOCADO SALSA

Preparation time: 15 minutes
Total cooking time: 1 minute
Serves 6

1 red onion
2 large avocados
¼ teaspoon lime juice
1 tomato
1 small red capsicum (pepper)
1 teaspoon ground coriander
1 teaspoon ground cumin
3 tablespoons chopped fresh
   coriander (cilantro) leaves
2 tablespoons olive oil
4–5 drops Tabasco

1 Finely chop the red onion. Cut avocados in half, remove stone and carefully peel. Finely chop flesh, place in a medium mixing bowl and toss lightly with lime juice.

2 Cut tomato in half horizontally and squeeze gently to remove seeds; chop finely. Remove seeds and membrane from capsicum, chop finely.

3 Place the ground coriander and cumin in a small pan, stir over medium heat 1 minute to enhance fragrance and flavour; cool. Add all ingredients to avocado in bowl and gently combine, so that the avocado retains its shape and is not mashed. Refrigerate until required. Serve at room temperature with corn chips.

COOK'S FILE

Storage time: This dish can be made up to four hours in advance.

Hints: For immediate use, choose an avocado that will just give to a gentle squeeze. Avocados should have skin without blemishes or brown patches. Green-skinned varieties should have shiny skins. Overripe avocados are sometimes offered at a low price, but on opening can be rancid and brown. Better still, buy avocados that are just underripe, and check them daily to use at their peak. Storing avocados with bananas will hasten the ripening process. Place avocados in a brown paper bag on top of the refrigerator to ripen them overnight.

1

2

3

ARTICHOKE DIP

Preparation time: 10 minutes
Total cooking time: 15 minutes
Serves 8

2 x 400 g (13 oz) cans artichoke
    hearts, drained
250 g (8 oz/1 cup) mayonnaise
75 g (2½ oz/¾ cup) grated
    Parmesan
2 teaspoons onion flakes
2 tablespoons grated Parmesan,
    extra
paprika, to sprinkle

1 Preheat the oven to moderate 180°C (350°F/Gas 4). Gently squeeze the artichokes to remove any remaining liquid. Chop and place in a bowl. Stir through the mayonnaise, Parmesan and onion flakes.

2 Spread into a 1-litre (4-cup) capacity shallow ovenproof dish. Sprinkle with the extra Parmesan and a little paprika. Bake for 15 minutes, or until heated through and lightly browned on top. Serve with crusty bread.

COOK'S FILE

Note: Use a hand-made mayonnaise for a great flavour, or ready-made mayonnaise if time is short.

Gently squeeze the artichoke hearts to remove any remaining liquid.

Mix the chopped artichoke with the mayonnaise, Parmesan and onion flakes.

Spread the dip in a shallow dish and sprinkle with Parmesan and paprika.

BOREKAS

Preparation time: 30 minutes
Total cooking time: 20 minutes
Makes 24

225 g (8 oz) feta, crumbled
200 g (7 oz) cream cheese,
    slightly softened
2 eggs, lightly beaten
¼ teaspoon ground nutmeg
20 sheets filo pastry
60 g (2¼ oz) butter, melted
3 tablespoons sesame seeds

1 Preheat the oven to moderate 180°C (350°F/Gas 4). Place the feta, cream cheese, egg and nutmeg in a bowl and mix until just combined—the mixture will be lumpy.

2 Work with five sheets of pastry at a time, keeping the rest covered with a damp tea towel. Lay each sheet on a work surface, brush with melted butter and lay them on top of each other. Use a ruler as guidance to cut the filo into six equal strips.

3 Place 1 tablespoon of the filling at one end of a strip, leaving a 1 cm (½ inch) border. Fold the pastry over to enclose the filling and form a triangle. Continue folding the triangle over until you reach the end of the pastry, tucking any excess pastry under. Repeat with the remaining ingredients to make 24 triangles, and place on a lined baking tray.

4 Lightly brush with the remaining melted butter and sprinkle with sesame seeds. Bake for 15–20 minutes, or until puffed and golden.

Mix together the feta, cream cheese, egg and nutmeg until just combined.

Using a straight edge for guidance, cut the filo sheets into six even strips.

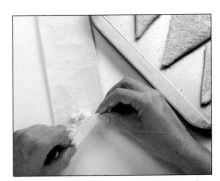

Fold the pastry over the filling, then continue folding until the end.

CREAMY BLUE CHEESE DIP WITH PEARS

Preparation time: 25 minutes +
  20 minutes refrigeration
Total cooking time: Nil
Serves 4

150 g (5 oz) creamy blue cheese
200 ml (6½ fl oz) thick cream
3 tablespoons thick plain
  yoghurt
2 tablespoons finely chopped
  chives
4 ripe pears, cored and cut into
  wedges

1 Mash the blue cheese with a fork to soften it slightly. Add the cream and yoghurt and season with freshly ground black pepper, mixing until smooth and well blended—do not overmix or it will become grainy and curdled. Spoon into a serving bowl, cover and refrigerate for 20 minutes, or until firm.
2 Scatter the chives over the dip. Serve with the pear wedges.

COOK'S FILE

Note: A creamy cheese such as Dolcelatte, Gorgonzola or King Island Blue will give the best result.

Use ripe pears for dipping. Any variety will suit—we used beurre bosc.

Mash the blue cheese with a fork to soften it slightly.

Add the cream and yoghurt and season to taste with ground black pepper.

MUSHROOM PÂTÉ WITH MELBA TOAST

Preparation time: 15 minutes +
  5 hours refrigeration + 10 minutes
  cooling
Total cooking time: 20 minutes
Makes 24

50 g (1¾ oz) butter
1 small onion, chopped
3 cloves garlic, crushed
375 g (13 oz) button mushrooms,
  quartered
125 g (4½ oz/1 cup) slivered
  almonds, toasted
2 tablespoons cream
2 tablespoons finely chopped
  fresh thyme
3 tablespoons finely chopped
  fresh flat-leaf (Italian)
  parsley
6 thick slices wholegrain or
  wholemeal (whole-wheat)
  bread

1 Heat the butter in a large frying pan. Cook the onion and garlic over medium heat for 2 minutes, or until soft. Increase the heat, add the mushrooms and cook for 5 minutes, or until the mushrooms are soft and most of the liquid has evaporated. Leave to cool for 10 minutes.

2 Place the almonds in a food processor or blender and chop roughly. Add the mushroom mixture and process until smooth. With the motor running, gradually pour in the cream. Stir in the herbs and season with salt and cracked black pepper. Spoon into two 250 ml (9 fl oz/1 cup) ramekins and smooth the surface. Cover and refrigerate for 4–5 hours to allow the flavours to develop.

3 To make the toast, preheat the oven to moderate 180°C (350°F/Gas 4). Toast one side of the bread under a hot grill (broiler) until golden. Remove the crusts and cut each slice into four triangles. Place on a large oven tray in a single layer, toasted-side-down, and cook for 5–10 minutes, or until crisp. Remove as they crisp. Spread with pâté and serve immediately.

Cook the onion, garlic and mushrooms until the mushrooms are soft.

Blend the almonds and mushroom mixture until smooth.

Spoon the pâté into the ramekins and smooth the surface.

EGGPLANT, CAPSICUM AND OLIVE SALSA

Preparation time: 45 minutes +
  cooling
Total cooking time: 20 minutes
Serves 6

1 medium eggplant (aubergine),
  diced
2 tablespoons olive oil
½ teaspoon salt
1 large red capsicum (pepper),
  diced
12 Kalamata olives, pitted and
  finely chopped
4 spring onions (scallions),
  finely chopped
1 small red chilli, chopped
2 cloves garlic, crushed
1 tablespoon olive oil
2 teaspoons red wine vinegar
2 teaspoons lemon juice
1 tablespoon chopped parsley
2 teaspoons chopped chives

1 Preheat the oven to moderate 180°C
(350°F/Gas 4). Toss the eggplant with
the olive oil and the salt, then place in
a single layer on a baking tray. Cook
for about 20 minutes, or until golden
and cooked. Remove from the oven
and allow to cool.
2 Gently mix the eggplant with the
capsicum, olives, spring onion, chilli,
garlic, olive oil, vinegar, lemon juice
and salt and freshly ground black
pepper, to taste.
3 Stir through the parsley and chives
and serve at room temperature.

COOK'S FILE

Note: Make sure the eggplant does
not have large hard or dark seeds—
these are unpalatable and will make
the salsa bitter. If you find them, cut
them out before roasting the eggplant.

*If you are very fond of olives, invest in an
olive pitter to make the task simple.*

*Toss the eggplant with the olive oil and salt
before roasting.*

*Add salt and pepper to the mixture, to your
taste.*

*Stir through the parsley and chives and
serve at room temperature.*

ASPARAGUS, APPLE AND AVOCADO DIP

Preparation time: 40 minutes +
    2 hours refrigeration
Total cooking time: 5 minutes
Serves 10–12

22 asparagus spears
3 green apples
2 tablespoons lemon juice
3 ripe avocados
300 g (10 oz) sour cream
4 drops Tabasco sauce

1 Wash and trim the woody ends from the asparagus. Steam or microwave until just cooked, then plunge into iced water and drain. Chop off the tips and set aside, to serve. Finely chop the remaining asparagus stalks.

2 Peel and grate the apples and sprinkle with 1 tablespoon lemon juice to prevent browning. Add the asparagus and mix together. In a separate dish, mash the avocado flesh. Mix in the remaining lemon juice and stir into the apple and asparagus. Add the sour cream and mix well. Add the Tabasco, cover with plastic wrap and refrigerate for 2 hours. Serve with the asparagus tips for dipping.

Remove the woody ends from the asparagus by snapping with your fingers.

As soon as you have grated the apple, sprinkle with lemon juice.

You will only need a little Tabasco to add spiciness to the dip.

MEXICAN LAYERED DIP

Preparation time: 50 minutes
Total cooking time: Nil
Serves 12

450 g (14 oz) can refried beans
35 g (1¼ oz) packet of taco
    seasoning mix
300 g (10 oz) sour cream
200 g (6½ oz) ready-made salsa
    sauce
60 g (2 oz/½ cup) grated
    Cheddar
2 tablespoons chopped pitted
    black olives
200 g (6½ oz) corn chips
1 tablespoon chopped coriander
    (cilantro)

Guacamole
3 ripe avocados
1 tomato
1–2 red chillies, finely chopped
1 small red onion, finely
    chopped
1 tablespoon chopped coriander
    (cilantro)
1 tablespoon lime or lemon juice
2 tablespoons sour cream
1–2 drops habanero sauce or
    Tabasco sauce

1 Using a fork, mix the refried beans and taco seasoning together in a small bowl.
2 To make the guacamole, cut the avocados in half, peel and discard the skin and stone (chop into the stone with a sharp knife and lift it out). Roughly chop the avocados and place in a bowl, then mash lightly with a fork. Cut the tomato in half horizontally, scoop out the seeds with a teaspoon and discard. Finely dice the flesh and add to the avocado. Stir in the chilli, onion, coriander, lime or lemon juice, sour cream and habanero or Tabasco sauce. Season with freshly cracked black pepper.
3 To assemble, spread the bean mixture in the middle of a large serving platter (we used a 30 x 35 cm/ 12 x 14 inch dish), leaving a clear border for the corn chips. Spoon the sour cream on top, leaving a small border of bean mixture showing. Repeat with the guacamole and salsa sauce so that you can see each layer. Sprinkle with cheese and olives.
4 Arrange the corn chips around the edge of the platter just before serving and garnish with the coriander.

COOK'S FILE

Note: Habanero sauce is a very hot condiment sauce made from habanero chillies. Use sparingly to add extra zing to the dip. It is available from delicatessens and speciality stores.
Hint: Always try to wear rubber gloves when you are chopping chillies. If this isn't possible, remember to scrub your hands thoroughly with warm soapy water after chopping. Be careful not to touch your eyes or any other delicate skin or you will cause burning and skin irritation.
Storage: The dip can be made 1–2 hours in advance and refrigerated, covered with plastic wrap.

Mash together the refried beans and the taco seasoning mix.

Remove the skin and stone from the avocado and mash the flesh.

Scoop out the seeds from the tomato and dice the flesh.

Season the guacamole with freshly ground black pepper.

Build up the layers of the dip, leaving a border around each so they can be seen.

Sprinkle the top of the layered dip with the grated cheese and chopped olives.

CHARGRILLED VEGETABLE SALSA

Preparation time: 30 minutes +
  2 hours marinating
Total cooking time: 30 minutes
Serves 4

2 Roma (plum) tomatoes
1 small red capsicum (pepper)
1 small green capsicum (pepper)
2 small zucchini (courgettes)
2 slender eggplants (aubergines)
3 tablespoons olive oil
1 tablespoon chopped flat-leaf
  (Italian) parsley
2 teaspoons chopped marjoram
2 teaspoons chopped oregano
2 tablespoons balsamic vinegar
1 tablespoon chopped flat-leaf
  (Italian) parsley, extra
2 teaspoons chopped marjoram,
  extra

1 Halve the tomatoes, capsicums, zucchini and eggplants lengthways. Place in a large shallow dish and pour over the combined olive oil and herbs. Toss well and leave to marinate for at least 2 hours or up to a day.

2 Heat the barbecue or chargrill pan and cook the vegetables until soft and a little blackened. Place the capsicum in a plastic bag for a few minutes, then peel away the skin. Cut all the vegetables into small pieces and mix with the vinegar and extra herbs.

Cut the tomatoes, capsicums, zucchini and eggplants in half lengthways.

Barbecue or chargrill the vegetables until soft and a little blackened.

Cut the vegetables into small chunks and mix with the herbs and vinegar.

FELAFEL WITH TOMATO SALSA

Preparation time: 40 minutes +
  4 hours soaking + 30 minutes
  standing
Total cooking time: 20 minutes
Serves 8

440 g (15½ oz/2 cups) dried
  chickpeas
1 small onion, finely chopped
2 cloves garlic, crushed
4 tablespoons chopped fresh
  flat-leaf (Italian) parsley
2 tablespoons chopped fresh
  coriander (cilantro) leaves
2 teaspoons ground cumin
½ teaspoon baking powder
oil, for deep-frying

Tomato salsa
2 tomatoes
¼ Lebanese (short) cucumber,
  finely chopped
½ green capsicum (pepper),
  diced
2 tablespoons chopped fresh
  flat-leaf (Italian) parsley
1 teaspoon sugar
2 teaspoons chilli sauce
½ teaspoon grated lemon rind
2 tablespoons lemon juice

1 Soak chickpeas in 1 litre (4 cups) water for 4 hours or overnight. Drain. Place in a food processor and blend for 30 seconds, or until finely ground. Add the onion, garlic, parsley, coriander, ground cumin, baking powder and 1 tablespoon water, then process for 10 seconds, or until a rough paste. Leave, covered, for 30 minutes.
2 To make the salsa, score a cross in the base of each tomato. Place in a bowl of boiling water for 30 seconds, then plunge into cold water and peel the skin away from the cross. Finely chop, then place in a bowl with all the other ingredients and mix well.
3 Using your hands, shape heaped tablespoons of the felafel mixture into even-sized balls. Squeeze out any excess liquid. Fill a large heavy-based saucepan one third full of oil and heat until a cube of bread dropped into the oil browns in 15 seconds. Lower the felafel balls into the oil and cook in batches of five for 3–4 minutes, or until well browned all over. Remove the felafel with a slotted spoon and drain on paper towels.
4 Serve hot or cold on a bed of salsa.

Grind the drained chickpeas in a food processor until finely chopped.

Shape heaped tablespoons of the felafel mixture into even-sized balls.

Cook until well browned, then remove them with a slotted spoon and drain.

ROASTED CAPSICUM AND CHILLI DIP

Preparation time: 40 minutes +
  30 minutes refrigeration
Total cooking time: 35 minutes
Serves 8

2 large red capsicums (peppers)
3 tablespoons olive oil
1–2 birds eye chillies
200 g (6½ oz) neufchatel cream
  cheese
3 tablespoons thick plain
  yoghurt
1 teaspoon red wine vinegar
½ teaspoon soft brown sugar
2 spring onions (scallions),
  chopped

1 Preheat the oven to moderately hot 200°C (400°F/Gas 6). Put the capsicums in a baking dish and drizzle with oil. Bake for 15 minutes. Make a small slit in each of the whole chillies (otherwise they will explode), add to the dish and bake for a further 20 minutes. (If the vegetables begin to burn, add about 1 tablespoon of water to the baking dish.) Allow to cool.

2 Peel the skin from the cooled capsicums. Cut them and the chillies in half and discard the seeds and membrane. Place the capsicum and chillies in a food processor and mix until pulpy.

3 Beat the cream cheese until soft, then add the capsicum chilli mixture, yoghurt, vinegar and sugar. Season to taste with salt and pepper, then cover and refrigerate for 30 minutes. Scatter with the spring onions to serve.

Roast the capsicums for 15 minutes, then add the chillies.

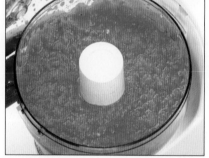

Put the capsicum and chillies in a food processor and mix until pulpy.

Mix together all the ingredients, then refrigerate for 30 minutes before serving.

HUMMUS

Preparation time: 15 minutes
Total cooking time: Nil
Serves 4–6

425 g (14 oz) can chickpeas

2–3 tablespoons lemon juice
2 tablespoons olive oil
2 cloves garlic, crushed
3 tablespoons tahini

1 Place the drained chickpeas, lemon juice, olive oil and garlic in a food processor. Season with salt and pepper. Process for 20–30 seconds, or until smooth.
2 Add the tahini and process for a further 10 seconds.

Drain the chickpeas to get rid of the canning brine.

Process the chickpeas, lemon juice, olive oil and garlic.

The hummus will be quite firm—if you prefer it softer, add a little water.

59

Soups

TOMATO SOUP WITH PASTA AND BASIL

Preparation time: 25 minutes
Total cooking time: 35 minutes
Serves 4

3 large ripe tomatoes
2 tablespoons olive oil
1 medium onion, finely chopped
1 clove garlic, crushed
1 small red capsicum (pepper), finely chopped
1 litre (32 fl oz/4 cups) vegetable stock
3 tablespoons tomato paste (concentrated purée)
salt and pepper
1 teaspoon sugar
3 tablespoons basil leaves, or 1½ teaspoons dried basil
155 g (5½ oz/1 cup) small shell pasta or macaroni
4 fresh basil leaves, extra

1 Cut a small cross in the top of each tomato. Plunge tomatoes into boiling water for 1–2 minutes. Remove. Peel skin downward from the cross and discard. Roughly chop tomatoes.
2 Heat oil in a large pan. Add onion, garlic and capsicum and cook, stirring, until all ingredients are soft. Add the chopped tomato and cook for another 10 minutes.

3 Add stock, tomato paste, salt, pepper and sugar. Cover and simmer for 15 minutes. Remove from heat, add basil leaves. Allow to cool. Pour mixture into food processor or blender and process in batches until smooth. Return mixture to pan, reheat gently.
4 Cook the shell pasta or macaroni separately in boiling salted water until tender. Drain. Add to soup and heat through. Serve sprinkled with fresh basil leaves.

COOK'S FILE

Storage time: Soup can be made a day ahead; add pasta before serving.
Note: Basil is added at the end of cooking, for the best flavour.

CREAMED FENNEL SOUP

Preparation time: 10 minutes
Total cooking time: 35 minutes
Serves 4

2 potatoes
1 medium fennel bulb
60 g (2¼ oz) butter
500 ml (17 fl oz/2 cups)
　　vegetable stock

125 g (4½ oz) cream cheese,
　　chopped
1 tablespoon chopped fresh
　　chives
1 tablespoon lemon juice

1 Chop potatoes. Slice and chop fennel. Heat butter in a medium pan; add fennel. Cook, covered, over low heat for 10 minutes, stirring occasionally. Do not allow fennel to colour. Add the potatoes and stock to pan, stir. Bring to the boil, reduce heat to low. Cover and cook for 10 minutes, or until vegetables are tender. Season to taste with salt and ground black pepper. Remove from heat; cool slightly.

2 Transfer mixture to a food processor bowl; add cheese. Process until mixture is smooth and creamy.

3 Return soup to pan. Add chives and juice, stir over low heat until just heated through.

1

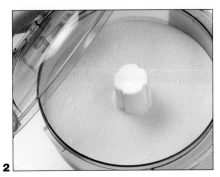

2

3

SWEET POTATO SOUP

Preparation time: 20 minutes
Total cooking time: 1 hour
Serves 8

1 kg (2 lb 4 oz) orange sweet
   potato
2 large onions
75 g (2½ oz) butter
1 garlic clove, crushed
1 tablespoon ground cumin
2 litres (8 cups) vegetable stock
310 g (11 oz/1¼ cups) crunchy
   peanut butter

1 tablespoon chilli sauce
3 tablespoons chopped
   peanuts
3 tablespoons chopped chives

1 Peel sweet potato. Peel and chop onions. Chop sweet potato into 5 mm (¼ inch) cubes. Heat butter in a deep heavy-based pan. Add onions, cook over medium-high heat 10 minutes, or until golden brown.
2 Add garlic and cumin, stir-fry for 30 seconds. Add sweet potato, stir until well coated. Cover, reduce heat, cook 10 minutes. Shake pan occasionally to prevent sticking. Add

stock, bring to boil, then reduce heat and simmer for 10 minutes.
3 Stir in peanut butter and chilli sauce. Simmer gently, uncovered, for 30 minutes, stirring occasionally. Add salt to taste. Serve immediately, sprinkled with chopped peanuts and chives.

COOK'S FILE

Hint: Spread sliced French sticks with butter creamed with curry powder to taste. Bake in moderate oven until golden. Serve hot with soup.

1

2

3

VEGETABLE SOUP

Preparation time: 20 minutes +
  overnight soaking
Total cooking time: 1 hour 5 minutes
Serves 6

105 g (3½ oz/½ cup) dried red
  kidney beans or borlotti
  beans
1 tablespoon olive oil
1 leek, halved lengthways and
  chopped
1 small onion, diced
2 carrots, chopped
2 celery sticks, chopped
1 large zucchini (courgette),
  chopped
1 tablespoon tomato paste
  (concentrated purée)
1 litre (4 cups) vegetable stock
400 g (14 oz) pumpkin, cut into
  2 cm (¾ inch) cubes
2 potatoes, cut into 2 cm
  (¾ inch) cubes
3 tablespoons chopped fresh
  flat-leaf (Italian) parsley

1 Place the beans in a bowl, cover with cold water and soak overnight. Rinse, then transfer to a saucepan, cover with cold water and cook for 45 minutes, or until just tender. Drain.
2 Heat the oil in a saucepan. Add the leek and onion and cook over medium heat for 2–3 minutes without browning, or until they start to soften. Add the carrot, celery and zucchini and cook for 3–4 minutes. Add the tomato paste and stir for 1 minute. Pour in the vegetable stock and 1.25 litres (5 cups) water and bring to

the boil. Reduce the heat to low and simmer for 20 minutes.
3 Add the pumpkin, potato, parsley and beans and simmer for a further 20 minutes, or until the vegetables are tender and the beans are cooked. Season. Serve with crusty bread.

COOK'S FILE

Note: To save time, use a 420 g (15 oz) can kidney beans instead of dried.

Using a sharp knife, cut the pumpkin into cubes.

Add the vegetables and beans and simmer until the vegetables are cooked.

PROVENCAL VEGETABLE SOUP WITH PESTO

Preparation time: 25–30 minutes
Total cooking time: 35–40 minutes
Serves 8

2 medium onions
1 leek
3 stalks fresh parsley
1 large sprig fresh rosemary
1 large sprig fresh thyme
1 large sprig fresh marjoram
3 tablespoons olive oil
1 bay leaf
375 g (13 oz) pumpkin, cut into
   small pieces
250 g (9 oz) potato, cut into
   small pieces
1 medium carrot, cut in half
   lengthways and thinly sliced

2 small zucchini (courgettes),
   finely chopped
2 litres (8 cups) water or
   vegetable stock
1 teaspoon salt
95 g (3¼ oz/½ cup) fresh or
   frozen broad (fava) beans
80 g (2¾ oz/½ cup) fresh or
   frozen peas
2 tomatoes, peeled and roughly
   chopped
80 g (2¾ oz/½ cup) short
   macaroni or shell pasta

Pesto
10 g (¼ oz/½ cup) fresh basil
   leaves
2 large cloves garlic, crushed
½ teaspoon black pepper
4 tablespoons grated parmesan
   cheese
4 tablespoons olive oil

1 Thinly slice onions and leek. Tie parsley, rosemary, thyme and marjoram with string. Heat oil in a heavy-based pan; add onion and leek. Cook over low heat 10 minutes or until soft. Add herbs, bay leaf, pumpkin, potato, carrot, zucchini, and water or stock; add salt. Cover, simmer 10 minutes or till vegetables are almost tender.

2 Add beans, peas, tomato and pasta. Cover, cook another 15 minutes or until vegetables are very tender (add more water if necessary). Remove herbs.

3 To make the pesto, process basil, garlic, pepper and cheese in food processor for 20 seconds or until finely chopped. Add oil gradually, process until smooth. Refrigerate. Ladle soup into bowls. Serve pesto separately for diners to help themselves.

1

2

3

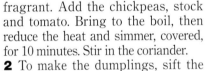

CHUNKY CHICKPEA AND HERB DUMPLING SOUP

Preparation time: 30 minutes
Total cooking time: 35 minutes
Serves 4

1 tablespoon oil
1 onion, chopped
2 cloves garlic, crushed
2 teaspoons ground cumin
1 teaspoon ground
   coriander
¼ teaspoon chilli powder
2 x 300 g (10½ oz) cans
   chickpeas, drained
875 ml (30 fl oz/3½ cups)
   vegetable stock

2 x 425 g (15 oz) cans chopped
   tomatoes
1 tablespoon chopped fresh
   coriander (cilantro) leaves
125 g (4½ oz/1 cup) self-raising
   flour
25 g (1 oz) butter, chopped
2 tablespoons grated Parmesan
2 tablespoons mixed chopped
   fresh herbs (flat-leaf (Italian)
   parsley, coriander (cilantro)
   leaves and chives)
3 tablespoons milk

1 Heat the oil in a saucepan, and cook the onion over medium heat for 2–3 minutes, or until soft. Add the garlic, cumin, ground coriander and chilli and cook for 1 minute, or until fragrant. Add the chickpeas, stock and tomato. Bring to the boil, then reduce the heat and simmer, covered, for 10 minutes. Stir in the coriander.

2 To make the dumplings, sift the flour into a bowl and add the chopped butter. Rub the butter into the flour with your fingertips until it resembles fine breadcrumbs. Stir in the cheese and mixed fresh herbs. Make a well in the centre, add the milk and mix with a flat-bladed knife until just combined. Bring together into a ball, divide into eight portions and roll into small balls.

3 Add the dumplings to the soup, cover and simmer for 20 minutes, or until a skewer comes out clean when inserted in the centre of the dumplings.

Stir the coriander into the simmering chickpea mixture.

Add the milk to the dumpling mixture and mix with a flat-bladed knife.

Pierce the dumplings with a skewer to test if they are cooked.

GREEN PEA SOUP

Preparation time: 20 minutes +
  2 hours soaking
Total cooking time: 1 hour 40 minutes
Serves 4–6

330 g (11½ oz/1½ cups) green
  split peas
2 tablespoons oil
1 onion, finely chopped
1 stalk celery, finely sliced
1 carrot, finely sliced
1 tablespoon ground cumin
1 tablespoon ground coriander
2 teaspoons grated fresh
  ginger

1.25 litres (5 cups) vegetable
  stock
310 g (11 oz/2 cups) frozen
  green peas
1 tablespoon chopped fresh mint
4 tablespoons plain yoghurt or
  sour cream, to serve

1 Soak split peas in cold water for
2 hours. Drain peas well. Heat oil in a
large heavy-based pan, add onion,
celery and carrot. Cook over medium
heat for 3 minutes, stirring
occasionally, until soft but not
browned. Stir in cumin, coriander and
ginger, cook 1 minute.
2 Add split peas and stock to pan.
Bring to boil; reduce heat to low.

Simmer, covered, for 1½ hours,
stirring occasionally.
3 Add frozen peas to pan and stir to
combine; set aside to cool. When cool,
purée soup in batches in a blender or
food processor until smooth. Return to
pan, gently reheat. Season to taste. Stir
in mint. Serve with a swirl of yoghurt
or sour cream in each bowl.

COOK'S FILE

Storage time: Soup may be made up
to one day in advance. Store in
refrigerator. Reheat gently and stir in
mint just before serving.
Hint: If soup becomes too thick after
refrigeration, thin with extra stock.

RICH RED ONION SOUP

Preparation time: 20 minutes
Total cooking time: 50 minutes
Serves 6

1 tablespoon oil
20 g (½ oz) butter
1 kg (2 lb 4 oz) red onions
1 tablespoon plain (all-purpose)
  flour
1 litre (4 cups) vegetable stock
250 ml (9 fl oz/1 cup) red wine
250 ml (9 fl oz/1 cup) puréed
  tomato
French bread, cut diagonally into

12 slices, 2 cm (¾ inch) thick
60 g (2¼ oz/½ cup) finely grated
  cheddar cheese

1 Heat oil and butter in a large heavy-
based pan. Slice onions thinly. Add
onions, stir-fry over a high heat for
3 minutes until soft and starting to
become golden. Reduce heat to
medium-low, and cook onions
25 minutes, stirring occasionally, until
very soft and golden.
2 Sprinkle flour over onions, stir well
with a wooden spoon. Cook for
2 minutes, stirring constantly. Add
stock, wine and puréed tomato, stir
until mixture boils and thickens

slightly. Season. Reduce heat and
simmer, uncovered, for 20 minutes.
3 Toast bread on both sides under a
grill (broiler). Top with grated cheese,
return to grill and cook until melted
and golden. To serve, ladle soup into
deep bowls and float-bread slices
on the top.

COOK'S FILE

Storage time: Rich red onion soup
may be made up to one day ahead.
Store in refrigerator. Reheat soup
gently, toast bread and grill (broil)
cheese just before serving.

*Green Pea Soup (top) and
Rich Red Onion Soup*

RED CAPSICUM SOUP

Preparation time: 20 minutes
Total cooking time: 50 minutes
Serves 6

4 red capsicums (peppers)
4 tomatoes
3 tablespoons oil
½ teaspoon dried marjoram
½ teaspoon dried mixed
   herbs
2 garlic cloves, crushed
1 teaspoon mild curry paste
1 red onion, sliced
1 medium leek, sliced
   (white part only)

250 g (9 oz) green cabbage,
   chopped
1 teaspoon sweet chilli sauce

1 Cut capsicum in quarters. Remove seeds and membrane. Place skin-side up on grill (broiler) tray. Brush with a little oil. Grill (broil) for 10 minutes, or until skin is black. Cover with a damp tea towel until cool. Peel off skin. Mark a small cross on the top of each tomato. Place in a bowl of boiling water for 1–2 minutes, then plunge into cold water. Peel skin off downwards from the cross. Cut tomatoes in half; gently squeeze out seeds.
2 Heat oil in a large pan. Add herbs, garlic and curry paste. Stir over low

heat for 1 minute, or until aromatic. Add onion and leek and cook 3 minutes, or until light golden. Add cabbage, tomatoes, capsicum and 1 litre (4 cups) water. Bring to boil, reduce heat and simmer 20 minutes. Remove from heat. Cool slightly.
3 Place soup in small batches in a food processor bowl. Using pulse action, process 30 seconds, or until smooth. Return soup to clean pan, stir through chilli sauce, season to taste. Reheat gently. Serve hot.

COOK'S FILE

Storage time: This soup can be made up to five days ahead and refrigerated. Reheat before serving.

SOBA NOODLE SOUP

Preparation time: 15 minutes +
    5 minutes standing
Total cooking time: 10 minutes
Serves 4

250 g (9 oz) packet soba noodles
2 dried shiitake mushrooms
2 litres (8 cups) vegetable stock
120 g (4 oz) snow peas
    (mangetout), cut into strips
2 small carrots, cut into thin
    5 cm (2 inch) strips
2 cloves garlic, finely chopped

6 spring onions (scallions), cut
    into 5 cm (2 inch) lengths and
    thinly sliced lengthways
3 cm (1¼ inch) piece ginger, cut
    into julienne strips
4 tablespoons soy sauce
3 tablespoons mirin or sake
90 g (3¼ oz/1 cup) bean sprouts

1 Cook the noodles according to the packet instructions. Drain.
2 Soak the mushrooms in 125 ml (4 fl oz/½ cup) boiling water until soft. Drain, reserving the liquid. Remove the stalk and slice the mushrooms.
3 Combine the vegetable stock, mushrooms, reserved liquid, snow peas, carrot, garlic, spring onion and ginger in a large saucepan. Bring slowly to the boil, then reduce the heat to low and simmer for 5 minutes, or until the vegetables are tender. Add the soy sauce, mirin and bean sprouts. Cook for a further 3 minutes.
4 Divide the noodles among four large serving bowls. Ladle the hot liquid and vegetables over the top and garnish with coriander.

Cut the ginger into julienne strips (thin strips the size and shape of matchsticks).

After soaking the mushrooms, drain and finely slice them.

Simmer the vegetables for 5 minutes, or until tender.

71

Stir in the curry powder, cumin and garam masala and cook until fragrant.

Simmer the lentils and vegetables over low heat until the lentils are tender.

Combine the yoghurt, coriander, garlic and Tabasco sauce.

LENTIL AND VEGETABLE SOUP WITH SPICED YOGHURT

Preparation time: 30 minutes
Total cooking time: 40 minutes
Serves 6

2 tablespoons olive oil
1 small leek (white part only), chopped
2 cloves garlic, crushed
2 teaspoons curry powder
1 teaspoon ground cumin
1 teaspoon garam masala
1 litre (4 cups) vegetable stock
1 bay leaf
185 g (6½ oz/1 cup) brown lentils
450 g (1 lb) butternut pumpkin (squash), peeled and cut into 1 cm (½ inch) cubes
2 zucchini (courgettes), cut in half lengthways and sliced
400 g (14 oz) can chopped tomatoes
200 g (7 oz) broccoli, cut into small florets
1 small carrot, diced
80 g (2¾ oz/½ cup) peas
1 tablespoon chopped mint

Spiced yoghurt
250 g (9 oz/1 cup) thick plain yoghurt
1 tablespoon chopped coriander (cilantro) leaves
1 clove garlic, crushed
3 dashes Tabasco sauce

1 Heat the oil in a saucepan over medium heat. Add the leek and garlic and cook for 4–5 minutes, or until soft and lightly golden. Add the curry powder, cumin and garam masala and cook for 1 minute, or until fragrant.

2 Add the stock, bay leaf, lentils and pumpkin. Bring to the boil, then reduce the heat to low and simmer for 10–15 minutes, or until the lentils are tender. Season well.

3 Add the zucchini, tomatoes, broccoli, carrot and 500 ml (17 fl oz/ 2 cups) water and simmer for 10 minutes, or until the vegetables are tender. Add the peas and simmer for 2–3 minutes.

4 To make the spiced yoghurt, place the yoghurt, coriander, garlic and Tabasco in a small bowl and stir until combined. Dollop a spoonful of the yoghurt on each serving of soup and garnish with the mint.

CHILLI, CORN AND RED CAPSICUM SOUP

Preparation time: 20 minutes
Total cooking time: 45 minutes
Serves 4

1 coriander (cilantro) sprig
4 corn cobs
30 g (1 oz) butter
2 red capsicums (peppers), diced
1 small onion, finely chopped
1 small red chilli, finely chopped
1 tablespoon plain (all-purpose)
   flour
500 ml (17 fl oz/2 cups)
   vegetable stock
125 ml (4 fl oz/½ cup) cream

1 Trim the leaves off the coriander and finely chop the root and stems. Cut the kernels off the corn cobs.
2 Heat the butter in a saucepan over medium heat. Add the corn kernels, capsicum, onion and chilli and stir to coat in the butter. Cook, covered, over low heat, stirring occasionally, for 10 minutes, or until soft. Increase the heat to medium and add the coriander root and stem and cook, stirring, for 30 seconds, or until fragrant. Sprinkle with the flour and stir for 1 minute. Remove from the heat and gradually stir in the vegetable stock. Add 500 ml (17 fl oz/2 cups) water and return to the heat. Bring to the boil, reduce the heat to low and simmer, covered, for 30 minutes, or until the vegetables are tender. Cool slightly.
3 Ladle 500 ml (17 fl oz/2 cups) of the soup into a blender and purée until smooth. Return the purée to the soup in the pan, pour in the cream and gently heat until warmed through. Season. Sprinkle with the coriander leaves and serve with grilled (broiled) cheese on pitta bread.

Using a sharp knife, cut all the kernels from the corn cob.

Trim the leaves and finely chop the root and stems of the coriander.

Simmer for 30 minutes, or until the vegetables are tender.

73

CARROT AND ORANGE SOUP WITH THYME

Preparation time: 20 minutes
Total cooking time: 35 minutes
Serves 4

500 g (1 lb 2 oz) carrots
30 g (1 oz) butter
125 ml (4 fl oz/½ cup) orange juice
1–1.25 litres (4–5 cups) vegetable stock
1 small onion, roughly chopped
3–4 teaspoons chopped fresh thyme, or 1 teaspoon dried
salt and pepper
sour cream, nutmeg, for serving

1 Peel and slice carrots. Place carrots and butter in a large heavy-based pan and cook over medium heat for 10 minutes, stirring occasionally.

2 Add the orange juice, stock and onion. Bring to boil, add thyme, salt and pepper. Cover and cook for 20 minutes, or until carrots are tender. Allow to cool.

3 Pour mixture into a food processor or blender and process in batches until smooth. Return mixture to pan and reheat. Serve in individual bowls. Top each with a dollop of sour cream sprinkled with nutmeg. Garnish with a small sprig of thyme, if desired.

COOK'S FILE

Storage time: Soup may be made up to 2 days in advance. Store, covered, in the refrigerator.

SPINACH AND SORREL SOUP

Preparation time: 30 minutes
Total cooking time: 25 minutes
Serves 4–6

500 g (1 lb 2 oz) English spinach
  leaves
3 tablespoons olive oil
1 large onion, finely chopped
1 small clove garlic, crushed
½ teaspoon white pepper
salt to taste

1.25 litres (5 cups) vegetable
  stock
8 small sorrel leaves, shredded
4 tablespoons cream

1 Wash spinach and shake dry. Trim roots and tear leaves into pieces. Place the spinach pieces in a large pan. Cook in two batches over low heat, turning spinach over until it is soft. Place in a food processor with any liquid from the pan; process until smooth.

2 Heat oil in a heavy-based pan. Add onion and garlic, cook over medium heat until soft and golden; add pepper, salt and stock. Cover and cook for 5 minutes; add spinach purée and cook for another 5 minutes.

3 Add sorrel and cream to soup, remove pan from heat (sorrel only takes seconds to cook). Serve soup immediately.

COOK'S FILE

Variation: Finely chop 2 hard-boiled eggs and combine with 1 teaspoon curry powder. Sprinkle this mixture on top of the soup in individual bowls before serving.

PUMPKIN AND RED LENTIL SOUP

Preparation time: 15 minutes
Total cooking time: 30 minutes
Serves 4

1 tablespoon olive oil
1 long red chilli, seeded
   and chopped
1 onion, finely chopped
500 g (1 lb 2 oz) butternut
   pumpkin (squash),
   chopped
350 g (12 oz) orange sweet
   potato, chopped
1 litre (4 cups) vegetable stock
125 g (4½ oz/½ cup) red lentils
1 tablespoon tahini

1 Heat the oil in a large saucepan over medium heat, add the chilli and onion and cook for 2–3 minutes, or until the onion is soft. Reduce the heat to low, add the pumpkin and sweet potato and cook, covered, for 8 minutes, stirring occasionally.
2 Increase the heat to high, add the stock and bring to the boil. Reduce the heat to low, and simmer, covered, for 10 minutes. Add the lentils and cook, covered, for 7 minutes, or until tender.
3 Blend the soup in batches in a blender or food processor, add the tahini and blend until smooth. Return to the saucepan and gently heat until warmed through. Garnish with chilli and serve with Turkish bread.

COOK'S FILE

Note: The soup can be made up to a day ahead. Keep covered with plastic wrap in the refrigerator and reheat in a saucepan or in the microwave.

Wearing rubber gloves, remove the seeds and membranes from the chilli and chop.

Stir the pumpkin and sweet potato into the onion mixture.

Blend the soup and tahini in a blender until smooth.

CORN AND CHEESE CHOWDER

Preparation time: 15 minutes
Total cooking time: 30 minutes
Serves 8

90 g (3¼ oz) butter
2 large onions, finely chopped
1 garlic clove, crushed
2 teaspoons cumin seeds
1 litre (4 cups) vegetable
    stock
2 medium potatoes, peeled and
    chopped
250 g (9 oz/1 cup) canned
    creamed corn

400 g (14 oz/2 cups) fresh corn
    kernels
3 tablespoons chopped fresh
    parsley
125 g (4½ oz/1 cup) grated
    Cheddar cheese
3 tablespoons cream, optional
2 tablespoons chopped fresh
    chives, to garnish

1 Heat butter in heavy-based pan. Add onion, cook over medium-high heat 5 minutes, or until golden. Add garlic and cumin seeds and cook 1 minute, stirring constantly. Add stock. Bring to the boil. Add the potato, reduce heat. Simmer, uncovered, 10 minutes.

2 Add creamed corn, corn kernels and parsley. Bring to boil, reduce heat and simmer for 10 minutes more.

3 Stir through cheese and cream and season to taste. Heat gently until cheese melts. Serve immediately, sprinkled with chopped chives.

COOK'S FILE

Storage time: Cook this dish up to one day in advance. Reheat and add cheese just before serving.

Variation: Corn kernels scraped from fresh young corn on the cob are best for this recipe—frozen or canned corn may be used if fresh is unavailable.

Starters & light meals

MUSHROOMS WITH HERB NUT BUTTER

Preparation time: 20 minutes
Total cooking time: 20 minutes
Serves 4–6

12 large mushroom caps
1 tablespoon olive oil
1 small onion, finely chopped
3 tablespoons blanched almonds
1 clove garlic, peeled and
　chopped
1 tablespoon lemon juice
3 tablespoons parsley sprigs
3 teaspoons chopped fresh
　thyme or 1 teaspoon dried
　thyme
3 teaspoons chopped fresh
　rosemary or 1 teaspoon dried
　rosemary
1 tablespoon chopped fresh
　chives
½ teaspoon salt
¼ teaspoon black pepper
75 g (2½ oz)butter, chopped

1 Preheat oven to 180°C (350°F/ Gas 4). Brush a shallow baking dish with oil or melted butter. Remove stalks from mushrooms. Chop stalks finely. Heat oil in a small pan, add onion. Cook over medium heat for 2–3 minutes or until soft and golden. Add chopped mushroom stalks. Cook another 2 minutes or until softened. Remove from heat.

2 Place almonds, garlic, lemon juice, parsley, thyme, rosemary, chives, salt, pepper and butter in food processor. Process for 20–30 seconds or until mixture is smooth.

3 Place mushroom caps in baking dish. Spoon equal amounts of onion and mushroom mixture into each cap; smooth surface. Top with almond and herb mixture. Bake for 10–15 minutes, or until mushrooms are cooked through and butter has melted.

COOK'S FILE

Storage: Mushrooms are best cooked just before serving.

EGGPLANT WITH TOMATO HERB SAUCE

Preparation time: 30 minutes
Total cooking time: 50 minutes
Serves 4

6–8 slender eggplant
   (aubergines)
olive oil for frying
2 tablespoons oil, extra
2 cloves garlic, crushed
1 onion, chopped
1 red capsicum (pepper), seeded
   and cut into small squares
2 ripe tomatoes, chopped
125 ml (4 fl oz/½ cup) vegetable
   stock

1 teaspoon finely chopped fresh
   thyme
1 teaspoon finely chopped fresh
   marjoram
2 teaspoons finely chopped fresh
   oregano
1 teaspoon sugar
3–4 teaspoons white wine
   vinegar
3 tablespoons small black olives
pepper and salt
3 tablespoons fresh basil leaves,
   shredded

1 Cut eggplant in half lengthways.
Pour enough oil into large frying pan
to cover base. Heat until oil is almost
smoking. Fry eggplant in batches over
medium-high heat for 2–3 minutes on
each side, or until golden brown.
Remove from pan with tongs, drain on
paper towels. Add more oil if
necessary to cook each batch. Cover
eggplant and keep warm.
2 Heat extra oil in pan, add garlic and
onion. Cook over medium heat for
2–3 minutes. Add chopped capsicum
and tomato and cook, stirring, for
1–2 minutes or until just softened.
3 Add stock to pan. Bring to boil,
reduce heat and simmer, stirring
occasionally, 5–10 minutes or until
liquid reduces and thickens. Stir in
thyme, marjoram, oregano, sugar and
vinegar. Cook for another 3–4 minutes.
Stir in olives; season with pepper and
salt. Serve warm eggplant topped with
tomato sauce and shredded basil.

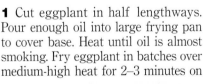

EGGPLANT AND ZUCCHINI POTS WITH CAPSICUM RELISH

Preparation time: 12 minutes +
20 minutes standing
Total cooking time: 40 minutes
Makes 6

1 large eggplant (aubergine), cut
into 1 cm (½ inch) cubes
200 g (7 oz) fresh ricotta
cheese
310 g (11 oz/1¼ cups) sour
cream
3 eggs
1 tablespoon cornflour
(cornstarch)
135 g (4¾ oz/1 cup) grated
zucchini (courgette)

½ teaspoon cracked black
pepper

Capsicum relish
185 ml (6 fl oz/¾ cup) brown
vinegar
4 tablespoons sugar
1 teaspoon yellow mustard
seeds
1 green apple, chopped
1 pear, chopped
1 red capsicum (pepper),
chopped
1 green capsicum (pepper),
chopped

1 Preheat oven to 210°C (415°F/
Gas 6–7). Brush six 60 ml (2 fl oz/
¼ cup) capacity ramekins with oil.
Place eggplant in colander and
sprinkle with 1 tablespoon salt; leave

20 minutes. Rinse under cold water,
then drain well.
2 Using electric beaters, beat ricotta
and cream until light and creamy. Add
eggs and cornflour, beat until smooth.
Transfer to large mixing bowl and
gently fold in eggplant, zucchini and
black pepper.
3 Spoon mixture evenly into pots.
Arrange in a deep baking dish. Fill
dish two-thirds up side of pots with
warm water; cover loosely with foil.
Bake 40 minutes, or until a skewer
comes out clean when inserted in
centre. Serve with capsicum relish.
4 To make capsicum relish, heat
vinegar, sugar and mustard seeds for
5 minutes, or until sugar dissolves and
mixture boils. Add remaining
ingredients. Bring to boil, reduce heat
and simmer, uncovered, 30 minutes.

1

2

3

82

VEGETABLE WONTONS WITH CHILLI SAUCE

Preparation time: 40 minutes +
  30 minutes soaking
Total cooking time: 20 minutes
Makes 25

8 dried Chinese mushrooms
1 tablespoon peanut oil
1 teaspoon sesame oil
1 teaspoon grated fresh ginger
2 spring onions (scallions),
  finely chopped
1 carrot, finely chopped
1 parsnip, finely chopped
80 g (2¾ oz) broccoli, cut into
  small florets
2 tablespoons breadcrumbs
1 tablespoon soy sauce
200 g (7 oz) packet wonton
  wrappers
oil, for deep-frying

Chilli sauce
1 tablespoon peanut oil
1 garlic clove, crushed
3 tablespoons sweet chilli sauce
2 tablespoons soy sauce
2 tablespoons sherry
1 tablespoon lemon juice

1 Soak mushrooms in hot water for 30 minutes. Drain mushrooms, squeeze to remove excess liquid. Remove stems, discard. Shred mushroom caps finely.

2 Heat oils in wok or heavy-based frying pan. Add ginger and spring onions. Cook 1 minute over medium heat. Add mushrooms, carrot, parsnip and broccoli and stir-fry for 3 minutes, or until vegetables are just softened. Add the breadcrumbs, soy sauce and 2 tablespoons water, stirring to combine. Remove from heat; cool.

3 Work with one wonton wrapper at a time, keeping the remainder covered with a damp tea towel to prevent them drying out. Place a heaped teaspoonful of vegetable mixture in the centre of each round. Moisten the edges of pastry with water, and pinch edges together to seal. Repeat procedure with remaining wrappers and filling. Heat the oil in a wok or deep-fryer. Cook wontons in batches (no more than four at a time) for 2 minutes, or until golden and crisp. Remove with tongs or a slotted spoon. Drain on paper towels. Serve immediately with chilli sauce.

4 To make chilli sauce, heat oil in a small pan, add garlic. Cook until just golden. Add chilli and soy sauces, sherry and juice, stir until smooth and heated through.

COOK'S FILE

Storage time: Vegetable mixture for wontons can be prepared up to Step 3, one day in advance. Store, covered, in refrigerator. Assemble and cook just before serving.

Hint: Wonton wrappers are available at Chinese food stores.

VEGETABLE FRITTATA WITH HUMMUS AND BLACK OLIVES

Preparation time: 35 minutes + cooling time
Total cooking time: 40 minutes
Makes 30 pieces

2 large red capsicums (peppers)
600 g (1 lb 5 oz) orange sweet potato, cut into 1 cm (½ inch) slices
3 tablespoons olive oil
2 leeks, finely sliced
2 cloves garlic, crushed
250 g (9 oz) zucchini (courgettes), thinly sliced
500 g (1 lb 2 oz) eggplant (aubergines), cut into 1 cm (½ inch) slices
8 eggs, lightly beaten
2 tablespoons finely chopped fresh basil
125 g (4½ oz/1¼ cups) grated Parmesan
200 g (7 oz) ready-made hummus
black olives, pitted and halved, to garnish

1 Cut the capsicums into large pieces, removing the seeds and membrane. Place, skin-side-up, under a hot grill (broiler) until the skin blackens and blisters. Cool in a plastic bag. Peel.
2 Cook the sweet potato in a saucepan of boiling water for 4–5 minutes, or until just tender. Drain.
3 Heat 1 tablespoon of the oil in a deep round 23 cm (9 inch) frying pan and stir the leek and garlic over medium heat for 1 minute, or until soft. Add the zucchini and cook for 2 minutes, then remove from the pan.

4 Heat the remaining oil and cook the eggplant in batches for 2 minutes each side, or until golden. Line the base of the pan with half the eggplant, then the leek. Cover with the capsicum, remaining eggplant and sweet potato.
5 Combine the eggs, basil, Parmesan and some pepper. Pour over the vegetables. Cook on low for 15 minutes, or until almost cooked. Place the pan under a hot grill for 2–3 minutes, or until golden and cooked. Cool, then invert onto a board. Trim and cut into 30 squares. Top with hummus and half an olive.

Lay the roasted capsicum pieces over the leek and zucchini mixture.

Pour the egg mixture over the vegetables so that they are covered.

Cook the frittata under a hot grill until it is golden brown on top.

SALT AND PEPPER TOFU PUFFS

Preparation time: 15 minutes
Total cooking time: 10 minutes
Serves 4–6

2 x 190 g (7 oz) packets fried
   tofu puffs
250 g (9 oz/2 cups) cornflour
   (cornstarch)
2 tablespoons salt
1 tablespoon ground white
   pepper
2 teaspoons caster (superfine)
   sugar
4 egg whites, lightly beaten
oil, for deep-frying (see Note)
125 ml (4 fl oz/½ cup) sweet
   chilli sauce
2 tablespoons lemon juice
lemon wedges, to serve

1 Cut the tofu puffs in half and pat
dry with paper towels.

2 Mix the cornflour, salt, pepper and
sugar together well in a large bowl.
3 Dip the tofu into the egg white in
batches, then toss in the cornflour
mixture, shaking off any excess.
4 Fill a deep heavy-based saucepan
or wok one third full of oil and heat
until a cube of bread dropped into the
oil browns in 15 seconds. Cook the tofu
in batches for 1–2 minutes, or until
crisp. Drain well on crumpled paper
towels.

*Dip the tofu puffs in the egg white, then in
the cornflour, shaking off any excess.*

5 Combine the sweet chilli sauce and
lemon juice. Serve immediately with
the tofu puffs and lemon wedges.

COOK'S FILE

Note: Use a good-quality peanut oil to
deep-fry the tofu puffs—the flavour
will be slightly nutty.

*Deep-fry the tofu in batches until crisp,
then remove with a slotted spoon.*

Using a sharp knife, cut the onions into very thin slices.

Simmer the spicy tomato mixture until it thickens.

Stir the coriander and onion into the batter.

Drop spoonfuls of the batter into the oil and cook in batches until golden.

ONION BHAJIS WITH SPICY TOMATO SAUCE

Preparation time: 30 minutes
Total cooking time: 35 minutes
Makes about 25

Spicy tomato sauce
2–3 red chillies, chopped
1 red capsicum (pepper), diced
425 g (15 oz) can chopped
   tomatoes
2 cloves garlic, finely chopped
2 tablespoons soft brown sugar
1½ tablespoons cider vinegar

125 g (4½ oz/1 cup) plain (all-purpose) flour
2 teaspoons baking powder
½ teaspoon chilli powder
½ teaspoon ground turmeric
1 teaspoon ground cumin

2 eggs, beaten
50 g (1¾ oz/1 cup) chopped
   fresh coriander (cilantro)
   leaves
4 onions, very thinly sliced
oil, for deep-frying

1 Combine sauce ingredients with 3 tablespoons water in a saucepan. Bring to the boil, then reduce heat and simmer for 20 minutes, or until it thickens. Remove from the heat.
2 To make the bhajis, sift the flour, baking powder, spices and 1 teaspoon salt into a bowl and make a well in the centre. Gradually add the combined egg and 3 tablespoons water, whisking to make a smooth batter. Stir in the coriander and onion.
3 Fill a deep heavy-based saucepan one third full of oil and heat until a cube of bread dropped into the oil browns in 15 seconds. Cook dessertspoons of the mixture in the oil in batches for 90 seconds each side, or until golden. Drain. Serve with sauce.

INDIVIDUAL SILVERBEET SOUFFLÉS

Preparation time: 20 minutes
Total cooking time: 25 minutes
Serves 4

4 tablespoons dry breadcrumbs
100 g (3½ oz) silverbeet (Swiss chard) leaves
40 g (1½ oz) butter
2 tablespoons plain (all-purpose) flour
250 ml (9 fl oz/1 cup) milk
4 eggs, separated
60 g (2¼ oz/½ cup) finely grated Cheddar cheese
2 tablespoons freshly grated Parmesan cheese
pinch cayenne pepper, to taste
1 tablespoon freshly grated Parmesan cheese, extra

1 Preheat oven to 180°C (350°F/ Gas 4). Brush four 185 ml (6 fl oz/ ¾ cup) soufflé dishes with melted butter or oil. Coat base and sides evenly with breadcrumbs, shake off excess.

2 Wash silverbeet leaves thoroughly. Shred finely, and steam for 1 minute, until just tender; cool. Using your hands, squeeze all excess moisture. Spread to separate strands. Set aside.

3 Heat butter in a medium pan; add flour. Stir over a low heat 2 minutes, or until lightly golden. Add milk gradually to pan, stirring until mixture is smooth. Stir constantly over medium heat 2 minutes until mixture boils and thickens; boil 1 minute more. Remove from heat. Add egg yolks, beat until smooth. Add cheeses and cayenne; season with salt. Stir until melted and almost smooth; stir in spinach.

4 Using electric beaters, beat egg whites in a clean dry bowl until stiff peaks form. Using a metal spoon, fold gently into silverbeet mixture.

5 Spoon into prepared soufflé dishes, bake for 20 minutes, or until well risen and browned. Sprinkle with the extra Parmesan and serve immediately.

1

2

3

4

CRISP POLENTA WITH MUSHROOMS

Preparation time: 20 minutes +
  10 minutes soaking + 30 minutes
  refrigeration
Total cooking time: 40 minutes
Serves 4

1 litre (4 cups) vegetable
  stock
150 g (5½ oz/1 cup) polenta
  (cornmeal)
2 tablespoons margarine
1 tablespoon grated fresh
  Parmesan cheese
rocket (arugula), to serve
fresh Parmesan cheese, shaved,
  to serve

Mushroom sauce
10 g (¼ oz) dried porcini
  mushrooms
1 tablespoon olive oil
800 g (1 lb 12 oz) mixed
  mushrooms (field, Swiss
  browns), thickly sliced
4 cloves garlic, finely chopped
2 teaspoons chopped thyme
185 ml (6 fl oz/¾ cup) dry white
  wine

125 ml (4 fl oz/½ cup) vegetable
  stock
30 g (1 oz/½ cup) chopped
  parsley

1 Bring the stock to the boil in a large
saucepan. Add the polenta in a thin
stream, stirring constantly. Simmer for
20 minutes over very low heat, stirring
frequently, or until the mixture starts
to leave the sides of the pan. Add the
margarine and Parmesan. Season.
Grease a shallow 20 cm (8 inch) square
cake tin. Pour in the polenta, smooth
the surface and refrigerate for
30 minutes, or until set.
2 For the mushroom sauce, soak the
porcini mushrooms in 125 ml (4 fl oz/

½ cup) boiling water for 10 minutes,
until soft. Drain well, reserving
4 tablespoons liquid.
3 Heat the oil in a large frying pan.
Add mixed mushrooms. Cook over
high heat for 4–5 minutes, or until
soft. Add the porcini, garlic and thyme.
Season and cook for 2–3 minutes. Add
the wine. Cook until it has evaporated.
Add the stock, then reduce the heat.
Cook for a further 3–4 minutes, or
until the stock has reduced and
thickened. Add the parsley.
4 Cut the polenta into 4 squares and
grill (broil) until golden on both sides.
Place one on each serving plate and
top with the mushrooms. Garnish with
rocket and Parmesan shavings.

*Cook the porcini and mixed mushrooms
over high heat until softened.*

*Cook squares of polenta until golden on
both sides.*

SALAD BASKETS WITH BERRY DRESSING

Preparation time: 20 minutes
Total cooking time: 15 minutes
Serves 4

12 sheets filo pastry
50 g (1¾ oz) butter, melted
160 g (5¾ oz) salad mix
8 cherry tomatoes, halved
½ small red capsicum (pepper), thinly sliced
1 small Lebanese (short) cucumber, thinly sliced
155 g (5½ oz/1 cup) blueberries, extra

Blueberry dressing
125 ml (4 fl oz/½ cup) olive oil
2 tablespoons balsamic vinegar
1 tablespoon soft brown sugar
4 tablespoons frozen blueberries, thawed, lightly crushed

1 Preheat oven to 180°C (350°F/ Gas 4).Brush the outer base of four 8 cm (3 inch) round, 125 ml (4 fl oz/ ½ cup) ramekin dishes with melted butter or oil. Line two oven trays with baking paper.
2 Place one sheet of filo pastry on work surface. Brush pastry lightly with melted butter, place another sheet on top. Repeat with a third layer. Fold pastry in half. Using a plate as a guide, cut a 21 cm (8½ inch) circle out of the pastry with a sharp knife. Place pastry over base of prepared ramekins. Carefully fold pastry around the ramekin to form a basket shape. Place on prepared trays. Repeat process for three more baskets. Bake 15 minutes, or until golden. Carefully remove filo basket from ramekin while hot; place baskets on wire rack to cool.
3 To make blueberry dressing, combine oil, vinegar and brown sugar in small bowl, add crushed berries. Mix well.
4 Combine salad mix, tomatoes, capsicum, cucumber and dressing in bowl. Mix well. Spoon into pastry baskets, top with extra blueberries.

COOK'S FILE

Storage time: Filo baskets can be prepared up to two hours ahead. Fill with salad mixture just before serving. Dressing can be prepared one day in advance. Store in an airtight container in refrigerator.

1

2

3

EGGPLANT AND SPINACH TERRINE

Preparation time: 1 hour + overnight
 refrigeration
Total cooking time: 55 minutes
Serves 6

3 large red capsicums (peppers)
1 large old potato, halved
40 g (1½ oz) butter
2 cloves garlic, crushed
800 g (1 lb 12 oz) English
 spinach leaves, shredded
3 tablespoons cream
1 egg yolk
4 tablespoons olive oil
2 eggplants (aubergines), cut
 into thin slices lengthways
30 g (1 oz/1 cup) fresh basil
350 g (12 oz) ricotta
2 cloves garlic, crushed, extra

1 Cut the capsicums into large pieces, removing the seeds and membranes. Cook, skin-side-up, under a hot grill (broiler) until the skin blisters. Cool, then peel.

2 Preheat the oven to moderate 180°C (350°F/Gas 4). Grease and line a 1.5 litre (6 cup) terrine. Bring a saucepan of salted water to the boil and cook the potato for 10 minutes. Drain and cool. Cut into thin slices.

3 Melt the butter in a large saucepan and cook the garlic for 30 seconds. Add the spinach and toss. Steam, covered, over low heat for 2–3 minutes, or until wilted. Cool slightly and place in a food processor or blender and process until smooth. Squeeze out any excess liquid, place in a bowl and stir the cream and egg in well.

4 Heat a chargrill plate or griddle over high heat and brush with some of the oil. Cook the eggplant for 2–3 minutes each side, or until golden, brushing with the remaining oil.

5 To assemble, arrange one third of the eggplant neatly in the base of the terrine, cutting to fit. Top with a layer of half the capsicum, spinach mixture, basil, all the potato, and all the combined ricotta and garlic. Repeat with the remaining ingredients, finishing with eggplant. Oil a piece of foil and cover the terrine, sealing well. Place in a baking dish and half fill with water. Bake for 25–30 minutes. Remove from the oven, put a piece of cardboard on top and weigh it down with small food cans. Chill overnight.

6 Turn out and cut into slices.

Grill the capsicum pieces until the skin blackens, cool in a plastic bag, then peel.

Blend the spinach mixture in a food processor until smooth.

Spread a layer of the spinach mixture over the second layer of capsicum.

STUFFED ZUCCHINI BLOSSOMS

Preparation time: 25 minutes
Total cooking time: 20 minutes
Serves 4

125 g (4½ oz/½ cup) ricotta
    cheese
60 g (2¼ oz/½ cup) finely
    grated Cheddar or mozzarella
    cheese
2 tablespoons chopped chives
12 zucchini (courgette) blossoms
4 tablespoons plain (all-purpose)
    flour

Batter
125 g (4½ oz/1 cup) plain
    (all-purpose) flour, extra
1 egg, lightly beaten
185 ml (6 fl oz/¾ cup) iced
    water
oil for deep frying

Tomato sauce
1 tablespoon olive oil, extra
1 small onion, finely chopped
1 clove garlic, crushed
425 g (15 oz) can tomatoes
½ teaspoon dried oregano

1 Combine ricotta, Cheddar or mozzarella, and chives in a small mixing bowl. Gently open out zucchini blossoms, remove stamens and spoon in cheese mixture. Close up blossoms and twist ends to seal. Dust lightly with flour then shake off excess.
2 To make batter, place flour in a medium bowl, make a well in centre. Add the egg and water and beat until all liquid is incorporated and batter is free of lumps. Heat oil in a large pan until moderately hot. Using tongs, dip each blossom into batter then lower into oil. Fry blossoms until just golden;

drain on paper towels. Serve immediately with tomato sauce.
3 To make tomato sauce, heat oil in a small pan, add onion. Cook over medium heat for 3 minutes, until onion is soft. Add garlic and cook for another minute. Add undrained, crushed tomatoes and oregano and stir to combine. Bring mixture to boil, reduce

heat and simmer gently for 10 minutes. Serve sauce hot.

COOK'S FILE

Note: Small zucchini blossoms often have a baby zucchini still attached to them; larger blossoms are sometimes available without zucchini. They are available from most greengrocers.

ARTICHOKES WITH TARRAGON MAYONNAISE

Preparation time: 30 minutes
Total cooking time: 30 minutes
Serves 4

4 medium globe artichokes
3 tablespoons lemon juice

Tarragon mayonnaise
1 egg yolk
1 tablespoon tarragon
   vinegar
½ teaspoon French mustard
170 ml (5½ fl oz/⅔ cup)
   olive oil

1 Trim stalks from the base of the artichokes. Using scissors, trim points from outer leaves. Using a sharp knife, cut top from artichoke. Brush all cut areas of artichokes with lemon juice to prevent discolouration.

2 Steam artichokes for 30 minutes, until tender. Top up pan with boiling water if necessary. Remove from heat and set aside to cool.

3 To make tarragon mayonnaise, place egg yolk, vinegar and mustard in a medium mixing bowl. Using a wire whisk, beat for 1 minute. At first, add oil a teaspoon at a time, whisking constantly until mixture is thick and creamy. As the mayonnaise thickens, pour oil in a thin, steady stream.

Continue whisking until all the oil is added. Season to taste. Place a cooled artichoke on each plate with a little tarragon mayonnaise.

COOK'S FILE

Storage time: Artichokes may be cooked up to four hours in advance. Mayonnaise may be made up to two hours in advance and refrigerated.

Hint: To eat artichokes, take off a leaf at a time, dip base of leaf in mayonnaise and scrape off fleshy base with teeth. Towards the centre of the artichoke, the leaves are more tender and more of the leaf is edible. Provide a bowl for discarded leaves.

TEMPURA VEGETABLES WITH WASABI MAYONNAISE

Preparation time: 20 minutes
Total cooking time: 20 minutes
Serves 4–6

Wasabi mayonnaise
2 tablespoons whole-egg
  mayonnaise
3 teaspoons wasabi paste
½ teaspoon grated lime rind

2 egg yolks
250 ml (9 fl oz/1 cup) chilled
  soda water
3 tablespoons cornflour
  (cornstarch)
110 g (4 oz/¾ cup) plain
  (all-purpose) flour
3 tablespoons sesame seeds,
  toasted
oil, for deep-frying
1 small (250 g/9 oz) eggplant
  (aubergine), cut into thin
  rounds
1 large onion, cut into thin
  rounds, with rings intact
300 g (10½ oz) orange sweet
  potato, cut into thin rounds

1 To make the wasabi mayonnaise, combine all the ingredients. Transfer to a serving bowl, cover with plastic wrap and refrigerate.
2 Place the egg yolks and soda water in a jug and mix lightly with a whisk. Sift the cornflour and flour into a bowl. Add the sesame seeds and a good sprinkling of salt and mix well. Pour the soda water and egg yolk mixture into the flour and stir lightly with chopsticks or a fork until just combined but still lumpy.

3 Fill a deep heavy-based saucepan or wok one-third full of oil and heat until a cube of bread dropped into the oil browns in 15 seconds. Dip pairs of the vegetables—eggplant and onion or eggplant and sweet potato—into the batter and cook in batches for 3–4 minutes, or until golden brown and cooked through. Drain on crumpled paper towels; season well. Keep warm, but do not cover or the tempura coating will go soggy.
4 Transfer the tempura to a warmed serving platter and serve immediately with the wasabi mayonnaise.

Gently stir the combined soda water and egg yolk into the flour mixture.

Dip assorted pairs of the vegetables into the batter.

Deep-fry the battered vegetables until they are golden brown and cooked through.

EGGPLANT AND CORIANDER TOSTADAS

Preparation time: 20 minutes
Total cooking time: 30 minutes
Serves 4

1 small eggplant (aubergine), cut into cubes
½ red capsicum (pepper), cut into cubes
½ red onion, cut into thin wedges
2 tablespoons olive oil
1 large clove garlic, crushed
1 small loaf wood-fired bread, cut into twelve 1.5 cm (⅝ inch) slices

1 small ripe tomato, halved
2 tablespoons chopped fresh mint
2 tablespoons chopped fresh coriander (cilantro) roots, stems and leaves
50 g (1¾ oz) slivered almonds, toasted

1 Preheat the oven to very hot 240°C (475°F/Gas 9). Place the eggplant, capsicum, onion and oil in a large bowl and mix until the vegetables are well coated in the oil. Spread the vegetables in a single layer in a large roasting tin. Bake for 15 minutes, then turn and bake for a further 10 minutes, or until tender. Transfer to a bowl, add the garlic and season.

2 Bake the bread on a baking tray for 4 minutes, or until crisp. Rub the cut side of the tomato onto one side of the bread slices, squeezing the tomato to extract as much liquid as possible, then finely chop the flesh. Add to the vegetables along with the herbs.

3 Spoon the vegetable mixture onto the tomato side of the bread and sprinkle with the almonds. Serve immediately.

COOK'S FILE

Note: You can roast the vegetables and toast the almonds up to a day ahead. Store the vegetables in an airtight container in the refrigerator.

Lay the vegetable mixture in a single layer in a large roasting tin.

Place the vegetable mixture and garlic in a bowl and mix together.

Rub the cut side of the tomato onto one side of each slice of bread.

TWO-CHEESE RISOTTO CAKES

Preparation time: 30 minutes + 1 hour 15 minutes refrigeration
Total cooking time: 30 minutes
Serves 6

810 ml (28 fl oz/3¼ cups) vegetable stock
1 tablespoon olive oil
20 g (½ oz) butter
1 small onion, finely chopped
275 g (9¾ oz/1¼ cups) short-grain rice
4 tablespoons freshly grated Parmesan cheese
30 g (1 oz) mozzarella cheese, cut into 1 cm (½ inch) cubes
3 tablespoons sun-dried (sun-blushed) tomatoes, chopped
oil, for deep-frying
70 g (2½ oz) mixed salad leaves, to serve

1 Boil stock in small pan. Reduce heat, cover; keep gently simmering. Heat oil and butter in a medium heavy-based pan. Add onion, stir over medium heat 3 minutes until golden; add rice. Reduce heat to low, stir 3 minutes, or until lightly golden. Add a quarter of the stock to pan. Stir 5 minutes, or until all liquid is absorbed.

2 Repeat process until all stock has been added and rice is almost tender, stirring constantly. Stir in Parmesan. Remove from heat. Transfer to a bowl to cool; refrigerate 1 hour.

3 With wetted hands gently roll 2 tablespoonfuls of the rice mixture into a ball. Make an indentation into the ball, and press in a cube of mozzarella and a couple of pieces of sun-dried tomato. Reshape ball to cover completely, then flatten slightly to a disc shape. Refrigerate for 15 minutes.

4 Heat oil in a medium heavy-based pan. Gently lower risotto cakes a few at a time into moderately hot oil. Cook 1–2 minutes, or until golden brown. Remove with a slotted spoon; drain on paper towel.

5 To serve, arrange salad leaves on each plate and place three risotto cakes on top. Serve immediately.

EGGPLANT, TOMATO AND GOAT'S CHEESE STACKS

Preparation time: 15 minutes
Total cooking time: 20 minutes
Serves 4

125 ml (4 fl oz/½ cup)
    olive oil
2 large cloves garlic, crushed
2 small eggplants (aubergines)
2 ripe tomatoes
150 g (5½ oz) goat's cheese
8 basil leaves
small rocket (arugula) leaves,
    to garnish

Dressing
285 g (9¾ oz) jar sun-dried
    (sun-blushed) tomatoes,
    drained, reserving
    1 tablespoon oil
1 clove garlic, crushed
2 tablespoons white wine
    vinegar
2 tablespoons whole-egg
    mayonnaise

1 Mix the oil and garlic together. Cut each eggplant into six 1 cm (½ inch) slices, then cut each tomato into four 1 cm (½ inch) slices. Using a sharp knife dipped in hot water, cut the cheese into eight 1 cm (½ inch) slices.

2 Brush the eggplant with half the oil mixture. Heat a frying pan and cook the eggplant in batches over high heat for 3–4 minutes each side, or until golden. Remove and keep warm. Brush the tomato with the remaining oil mixture. Cook for 1 minute each side, or until sealed and warmed through.

3 To make the dressing, blend the sun-dried tomatoes, reserved oil and the garlic in a food processor until smooth. Add the vinegar and process until combined. Transfer to a bowl and stir in the mayonnaise. Season.

4 To assemble, place an eggplant slice on each plate. Top with a slice of tomato, then a basil leaf and a slice of cheese. Repeat with the remaining ingredients to give two layers, then finish with a third piece of eggplant. Add a dollop of dressing and arrange the rocket leaves around each stack. Serve immediately.

Cut the eggplant, tomato and cheese into 1 cm (½ inch) slices.

Cook the eggplant over high heat for 3–4 minutes each side, or until golden.

Cook the tomato slices on both sides until sealed and warmed through.

Stir the mayonnaise into the sun-dried tomato mixture.

VEGETABLE FRITTERS WITH TOMATO SAUCE

Preparation time: 30 minutes
Total cooking time: 36 minutes
Makes 12

2 potatoes
1 carrot
2 zucchini (courgettes)
120 g (4¼ oz) sweet potato,
    peeled
1 small leek
2 tablespoons plain (all-purpose)
    flour
3 eggs, lightly beaten
oil, for frying

Fresh tomato sauce
1 tablespoon oil
1 small onion, finely chopped
1 garlic clove, crushed
½ teaspoon ground paprika
3 ripe tomatoes, finely chopped
3 tablespoons finely shredded
    fresh basil

1 Finely grate potatoes, carrot, zucchini and sweet potato. Finely slice leek (white part only). Cup small handfuls of the vegetables in both hands and squeeze out as much excess moisture as possible. Combine well in a large mixing bowl.

2 Sprinkle flour over vegetables, and combine. Add eggs and mix well. Heat about 5 mm (¼ inch) of oil in a frying pan and drop 3 tablespoons of mixture in a neat pile. Use a fork to gently form mixture into a 10 cm (4 inch) round. Fry 2–3 at a time for 3 minutes each side over medium heat until golden. Drain on paper towels; keep warm. Repeat with remaining mix.

3 To make tomato sauce, heat oil in a small pan. Add onion, garlic and paprika; cook over medium heat 3 minutes, or until soft. Add tomatoes, reduce heat to low, and cook 10 minutes, stirring occasionally. Stir in basil. Serve warm.

COOK'S FILE

Storage time: Make fritters just before serving. Tomato sauce can be made up to eight hours in advance.

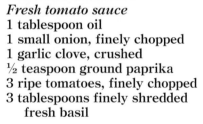

SPINACH CROQUETTES WITH MINTED YOGHURT SAUCE

Preparation time: 50 minutes
Total cooking time: 25 minutes +
  1 hour refrigeration
Makes 18

330 g (11½ oz/1½ cups) short-
  grain rice
250 g (9 oz) feta cheese,
  crumbled
3 tablespoons grated Parmesan
  cheese
2 eggs, lightly beaten
1 garlic clove, crushed
2 teaspoons grated lemon
  zest
60 g (2¼ oz/½ cup) chopped
  spring onions (scallions)
250 g (9 oz) packet frozen
  spinach, drained, squeezed
  of excess moisture
1 tablespoon chopped dill
200 g (7 oz/2 cups) dry
  breadcrumbs
2 eggs, lightly beaten, extra
oil, for deep-frying

Yoghurt sauce
200 g (7 oz) plain yoghurt
2 tablespoons chopped fresh
  mint
2 tablespoons lemon juice

1 Cook rice in a large pan of boiling water until just tender; drain, rinse under cold water, drain again. Combine rice, cheeses, eggs, garlic, lemon, onions, spinach and dill in a large bowl. Using wet hands, divide the mixture into 18 portions. Roll each portion into even-sized sausage shapes. Place on tray. Refrigerate for 30 minutes.

2 Spread breadcrumbs on a sheet of greaseproof paper. Dip croquettes into extra beaten egg mixture. Coat with breadcrumbs; shake off excess. Refrigerate a further 30 minutes.

3 To make yoghurt sauce, combine the yoghurt, mint, lemon juice, salt and pepper in a bowl. Mix well. Cover, refrigerate until needed.

4 Heat oil in a deep heavy-based pan. Gently lower batches of croquettes into moderately hot oil with tongs or slotted spoon. Cook over medium high heat 2–3 minutes, or until golden and crisp and cooked through. Drain on paper towels. Repeat with remaining croquettes. Serve croquettes hot or cold with the yoghurt sauce.

COOK'S FILE

Storage time: Croquettes can be made up to two days in advance. Cook just before serving.

Variation: Use fresh, lightly steamed spinach in place of frozen spinach if preferred. Use the same gram weight.

ROAST SWEET POTATO WITH CORIANDER PESTO AND SPRING SALAD

Preparation time: 30 minutes
Total cooking time: 35–40 minutes
Serves 6

850 g (1 lb 14 oz) orange sweet
   potato, peeled
2 tablespoons lemon juice
12 asparagus spears
1 red capsicum (pepper)
1 small Lebanese (short)
   cucumber
160 g (5¾ oz) salad mix

Coriander pesto
100 g (3½ oz/⅔ cup) pine nuts
1 red chilli, seeded
2 garlic cloves
45 g (1½ oz) coriander (cilantro)
   leaves and roots, chopped
2 teaspoons lime juice
2 tablespoons oil

1 Preheat oven to 180°C (350°F/Gas 4). Peel sweet potato and cut into 1 cm (½ inch) slices. Place in a bowl, cover with iced water and lemon juice. Leave for 5 minutes, drain and pat dry with paper towels.

2 Heat oil in a deep baking dish on top of stove. Add potato, lightly coat with oil. Transfer dish to oven. Bake 30 minutes, or until golden. Remove; keep warm.

3 To make coriander pesto, place pine nuts in small pan. Stir over medium heat until golden. Remove from heat, cool slightly. Place pine nuts, chilli, garlic, coriander, juice and oil in a food processor. Using the pulse action, process for 30 seconds, or until smooth. If mixture is too thick, add a little extra oil to thin. Cover, set aside.

4 Plunge asparagus into a pan of boiling water. Cook for 1 minute, or until just tender, drain. Plunge into bowl of iced water, drain. Pat dry with paper towels. Cut asparagus into 5 cm (2 inch) pieces. Cut capsicum into quarters. Remove seeds and membrane. Place skin-side up on grill (broiler) tray; brush with oil. Grill (broil) 10 minutes, or until skin is black. Cover with damp tea towel until cool. Peel off skin. Cut capsicum into long thin strips. Cut cucumber into matchstick thin strips. Arrange salad mix, asparagus, capsicum and cucumber in a serving bowl. Serve sweet potato separately; top with coriander pesto.

COOK'S FILE

Storage time: Except for roast capsicum, which can be made one day ahead, cook and assemble this dish just before serving.

CHILLI PUFFS WITH CURRIED VEGETABLES

Preparation time: 20 minutes
Total cooking time: 1 hour 5 minutes
Makes 12

90 g (3¼ oz) butter
155 g (5½ oz/1¼ cups) plain
    (all-purpose) flour, sifted
¼ teaspoon chilli powder
4 eggs, lightly beaten
4 yellow squash
100 g (3½ oz) snow peas
    (mangetout)
1 carrot
50 g (1¾ oz) butter, extra
2 medium onions, sliced
2 tablespoons mild curry paste
300 g (10½ oz) small oyster
    mushrooms
1 tablespoon lemon juice

1 Preheat oven to 240°C (475°F/Gas 8). Grease and line two 32 x 28 cm (13 x 11 inch) oven trays. Combine the butter and 310 ml (10¾ fl oz/1¼ cups) water in a medium pan. Stir over low heat 5 minutes, or until butter has melted and mixture reaches the boil. Remove from heat; add flour and chilli all at once, stir with a wooden spoon until just combined.

2 Return pan to heat, beating constantly over low heat 3 minutes, or until it thickens and comes away from side and base of pan. Transfer mixture to a large bowl. Using electric beaters, beat mixture on high speed for 1 minute. Add eggs gradually, beating until mixture is glossy. (This stage could take up to 5 minutes.)

3 Place 2 heaped tablespoons of mixture at a time onto prepared trays about 10 cm (4 inches) apart. Bake on top shelf for 20 minutes. Reduce heat to 210°C (415°F/Gas 6–7) and bake for

30 minutes, or until crisp and well browned. (Cut a small slit into each puff halfway during cooking to allow excess steam to escape and puff to dry out.) Cool puffs on a wire rack.

4 Slice squash thinly. Cut snow peas in half diagonally. Cut carrot into thin strips. Heat butter in pan, add onion. Cook over low heat 5 minutes, or until golden; stir in curry paste. Add mushrooms and vegetables, stir over high heat for 1 minute. Add lemon

juice, remove from heat, stir. Cut puffs in half (see Note) and fill with the vegetables. Serve immediately.

COOK'S FILE

Note: A small amount of uncooked choux mixture in the centre of cooked curry puffs is a result of the large size of the puffs. Remove mixture using a spoon, then dry out the shells in a warm oven.

1

2

3

ROASTED TOMATOES AND EGGPLANT WITH RED LENTIL PURÉE

Preparation time: 20 minutes
Total cooking time: 1 hour 10 minutes
Serves 6

3 tablespoons extra virgin olive
   oil
1 tablespoon balsamic vinegar
700 g (1 lb 9 oz) Roma (plum)
   tomatoes, halved lengthways
500 g (1 lb 2 oz) eggplant
   (aubergine), cut into 1.5 cm
   (⅝ inch) slices
150 g (5½ oz) rocket (arugula)
3 tablespoons pine nuts, toasted

Red lentil purée
625 ml (21½ fl oz/2½ cups)
   vegetable stock
200 g (7 oz) red lentils
1 teaspoon paprika
1 clove garlic, crushed

1 Preheat the oven to moderate 180°C (350°F/Gas 4). Line a large baking tray with foil and grease with oil. To make the balsamic vinaigrette, whisk together the oil, vinegar, ¼ teaspoon each of salt and cracked black pepper.
2 Place the tomatoes, cut-side-up, and eggplant on the baking tray and brush with 1 tablespoon of the balsamic vinaigrette. Bake for 40 minutes. Transfer the eggplant to a plate and keep warm. Return the tomatoes to the oven and bake for 30 minutes, or until starting to brown on the edges. Transfer to a plate.
3 Meanwhile, to make the lentil purée, place the stock in a saucepan and bring to the boil. Add the lentils and paprika, return to the boil, then

reduce the heat and simmer for 10 minutes, or until the lentils are tender. Add 1 tablespoon of the balsamic vinaigrette, then the garlic and continue stirring for 5 minutes, or until the lentils break up and form a thick purée. Season.

4 To serve, divide the red lentil purée among six serving plates. Top with the rocket leaves, then the eggplant and tomato. Drizzle with the remaining balsamic vinaigrette and sprinkle with pine nuts. Serve with crusty bread.

Place the oil, vinegar, salt and pepper in a small bowl and whisk.

Bake the tomatoes until they are shrivelled and just brown on the edges.

Cook the lentil mixture until the lentils break up and form a thick purée.

VEGETARIAN CALIFORNIA ROLLS

Preparation time: 35 minutes +
  15 minutes standing
Total cooking time: 15 minutes
Makes 30

500 g (1 lb 2 oz/2¼ cups) short-
  grain white rice
3 tablespoons rice vinegar
1 tablespoon caster (superfine)
  sugar
5 nori sheets
1 large Lebanese (short)
  cucumber, cut lengthways
  into long batons
1 avocado, thinly sliced
1 tablespoon black sesame
  seeds, toasted
30 g (1 oz) pickled ginger
  slices
3 teaspoons wasabi paste
125 g (4½ oz/½ cup) whole-egg
  mayonnaise
2 teaspoons soy sauce

1 Wash the rice under cold running water, until the water runs clear. Put the rice and 750 ml (26 fl oz/3 cups) water in a saucepan, bring to the boil over low heat and cook for 5 minutes, or until tunnels form. Remove from the heat, cover and leave for 15 minutes.
2 Stir the vinegar, sugar and 1 teaspoon salt in a saucepan over low heat until the sugar and salt dissolve.
3 Transfer the rice to a non-metallic bowl and separate the grains. Make a slight well in the centre, slowly stir in the vinegar dressing, then leave to cool a little.
4 To assemble, lay a nori sheet, shiny-side-down, on a bamboo mat or flat surface and spread out one fifth of the rice, leaving a 2 cm (¾ inch) border at one end. Arrange one fifth of the cucumber, avocado, sesame seeds and ginger lengthways over the rice, 3 cm (1¼ inches) from the border. Spread on some combined wasabi, mayonnaise and soy sauce and roll to cover the filling, then roll tightly to join the edge. Hold in place for a few seconds. Trim the ends and cut into 2 cm (¾ inch) slices. Repeat. Serve with remaining wasabi mayonnaise.

Cook the rice until tunnels appear, then cover and leave for 15 minutes.

Slowly pour the vinegar dressing into the rice and stir it through.

Spread the wasabi mayonnaise mixture over the vegetables and start rolling.

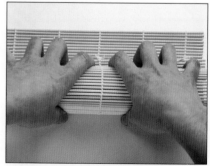

Roll the mat tightly to join the edge, then hold in place for a few seconds.

VIETNAMESE SPRING ROLLS

Preparation time: 30 minutes +
10 minutes standing
Total cooking time: 10 minutes
Serves 4 (Makes 16)

75 g (2½ oz) dried rice
vermicelli
200 g (7 oz) firm tofu
1 teaspoon sesame oil
1 tablespoon peanut oil
1 packet 15 cm (6 inch) square
rice-paper wrappers
½ small Lebanese (short)
cucumber, cut into strips
½ carrot, cut into strips
1 handful fresh mint
4 tablespoons roasted salted
cashews, roughly chopped
3 tablespoons hoisin sauce
2 tablespoons kecap manis
1 tablespoon lime juice

1 Place the vermicelli in a bowl, cover with boiling water and leave for 10 minutes. Drain well.

2 Pat the tofu dry and cut into four 2 x 7 cm (¾ x 2¾ inch) slices. Heat the oils in a large frying pan and cook the tofu over medium heat for 3 minutes each side, or until golden brown. Drain on paper towels. Cut each tofu slice into four widthways.

3 Fill a bowl with warm water. Dip one wrapper at a time into the water for about 15 seconds, or until pliable.

4 Place a wrapper on a work surface, top with some vermicelli, tofu, cucumber, carrot, mint and cashews. Roll tightly, folding in the sides and place on a plate, seam-side-down. Cover with a damp cloth and repeat.

5 Mix the hoisin sauce, kecap manis and lime juice in a bowl. Serve immediately with the spring rolls.

Cook the tofu over medium heat, turning once, until golden brown on both sides.

Dip one wrapper at a time into the water until soft and pliable.

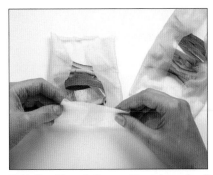

Fold the sides of the wrappers in and roll up tightly, enclosing the filling.

INDIVIDUAL VEGETABLE TERRINES WITH A SPICY TOMATO SAUCE

Preparation time: 40 minutes
Total cooking time: 50 minutes
Serves 4

125 ml (4 fl oz/½ cup) oil
2 zucchini (courgettes), sliced on the diagonal
500 g (1 lb 2 oz) eggplant (aubergines), sliced
1 small fennel bulb, sliced
1 red onion, sliced
300 g (10½ oz) ricotta
50 g (1¾ oz/½ cup) grated Parmesan
1 tablespoon chopped fresh flat-leaf (Italian) parsley
1 tablespoon chopped fresh chives
1 red and 1 yellow capsicum (pepper), grilled (broiled), peeled, cut into large pieces

Spicy tomato sauce
1 tablespoon oil
1 onion, finely chopped
2 cloves garlic, crushed
1 red chilli, seeded and chopped
425 g (15 oz) can chopped tomatoes
2 tablespoons tomato paste (concentrated purée)

1 Heat 1 tablespoon of the oil in a large frying pan. Cook the vegetables in batches over high heat for 5 minutes, or until golden, adding oil as needed. Drain separately on paper towels.
2 Preheat the oven to moderately hot 200°C (400°F/Gas 6). Mix the cheeses and herbs together well. Season.

3 Lightly grease and line four 315 ml (11 fl oz/1¼ cup) ramekins. Using half the eggplant, layer the base of each dish. Continue layering with the zucchini, capsicum, cheese mixture, fennel and onion. Cover with the remaining eggplant and press down firmly. Bake for 10–15 minutes, or until hot. Leave for 5 minutes before turning out.

4 Meanwhile, to make the sauce, heat the oil in a saucepan and cook the onion and garlic for 2–3 minutes, or until soft. Add the chilli, tomato and tomato paste and simmer for 5 minutes, or until thick and pulpy. Purée in a food processor. Return to the saucepan and keep warm. Spoon over the terrines.

Cook the capsicums under a hot grill (broiler) until blackened.

Layer the fennel over the cheese mixture, then add a layer of onion.

Simmer the tomato sauce for 5 minutes, or until thick and pulpy.

TOFU WITH CARROT AND GINGER SAUCE

Preparation time: 25 minutes +
  overnight refrigeration
Total cooking time: 30 minutes
Serves 6

600 g (1 lb 5 oz) firm tofu
125 ml (4 fl oz/½ cup) orange juice
1 tablespoon soft brown sugar
1 tablespoon soy sauce
2 tablespoons chopped fresh
  coriander (cilantro) leaves
2 cloves garlic, crushed
1 teaspoon grated fresh ginger
2–3 tablespoons oil
1 kg (2 lb 4 oz) baby bok choy,
  quartered lengthways

Carrot and ginger sauce
300 g (10½ oz) carrots, chopped
2 teaspoons grated fresh ginger
170 ml (5½ fl oz/⅔ cup) orange
  juice
125 ml (4 fl oz/½ cup) vegetable
  stock

1 Drain the tofu, then slice each block into six lengthways. Place in a single layer in a flat non-metallic dish. Mix the juice, sugar, soy sauce, coriander, garlic and ginger in a jug, then pour over the tofu. Cover and refrigerate overnight, turning once.
2 Drain the tofu, reserving the marinade. Heat the oil in a large frying pan and cook the tofu in batches over high heat for 2–3 minutes each side, or until golden. Remove and keep warm.

Bring the marinade to the boil in a saucepan, then reduce the heat and simmer for 1 minute. Remove from the heat and keep warm.
3 Heat a wok, add the bok choy and 1 tablespoon water and cook, covered, over medium heat for 2–3 minutes, or until tender. Remove and keep warm.
4 Add all the sauce ingredients to a saucepan, bring to the boil, then reduce the heat and simmer, covered, for 5–6 minutes, or until the carrot is tender. Transfer to a food processor and blend until smooth.
5 To serve, divide the bok choy among six plates. Top with some sauce, then the tofu and drizzle on a little of the marinade before serving.

Lay the tofu slices in a flat dish and pour on the marinade.

Cook the tofu slices in batches until golden brown on both sides.

Blend the carrot mixture in a food processor until smooth.

CAULIFLOWER FRITTERS WITH TOMATO RELISH

Preparation time: 35 minutes
Total cooking time: 30 minutes
Serves 4–6

1 small cauliflower
90 g (3¼ oz/½ cup) peasemeal (see Note)
3 tablespoons self-raising flour
1 teaspoon ground cumin
¼ teaspoon bicarbonate of soda
1 egg
200 g (7 oz) plain yoghurt
vegetable oil, for deep-frying

Tomato relish
2 tablespoons vegetable oil
1 onion, finely chopped
400 g (14 oz) tomatoes, peeled and chopped
125 ml (4 fl oz/½ cup) white wine vinegar
185 g (6½ oz/¾ cup) sugar
1 garlic clove, crushed
1 teaspoon ground cumin
80 g (2¾ oz/½ cup) sultanas
35 g (1¼ oz/¾ cup) finely chopped fresh coriander (cilantro)

1 Cut cauliflower into large florets. Remove as much of the stem as possible without breaking florets. Wash and drain well. Pat dry with paper towels.
2 Combine peasemeal, flour, cumin and soda in a mixing bowl and make a well in the centre. Beat together the egg, yoghurt and 170 ml (5½ fl oz/⅔ cup) water. Pour onto the dry ingredients. Using a wooden spoon, stir until batter is smooth and free of lumps. Leave for 10 minutes.
3 To make tomato relish, place the oil, onion, tomato, vinegar, sugar, garlic, cumin and sultanas in a pan. Cover, cook over medium heat for 10 minutes. Bring to boil, reduce heat and simmer, uncovered, 5 minutes, or until mixture thickens and darkens slightly. Remove from heat. Stir in the coriander.
4 Heat oil in deep heavy-based pan. Dip florets in batter, drain off excess. Using a metal spoon or tongs, gently lower cauliflower into hot oil in small batches. Cook until golden brown, 3–5 minutes. Lift out with a slotted spoon and drain on paper towels. Serve hot with tomato relish.

COOK'S FILE

Storage time: Tomato relish can be prepared up to three days in advance. Store, covered, in the refrigerator.
Note: Peasemeal is a flour made from yellow split peas. It is available in health food stores or Indian food stores. Fine cornmeal or besan flour may be used as a substitute.

1

2

3

EGGPLANT AND MUSHROOM SKEWERS WITH TOMATO CONCASSÉ

Preparation time: 20 minutes +
15 minutes marinating
Total cooking time: 25 minutes
Serves 4

12 long rosemary sprigs
18 Swiss brown mushrooms
1 small eggplant (aubergine), cut
   into 2 cm (¾ inch) cubes
3 tablespoons olive oil
2 tablespoons balsamic vinegar
2 cloves garlic, crushed
1 teaspoon sugar
olive oil, for brushing
sea salt, to sprinkle (optional)

Tomato concassé
5 tomatoes
1 tablespoon olive oil
1 small onion, finely chopped
1 clove garlic, crushed
1 tablespoon tomato paste
   (concentrated purée)
2 teaspoons sugar
2 teaspoons balsamic vinegar
1 tablespoon chopped fresh
   flat-leaf (Italian) parsley

1 Remove the leaves from the rosemary sprigs, leaving 5 cm (2 inch) on the tip. Reserve 1 tablespoon of the leaves. Cut the mushrooms in half, stems intact. Place the mushrooms and eggplant in a non-metallic bowl. Pour on the combined oil, vinegar, garlic and sugar, then season and toss. Marinate for 15 minutes.

2 Score a cross in the base of each tomato. Put in a bowl of boiling water for 30 seconds then plunge into cold water. Peel the skin away from the cross. Cut in half and scoop out the seeds with a teaspoon. Dice.

3 Heat the oil in a saucepan. Cook the onion and garlic over medium heat for 2–3 minutes, or until soft. Reduce the heat, add the tomato, tomato paste, sugar, vinegar and parsley and simmer for 10 minutes, or until the liquid has evaporated. Keep warm.

4 Thread alternating mushroom halves and eggplant cubes onto the rosemary sprigs, so there are three mushroom halves and two cubes of eggplant on each. Lightly oil a chargrill plate or barbecue and cook the skewers for 7–8 minutes, or until the eggplant is tender, turning occasionally. Serve with concassé and sprinkle with sea salt and the reserved rosemary.

Simmer the tomato sauce until it is thick and pulpy.

Thread alternating mushrooms and eggplant cubes onto the skewers.

107

Salads

TABOULI WITH LEMON THYME

Preparation time: 20 minutes
Total cooking time: Nil
Serves 4–6

25 g (1 oz/2 cups) flat-leaf
   (Italian) parsley
3 tablespoons mint leaves
90 g (3¼ oz/½ cup) burghul
   (cracked wheat)
125 ml (4 fl oz/½ cup) hot water

125 g (4½ oz) cherry
   tomatoes
125 g (4½ oz) yellow pear
   tomatoes
3 spring onions (scallions),
   chopped
2 tablespoons lemon thyme
   leaves
2 tablespoons lemon juice
2 tablespoons olive oil
salt and pepper

1 Wash and dry parsley and mint. Combine burghul and hot water in a bowl. Leave to stand for 15 minutes, until all the water is absorbed.

2 Cut tomatoes in half. Chop parsley and mint coarsely with a sharp knife or in food processor (do not overprocess).

3 Place tomatoes in a large bowl with burghul, parsley, mint and spring onion. Sprinkle with lemon thyme, juice and oil. Toss gently to combine, season with salt and pepper and refrigerate.

1

2

3

BEAN SALAD WITH CUMIN AND CORIANDER DRESSING

Preparation time: 25 minutes
Total cooking time: 15 minutes
Serves 6

300 g (10 oz) vegetable spiral
　　pasta
2 tablespoons sunflower oil
1 leek, sliced
1 red capsicum (pepper), seeded
　　and diced
130 g (4½ oz/2 cups) finely
　　shredded English spinach
150 g (5 oz) button mushrooms,
　　halved
300 g (10 oz) can red kidney
　　beans, rinsed and drained
300 g (10 oz) can butter beans,
　　rinsed and drained
2 tablespoons snipped chives
½ teaspoon coarsely ground
　　black pepper
60 g (2 oz/½ cup) sunflower
　　seeds, toasted

Cumin and coriander dressing
2 cloves garlic, crushed
½ teaspoon ground cumin
½ teaspoon ground coriander
2 tablespoons cider vinegar
125 ml (4 fl oz/½ cup)
　　olive oil

1 Cook the pasta in a large pan of boiling water for 8–10 minutes, or until *al dente*. Drain.
2 Heat the oil in a large pan, add the leek and capsicum and stir-fry over medium heat for 2–3 minutes. Add the spinach and mushrooms and toss together for about 1 minute, or until the spinach just wilts.

3 To make the dressing, mix the garlic, cumin, coriander and vinegar together. Gradually add the olive oil and whisk to combine.
4 In a large bowl, combine the pasta, vegetables, beans, chives and black

pepper. Pour in the dressing and toss through. Transfer to a large serving bowl and sprinkle with the toasted sunflower seeds.

Add the spinach and mushrooms to the leek and capsicum.

Gradually whisk the oil into the combined garlic, cumin, coriander and vinegar.

Pour the dressing into the salad and toss gently to mix through.

111

SPICY BASMATI RICE, CASHEW AND GREEN PEA SALAD

Preparation time: 30 minutes +
 30 minutes standing
Total cooking time: 20 minutes
Serves 6

40 g (1¼ oz) butter or ghee
½ teaspoon turmeric
300 g (10 oz) basmati rice
½ teaspoon salt
200 g (6½ oz) fresh or frozen
 peas, thawed
3 tablespoons peanut oil
1 teaspoon yellow mustard seeds
1 teaspoon cumin seeds
3 tablespoons currants
1 clove garlic, crushed
1–2 small green chillies, finely
 chopped
1 teaspoon Madras curry powder
100 ml (3½ fl oz) coconut cream
50 g (1¾ oz) glacé ginger, cut
 into thin strips
¼ small red onion, finely
 chopped
1 tablespoon chopped mint
 leaves
1 tablespoon chopped coriander
 (cilantro)
30 g (1 oz/½ cup) shredded
 coconut
100 g (3¼ oz) roasted cashew
 nuts, coarsely chopped
2 teaspoons shredded coconut,
 to garnish

1 Melt the butter or ghee in a heavy-based pan and stir in the turmeric. Add the rice and salt, and stir for 10–15 seconds, then pour in 375 ml (12 fl oz/1½ cups) of water. Stir over high heat until boiling, then reduce the heat until gently simmering. Simmer, tightly covered, and cook for 13 minutes without removing the lid. Remove the pan from the heat and leave for 10 minutes without removing the lid, then fluff gently with a fork. Add the peas, transfer to a large bowl and allow to cool.

2 Heat 2 teaspoons of the oil in a pan and stir in the mustard and cumin seeds. When the mustard seeds start to pop, add the currants, garlic, chilli and curry powder. Stir to combine, but do not brown. Stir in the coconut cream, remove from the heat and transfer to the bowl of rice and peas.

3 Add the ginger, onion, herbs and the remaining oil. Toss well, and set aside for at least 30 minutes. Just before serving, toss through the coconut and cashew nuts. Garnish with the shredded coconut.

COOK'S FILE

Note: Rice salads often improve if made in advance, and this one is no exception. It may be prepared up to 24 hours in advance, but add the cashew nuts and coconut just before serving to ensure a crisp texture.

Cut the glacé ginger into thin strips, and chop the red onion and mint.

Add the rice and salt to the melted butter and turmeric.

Add the currants, garlic, chilli and curry powder to the mustard and cumin seeds.

JAPANESE SPINACH SALAD

Preparation time: 25 minutes
Total cooking time: 5 minutes
Serves 4

2 eggs
1 sheet nori, cut into
    matchsticks
100 g (3¼ oz) baby English
    spinach leaves
1 small red onion, finely sliced
½ small daikon radish, finely
    sliced
2 Lebanese (short) cucumbers,
    sliced
30 g (1 oz) pickled ginger, sliced
1 tablespoon toasted sesame
    seeds

Dressing
4 tablespoons light olive oil
1 tablespoon rice vinegar
1 tablespoon light soy sauce

1 Preheat the grill (broiler) to hot. Beat the eggs lightly in a small bowl, add 1 tablespoon water and the nori. Season with salt and pepper. Heat and grease a 20 cm (8 inch) omelette pan. Pour in the egg mixture to make a thin omelette. When lightly browned underneath, place under the grill to set the top, without colouring. Turn out onto a board and leave to cool. Cut the omelette into thin strips.
2 To make the dressing, put the olive oil, vinegar and soy sauce in a small bowl. Whisk gently to combine with a small wire whisk or a fork.
3 Put the spinach leaves, onion, daikon, cucumber, pickled ginger, toasted sesame seeds and omelette strips in a large serving bowl. Add the

dressing and toss the salad gently to combine. Serve immediately.

COOK'S FILE

Note: If light soy sauce is not available, use half soy sauce and half water. Pickled ginger is available from Asian supermarkets.
Hint: Use scissors to cut the nori.

Peel the daikon radish and cut it into fine slices using a sharp knife.

Add 1 tablespoon water and the nori to the lightly beaten eggs.

Once the omelette has cooled, slice it into thin strips.

WARM RADICCHIO SALAD WITH CRUSHED TOMATO VINAIGRETTE

Preparation time: 40 minutes
Total cooking time: 25 minutes
Serves 4

3 tablespoons oil
6 cloves garlic, thinly sliced
1–2 tablespoons olive oil
7 Roma (plum) tomatoes, cored and halved
3 tablespoons extra virgin olive oil
2 tablespoons red wine vinegar
1 teaspoon honey

920 g (1 lb 14 oz) witlof (chicory/Belgian endive)
1 onion, halved and sliced
1 radicchio lettuce

1 Heat the oil in a small pan, add the garlic and fry over moderately high heat for a few minutes, or until lightly browned. Drain on paper towels.

2 Heat a little of the olive oil in a frying pan and cook the tomatoes, cut-side-down, over moderate heat until browned and very soft. Turn to brown the other side. Transfer to a bowl to cool, then peel and discard the skins. Coarsely mash the flesh with a fork.

3 To make the vinaigrette, whisk about half of the crushed tomatoes, the extra virgin olive oil, vinegar and honey until combined. Season with salt and freshly ground black pepper.

4 Trim the coarse stems from the chicory, wash the leaves very well and drain. Cut into short lengths. Heat a little more olive oil in the frying pan, add the onion and cook until transparent. Add the chicory and stir until just wilted. Add the remaining tomatoes and stir until well combined. Season with salt and black pepper.

5 Tear any large radicchio leaves into smaller pieces. Toss through the chicory mixture. Transfer to a large serving bowl, drizzle with the tomato vinaigrette and sprinkle with the garlic. Serve immediately.

Fry the garlic in the oil over moderate heat until lightly browned.

Cook the tomatoes until they are browned and very soft.

Tear any large radicchio leaves into smaller pieces.

LEMON AND CHERVIL PASTA SALAD

Preparation time: 20 minutes
Total cooking time: 15 minutes
Serves 4

250 g (9 oz) pasta bows
1 tablespoon olive oil
250 g (9 oz) broccoli, cut
  into small florets
125 g (4½ oz) snow peas
  (mangetout), topped
  and tailed

150 g (5½ oz) small yellow
  button squash, cut into
  quarters
2 tablespoons sour cream
1 tablespoon lemon juice
2 teaspoons finely grated lemon
  rind
3 tablespoons olive oil, extra
salt and white pepper
1 stick celery, finely sliced
1 tablespoon chopped chervil
chervil sprigs, to garnish

1 Cook pasta until tender. Drain well, toss with olive oil and set aside to cool.

2 Place broccoli, snow peas and squash in a large bowl, cover with boiling water and leave for 2 minutes. Drain, plunge into iced water, drain again and pat dry with paper towels.
3 Place sour cream, juice, rind and extra oil in a screwtop jar and shake for 30 seconds or until combined. Season with salt and pepper, to taste.
4 Combine pasta, celery and drained vegetables in a large bowl; sprinkle with chervil. Drizzle over dressing and toss to combine. Garnish with chervil. Serve at room temperature.

1

2

3

VIETNAMESE SALAD

Preparation time: 30 minutes +
  10 minutes standing + 30 minutes
  refrigeration
Total cooking time: Nil
Serves 4–6

200 g (7 oz) dried rice vermicelli
10 g (¼ oz/½ cup) firmly packed
  torn fresh Vietnamese mint
15 g (½ oz/½ cup) firmly packed
  fresh coriander (cilantro)
  leaves
½ red onion, cut into thin
  wedges
1 green mango, cut into strips

1 Lebanese (short) cucumber,
  halved lengthways and thinly
  sliced on the diagonal
140 g (5 oz/1 cup) crushed
  peanuts

Lemon grass dressing
125 ml (4 fl oz/½ cup) lime juice
1 tablespoon shaved palm sugar
  (jaggery)
3 tablespoons seasoned rice
  vinegar
2 stems lemon grass, finely
  chopped
2 red chillies, seeded and finely
  chopped
3 makrut (kaffir) lime leaves,
  shredded

1 Place the rice vermicelli in a bowl
and cover with boiling water. Leave
for 10 minutes, or until soft, then
drain, rinse under cold water and cut
into short lengths.
2 Place the vermicelli, mint, coriander,
onion, mango, cucumber and three-
quarters of the nuts in a large bowl
and toss together.
3 To make the dressing, place all the
ingredients in a jar with a lid and
shake together.
4 Toss the dressing through the salad
and chill for 30 minutes. Sprinkle with
the remaining nuts.

*Cut the green mango into julienne strips
(the size and shape of matchsticks).*

*Using scissors, cut the rice vermicelli into
short lengths.*

*Toss the salad ingredients together in a
large bowl.*

TORTELLINI SALAD WITH BALSAMIC VINAIGRETTE

Preparation time: 15 minutes +
  20 minutes standing
Total cooking time: 8 minutes
Serves 4

Balsamic vinaigrette
3 tablespoons olive oil
2 tablespoons balsamic vinegar
1 clove garlic, crushed

375 g (12 oz) spinach and ricotta
  tortellini
6 spring onions (scallions),
  thinly sliced
100 g (3¼ oz) pitted black and
  green olives, finely diced
6 Roma (plum) tomatoes, finely
  diced
2 tablespoons chopped parsley
8–12 black olives, to garnish

1 To make the vinaigrette, combine the oil, vinegar and garlic, and season to taste with salt and freshly ground black pepper.
2 Cook the tortellini in a large pan with plenty of salted boiling water until tender. Drain the tortellini and rinse under cold water. Drain again.
3 Combine the sliced spring onion, diced olives and tomato, and toss with the dressing in a large bowl.
4 Add the tortellini and set aside for at least 20 minutes to allow the flavours to develop. Toss the parsley through the salad and season with salt and freshly ground black pepper. Transfer to a serving bowl and serve garnished with the black olives.

Slice the spring onions thinly, and finely dice the pitted olives.

Add the dressing to the combined spring onion, olives and tomato.

Add the cooked tortellini to the tossed salad and dressing.

117

SPICY INDIAN-STYLE LENTIL SALAD

Preparation time: 30 minutes
Total cooking time: 1 hour 10 minutes
Serves 6

220 g (7 oz/1 cup) brown rice
185 g (6 oz/1 cup) brown
    lentils
1 teaspoon turmeric
1 teaspoon ground cinnamon
6 cardamom pods
3 star anise
2 bay leaves
3 tablespoons sunflower oil
1 tablespoon lemon juice
250 g (8 oz) broccoli florets
2 carrots, cut into julienne strips
1 onion, finely chopped
2 cloves garlic, crushed
1 red capsicum (pepper), finely
    chopped
1 teaspoon garam masala
1 teaspoon ground coriander
235 g (7¼ oz/1½ cups) fresh or
    frozen peas, thawed

Mint and yoghurt dressing
250 g (8 oz/1 cup) plain yoghurt
1 tablespoon lemon juice
1 tablespoon finely chopped
    fresh mint
1 teaspoon cumin seeds

1 Put 750 ml (24 fl oz/3 cups) water with the rice, lentils, turmeric, cinnamon, cardamom, star anise and bay leaves in a medium pan. Stir to combine and bring to the boil. Reduce the heat, cover and simmer gently for 50–60 minutes, or until the liquid is absorbed. Remove the whole spices and discard. Transfer the mixture to a large bowl. Whisk 2 tablespoons of the oil with the lemon juice and fork through the rice mixture.
2 Boil, steam or microwave the broccoli and carrots until tender. Drain and refresh in cold water.
3 Heat the remaining oil in a large pan and add the onion, garlic and capsicum. Stir-fry for 2–3 minutes, then add the garam masala and coriander, and stir-fry for a further 1–2 minutes. Add the vegetables and toss to coat in the spice mixture. Add to the rice mixture and fork through to combine. Cover and refrigerate.
4 To make the dressing, mix the yoghurt, lemon juice, mint and cumin seeds together, and season with salt and pepper. Spoon the salad into individual serving bowls or onto a platter and serve with the dressing.

Add the cardamom pods, star anise and bay leaves to the pan.

Add the vegetables and toss to coat with the spice mixture.

Mix the yoghurt, lemon juice, mint and cumin seeds together.

PAPAYA AND GORGONZOLA SALAD

Preparation time: 20 minutes
Total cooking time: 20 minutes
Serves 4

250 ml (8 fl oz/1 cup) orange
    juice
1 tablespoon oil
1 tablespoon soft brown sugar
1 fennel bulb, sliced
2 heads witlof (chicory/Belgian
    endive), quartered
250 g (8 oz) watercress, ends
    trimmed
1 papaya, sliced
200 g (6½ oz) Gorgonzola
    cheese, crumbled
70 g (2¼ oz/½ cup) hazelnuts,
    roughly chopped

Dressing
30 g (1 oz/1 cup) loosely packed
    basil leaves
125 ml (4 fl oz/½ cup) olive oil

1 Put the orange juice in a frying pan and cook over high heat until reduced by a third.

2 Stir the oil and brown sugar in a frying pan over low heat until the sugar dissolves. Add the fennel, witlof and orange juice, cover and cook for 15 minutes, or until the vegetables have caramelised. Check the liquid a couple of times during cooking; if it is looking too dry add a little water.

3 Divide the watercress among four serving plates, top with the papaya, caramelized vegetables, Gorgonzola and hazelnuts.

4 To make the dressing, process the basil and oil in a food processor until combined, then strain and drizzle over the salad.

COOK'S FILE

Note: Gorgonzola is a blue-veined cheese with a strong, sharp flavour. It is named after the Italian town where it originated, and is made from pressed cows milk. If Gorgonzola cheese is not available, you can substitute Roquefort or Blue Castello in this recipe.

Using a large sharp knife, cut the fennel bulb into slices.

Cut the papaya in half, scrape out the seeds and slice the flesh.

Cook, the orange juice over high heat until it is reduced by a third.

Add the fennel and witlof to the oil and sugar mixture.

MEDITERRANEAN PASTA SALAD WITH BLACK OLIVE DRESSING

Preparation time: 30 minutes
Total cooking time: 25 minutes
Serves 4

250 g (8 oz) fusilli pasta
1 red capsicum (pepper)
1 yellow or green capsicum
   (pepper)
1 tablespoon sunflower oil
2 tablespoons olive oil
2 cloves garlic, crushed
1 eggplant (aubergine), cubed
2 zucchini (courgettes), thickly
   sliced
2 large ripe tomatoes, peeled,
   seeded and chopped
3 tablespoons chopped flat-leaf
   (Italian) parsley
1 teaspoon seasoned pepper
150 g (5 oz) feta cheese,
   crumbled

Black olive dressing
6 large marinated black olives,
   pitted
125 ml (4 fl oz/½ cup) olive oil
2 tablespoons balsamic vinegar

1 Add the fusilli pasta to a large pan of gently boiling water and cook for 10–12 minutes, or until *al dente*. Drain, spread in a single layer on a baking tray to dry, then refrigerate, uncovered, until chilled.

2 Cut the red and yellow capsicum in half lengthways, removing the seeds and white membrane, then cut into large pieces. Place, skin-side-up, under a hot grill (broiler) until the skin blackens and blisters. Leave under a tea towel or in a plastic bag to cool, then peel away and discard the skin. Slice the flesh into thick strips.

3 Heat the sunflower and olive oil in a frying pan. Add the garlic and eggplant and fry quickly, tossing constantly, until lightly browned. Remove from the heat and place in a large bowl. Steam or microwave the zucchini for 1–2 minutes, or until just tender. Rinse under cold water, drain, and add to the eggplant.

4 To make the dressing, process the olives in a food processor until finely chopped. Gradually add the olive oil, processing until thoroughly combined after each addition. Add the vinegar, season with salt and freshly ground black pepper and process to combine.

5 Combine the pasta, capsicum, eggplant, zucchini, tomato, parsley and pepper in a large bowl. Spoon onto individual serving plates or a large salad platter, top with the feta cheese and drizzle with the dressing.

Drain the cooked pasta and spread on a tray to dry.

Remove the seeds and white membrane from the halved capsicums.

Fry the cubed eggplant quickly until it is lightly browned.

HERBED FETA SALAD

Preparation time: 20 minutes
Total cooking time: 10 minutes
Serves 6–8

2 slices thick white bread
200 g (7 oz) feta cheese
1 clove garlic, crushed
1 tablespoon finely chopped
   marjoram
1 tablespoon finely chopped
   chives
1 tablespoon finely chopped
   basil
2 tablespoons white wine
   vinegar
4 tablespoons olive oil
1 red coral lettuce
1 green mignonette or oak leaf
   lettuce

1 Preheat oven to moderate 180°C (350°F/Gas 4). Remove crusts from bread, cut bread into small cubes. Place on an oven tray in a single layer; bake for 10 minutes until crisp and lightly golden. Transfer to a bowl, cool completely.

2 Cut feta into 1.5 cm (⅝ inch) cubes; place in a bowl. Combine garlic, marjoram, chives, basil, vinegar and oil in small screwtop jar and shake for 30 seconds. Pour over feta; cover with plastic wrap, leave for at least 30 minutes, stirring occasionally.

3 Wash and dry lettuces. Tear leaves into pieces, place in bowl. Add feta with dressing, and bread cubes; toss.

COOK'S FILE

Storage time: This salad is best eaten as soon as it is made.

1

2

3

TOMATO AND BOCCONCINI SALAD

Preparation time: 15 minutes
Total cooking time: Nil
Serves 4

6 Roma (plum) tomatoes
5 bocconcini
20 g (¾ oz/⅔ cup) loosely
   packed basil leaves

Dressing
3 tablespoons extra virgin olive
   oil
2 tablespoons balsamic vinegar

1 Cut the tomatoes lengthways into 3–4 slices (discard the thin outside slices, which won't lie flat). Slice the bocconcini lengthways into 3–4 slices.
2 Arrange some tomato slices on a serving plate, place a bocconcini slice on top of each tomato and scatter with some of the basil leaves. Repeat the layers until all the tomato, bocconcini and basil have been used. Season with salt and pepper.
3 To make the dressing, whisk the oil and vinegar. Drizzle over the salad.

COOK'S FILE

Variation: Try the salad with a pesto dressing. Process 25 g (¾ oz/½ cup) basil leaves, 1 tablespoon pine nuts, 3 tablespoons grated Parmesan and 1 crushed clove garlic in a food processor until finely chopped. With the motor running, add 3 tablespoons olive oil and 1 tablespoon lemon juice in a steady stream.

Slice the tomatoes lengthways, discarding the thin outside slices.

Slice the bocconcini lengthways into three or four slices.

Whisk together the olive oil and balsamic vinegar in a small jug.

POTATO SALAD

Preparation time: 30 minutes
Total cooking time: 5 minutes
Serves 4

600 g (1¼ lb) potatoes, cut into
    bite-sized pieces
1 small onion, finely chopped
1 small green capsicum
    (pepper), chopped
2–3 celery sticks, finely
    chopped
3 tablespoons finely chopped
    parsley

Dressing
185 g (6 oz/¾ cup) mayonnaise
1–2 tablespoons vinegar or
    lemon juice
2 tablespoons sour cream

1 Cook the potato in a large pan of boiling water for 5 minutes, or until just tender (pierce with a small sharp knife—if the potato comes away easily it is ready). Drain and cool completely.

2 Combine the onion, capsicum, celery and parsley, reserving some for garnishing, with the cooled potato in a large salad bowl.

3 To make the dressing, mix together the mayonnaise, vinegar and sour cream. Season with salt and pepper. Pour over the salad and toss gently to combine, without breaking the potato. Garnish with the remaining parsley.

COOK'S FILE

Note: Any potato is suitable for this recipe. Most potatoes are delicious with their skins left on.

Cut the potatoes into bite-sized pieces, leaving the skins on.

Combine the onion, capsicum, celery and parsley with the cooled potato.

Mix together the mayonnaise, vinegar and sour cream and season, to taste.

ROASTED VEGETABLE AND FETA SALAD

Preparation time: 20 minutes
Total cooking time: 50 minutes
Serves 4

150 g (5½ oz) reduced-fat feta
  cheese, grated
4 tablespoons skim milk
3 tablespoons olive oil
6 Roma (plum) tomatoes, cut in
  half lengthways
400 g (14 oz) pumpkin, peeled,
  seeded and cut into large
  chunks
1 red onion, cut into eight
  wedges
4 small zucchini (courgettes),
  cut in half
8 cloves garlic, unpeeled
1 teaspoon thyme
50 g (1¾ oz) rocket (arugula)
  leaves
1 tablespoon pine nuts, toasted

1 To make the dressing, blend the feta and milk in a food processor for 20–30 seconds to combine well. Gradually pour in 1 tablespoon of the oil and process until combined. Season lightly with salt. Store in a sealed container in the refrigerator until ready to use.

2 Preheat the oven to 200°C (400°F/ Gas 6). Place the tomatoes, pumpkin, onion, zucchini, garlic and thyme in a large bowl with the remaining olive oil and season with salt and freshly ground black pepper, then toss to coat. Arrange the vegetables on a greased baking tray and then roast for 45–50 minutes, or until the pumpkin is cooked through. Remove all the vegetables and cool slightly.

3 Place the rocket leaves on a large serving platter and arrange the roasted vegetables on top. Spoon the feta dressing over the vegetables and sprinkle with pine nuts.

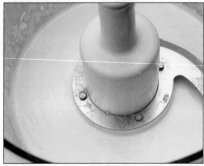

Blend the grated feta and milk together in a food processor, then add the oil.

Toss the vegetables and thyme in the remaining oil and seasonings.

FRESH BEETROOT AND GOAT'S CHEESE SALAD

Preparation time: 20 minutes
Total cooking time: 30 minutes
Serves 4

1 kg (2 lb 4 oz) (4 bulbs with
 leaves) fresh beetroot
200 g (7 oz) green beans
1 tablespoon red wine
 vinegar
2 tablespoons extra virgin
 olive oil
1 clove garlic, crushed
1 tablespoon drained capers,
 coarsely chopped
100 g (3½ oz) goat's cheese

1 Trim the leaves from the beetroot. Scrub the bulbs and wash the leaves thoroughly. Add the whole bulbs to a large saucepan of boiling water, reduce the heat and simmer, covered, for 30 minutes, or until tender when pierced with the point of a knife.

(The cooking time may vary depending on the size of the bulbs.)
2 Meanwhile, bring a saucepan of water to the boil, add the beans and cook for 3 minutes, or until just tender. Remove with a slotted spoon and plunge into a bowl of cold water. Drain well. Add the beetroot leaves to the same saucepan of boiling water and cook for 3–5 minutes, or until the leaves and stems are tender. Drain, plunge into a bowl of cold water, then drain well.

Remove the skin from the beetroot, then cut into thin wedges.

3 Drain and cool the beetroots, then peel the skins off and cut the bulbs into thin wedges.
4 To make the dressing, put the red wine vinegar, oil, garlic, capers, ½ teaspoon salt and ½ teaspoon pepper in a screw-top jar and shake.
5 To serve, divide the beans, beetroot leaves and bulbs among four serving plates. Crumble goat's cheese over the top and drizzle with the dressing.

Cook the beetroot leaves until the leaves and stems are tender.

125

ASPARAGUS AND MUSHROOM SALAD

Preparation time: 20 minutes
Total cooking time: 10 minutes
Serves 4

155 g (5½ oz) asparagus spears
1 tablespoon wholegrain
    mustard
3 tablespoons orange juice
2 tablespoons lemon juice
1 tablespoon lime juice
1 tablespoon orange zest
2 teaspoons lemon zest

2 teaspoons lime zest
2 cloves garlic, crushed
3 tablespoons honey
400 g (14 oz) button mushrooms,
    halved
150 g (5½ oz) rocket
    (arugula)
1 red capsicum (pepper), cut
    into strips

1 Trim the ends from the asparagus and cut in half on the diagonal. Place in a saucepan of boiling water and cook for 1 minute, or until just tender. Drain, then plunge into cold water. Set aside.

2 Place the mustard, juices, zests, garlic and honey in a large saucepan. Season with pepper. Bring to the boil, then reduce heat and add the mushrooms. Toss for 2 minutes. Cool.
3 Remove the mushrooms from the sauce with a slotted spoon. Return the sauce to the heat, bring to the boil, then reduce the heat and simmer for 3–5 minutes, or until reduced and syrupy. Cool slightly.
4 Toss the mushrooms, rocket, capsicum and drained asparagus together. Serve drizzled with the sauce.

Use a zester to remove the zest of the orange, lemon and lime.

Toss the mushrooms in the mustard, juices, zest, garlic and honey.

Simmer the sauce until it is reduced and syrupy.

MARINATED TOFU AND CARROT SESAME SALAD

Preparation time: 30 minutes + 1 hour
  marinating
Total cooking time: 15 minutes
Serves 4

500 g (1 lb) firm tofu
2 tablespoons grated fresh
  ginger
2 spring onions (scallions),
  finely sliced
1 tablespoon mirin
3 tablespoons soy sauce
1 teaspoon sesame oil
oil, for cooking
2 Lebanese (short) cucumbers
2 carrots, peeled
¼ Chinese cabbage, shredded
100 g (3¼ oz) crispy fried egg
  noodles
50 g (1¾ oz) roasted peanuts,
  roughly chopped
mint leaves, to garnish

Dressing
1 tablespoon grated lime rind
1 tablespoon sugar
2 tablespoons lime juice
3 tablespoons olive oil
2 tablespoons shredded mint
  leaves

1 Cut the tofu into 1 cm (½ inch) thick triangles. Put in a shallow dish with the ginger, spring onion, mirin, soy sauce and sesame oil. Cover and refrigerate for 1 hour.
2 Heat 2 tablespoons of the oil in a large non-stick frying pan. Add the tofu and cook, in batches, over high heat until it is crisp and golden. Remove from the pan and drain on paper towels.

3 Using a sharp vegetable peeler, cut the cucumbers and carrots into paper-thin ribbons. Arrange the cabbage on a large platter and top with the cucumber, carrot and tofu.
4 To make the dressing, gently whisk the ingredients in a bowl to combine.

Drizzle the dressing over the salad and sprinkle with the noodles and nuts. Garnish with the mint leaves and serve immediately.

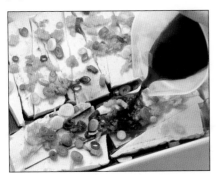

Marinate the tofu in the ginger, spring onion, mirin, soy sauce and sesame oil.

Fry the marinated tofu in batches until crisp and golden.

Use a sharp vegetable peeler to cut the cucumbers and carrots into ribbons.

SUMMER BREAD SALAD

Preparation time: 20 minutes
Total cooking time: 15 minutes
Serves 6–8

2 red capsicums (peppers)
2 yellow capsicums (peppers)
6 Roma (plum) tomatoes, cut
   into large chunks
100 g (3¼ oz) capers, drained
100 g (3¼ oz) anchovies, halved
100 g (3¼ oz) black olives
150 g (5 oz) bocconcini, halved
1 Italian wood-fired loaf

60 g (2 oz/2 cups) basil leaves

Dressing
4 cloves garlic, finely chopped
3 tablespoons red wine
   vinegar
125 ml (4 fl oz/½ cup) extra
   virgin olive oil

1 Cut the capsicums into large pieces, removing the seeds and white membrane. Place, skin-side-up, under a hot grill (broiler), until the skin blackens and blisters. Cool in a plastic bag or under a tea towel, then peel away the skin and cut into thick strips.

2 Put the capsicum, tomato, capers, anchovies, olives and bocconcini in a bowl and toss to combine.
3 To make the dressing, put the ingredients in a screwtop jar and shake to combine.
4 Cut the bread into large pieces, and place in a serving bowl. Drizzle with the dressing and mix until the bread is coated. Add the capsicum mixture and basil leaves, and toss gently.

COOK'S FILE

Note: This salad is based on the Tuscan favourite which uses leftover crusty bread to make a salad.

Put the capsicum pieces in a plastic bag until cool enough to handle.

Combine the capsicum, tomato, capers, anchovies, olives and bocconcini.

Using a bread knife, cut the wood-fired loaf into large pieces.

TOMATO, HALOUMI AND SPINACH SALAD

Preparation time: 15 minutes +
2 hours marinating
Total cooking time: 1 hour
Serves 4

200 g (7 oz) haloumi cheese
3 tablespoons olive oil
2 cloves garlic, crushed
1 tablespoon chopped fresh
oregano
1 tablespoon chopped fresh
marjoram

8 Roma (plum) tomatoes, halved
1 small red onion, cut into eight
wedges with base intact
3 tablespoons olive oil, extra
2 tablespoons balsamic vinegar
150 g (5½ oz) baby English
spinach leaves

1 Cut the haloumi into 1 cm (½ inch) slices lengthways and place in a shallow dish. Mix the oil, garlic and herbs and pour over the haloumi. Marinate, covered, for 1–2 hours.
2 Preheat the oven to moderately hot 200°C (400°F/Gas 6). Place the tomato and onion in a single layer in a

roasting tin, drizzle with 2 tablespoons of the extra oil and 1 tablespoon of the vinegar and sprinkle with salt and cracked black pepper. Bake for 50–60 minutes, or until golden.
3 Meanwhile, heat a non-stick frying pan over medium heat. Drain the haloumi and cook for 1 minute each side, or until golden brown.
4 Divide the spinach leaves among four serving plates and top with the tomato and onion. Whisk together the remaining olive oil and balsamic vinegar in a small bowl and drizzle over the salad. Top with the haloumi.

Cut the onion into eight wedges, keeping the base intact.

Bake the tomatoes and onion in a roasting tin until golden.

Cook both sides of the drained haloumi in a frying pan until golden brown.

129

RICE SALAD

Preparation time: 30 minutes + 1 hour
   refrigeration
Total cooking time: 20 minutes
Serves 6–8

300 g (10 oz/1½ cups) long-grain
   rice
80 g (2¾ oz/½ cup) fresh or
   frozen peas
3 spring onions (scallions),
   sliced
1 green capsicum (pepper),
   finely diced
1 red capsicum (pepper), finely
   diced
310 g (10 oz) can corn kernels
3 tablespoons chopped mint

Dressing
125 ml (4 fl oz/½ cup) extra
   virgin olive oil
2 tablespoons lemon juice
1 clove garlic, crushed
1 teaspoon sugar

1 Bring a large pan of water to the
boil and stir in the rice. Return to the
boil and cook for 12–15 minutes, or
until tender. Drain and cool.
2 Cook the peas in a small pan of
boiling water for about 2 minutes.
Rinse under cold water and drain well.
3 To make the dressing, combine the
oil, lemon juice, garlic and sugar in a
small jug and whisk until well blended.
Season with salt and pepper.
4 Combine the rice, peas, spring
onion, capsicum, corn and mint in a
large bowl. Add the dressing and mix
well. Cover and refrigerate for 1 hour.
Transfer to a serving dish to serve.

*Slice the spring onions and finely dice the
capsicums, removing the white membrane.*

*Cook the peas in a pan of boiling water for
2 minutes.*

*Combine the rice, vegetables and mint and
drizzle with the dressing.*

BROAD BEAN AND EGGPLANT SALAD WITH GARLIC CROUTONS

Preparation time: 30 minutes
Total cooking time: 30 minutes
Serves 4

350 g (11¼ oz) slender eggplant (aubergine), diagonally sliced
1 teaspoon salt
500 g (1 lb) fresh broad (fava) beans, shelled, or 250 g (8 oz) frozen shelled beans
155 g (5 oz) fresh asparagus, cut into short lengths
4 tablespoons extra virgin olive oil
1 clove garlic, crushed
3 slices pumpkin or corn bread, or 1 large bread roll, cut into small cubes
¼ small yellow capsicum (pepper), finely sliced
3 spring onions (scallions), finely chopped
6–8 torn red oakleaf lettuce leaves
30 g (1 oz/1 cup) watercress
2 tablespoons finely sliced opal or green basil leaves
2 tablespoons toasted pistachio nuts, coarsely chopped

Dressing
4 tablespoons extra virgin olive oil
2 tablespoons balsamic vinegar

1 Preheat the oven to moderately hot 200°C (400°F/Gas 6). Toss the eggplant with the salt and place in a colander. Set aside to drain.

2 Cook the broad beans in a large pan of boiling water for 5 minutes (3 minutes if using frozen beans), and transfer to a bowl of cold water. When cool, peel and discard the skins. Plunge the asparagus into the boiling water and cook for 2 minutes, then drain and rinse under cold water.

3 Heat the olive oil in a small pan over low heat, add the garlic and sauté for 1 minute. Shake the eggplant slices dry but do not rinse. Place in a single layer on a baking tray, brush lightly with the garlic oil and bake for 10 minutes.

4 Toss the bread cubes lightly in 1 tablespoon of the garlic oil. Spread on a baking tray. When the eggplant has baked for 10 minutes, turn the slices over and brush with the remaining garlic oil. Return to the oven along with the croutons. Reduce the temperature to moderate 180°C (350°F/Gas 4) and bake for 10 minutes, or until the croutons are golden and the eggplant is tender. Remove and cool on the trays.

5 To make the dressing, put the oil and vinegar in a small bowl, season with salt and freshly ground black pepper, and mix well.

6 Place the eggplant, broad beans, asparagus, croutons, capsicum, spring onion, lettuce, watercress and basil in a serving bowl. Pour in the dressing and toss lightly. Scatter with the pistachios before serving.

Sprinkle the eggplant with the salt and leave to drain in a colander.

When the broad beans are cool, peel away and discard the skins.

BLACK BEAN AND AVOCADO SALAD

Preparation time: 20 minutes +
  overnight soaking
Total cooking time: 55 minutes
Serves 6

220 g (7 oz/1 cup) black beans
1 fresh corn cob
1 tomato, chopped
15 g (½ oz/½ cup) coriander
  (cilantro) leaves
1 red onion, sliced
1 red capsicum (pepper), thinly
  sliced

2 avocados, thinly sliced

Lime dressing
100 ml (3¼ fl oz) lime juice
3 tablespoons olive oil
1 tablespoon chopped coriander
  (cilantro)

1 Place the beans in a large bowl and cover with cold water. Leave to soak overnight. Drain and place in a large pan of water. Bring to the boil, then simmer for 45 minutes, or until the beans are tender. Drain and leave to cool.
2 Cook the corn in a large pan of boiling water for 8–10 minutes, or until tender. Drain and cool. Cut off the kernels with a sharp knife.
3 Place the beans, tomato, coriander, corn, red onion and capsicum in a large bowl. Toss until well combined.
4 To make the dressing, put the lime juice, olive oil and chopped coriander in a screw-top jar and shake until combined. Pour into the bean salad and toss gently to combine. Arrange the avocado slices on individual plates or a large serving platter and top with the black bean salad.

COOK'S FILE

Note: Black beans are available from supermarkets and health food stores.

Cover the black beans with cold water in a large bowl.

Cut the cooked corn kernels off the cob with a large sharp knife.

Combine the beans, tomato, coriander, corn, red onion and capsicum.

ROAST SWEET POTATO AND CAPSICUM SALAD

Preparation time: 15 minutes
Total cooking time: 40 minutes
Serves 4

125 ml (4 fl oz/½ cup) olive oil
1 tablespoon chopped oregano or
    marjoram
1 clove garlic, crushed
3 red capsicums (peppers)
500 g (1 lb) orange sweet potato
flaked sea salt
1 tablespoon balsamic vinegar
oregano leaves, to garnish

1 Preheat the oven to moderate 180°C (350°F/Gas 4). Place the oil, oregano or marjoram and garlic in a jug. Season with freshly ground black pepper and whisk with a small wire whisk or fork to combine.

2 Halve the capsicums lengthways and remove the seeds and white membrane. Cut the sweet potato lengthways into slices.

3 Brush the capsicum and sweet potato slices lightly with the herb oil mixture and place in a single layer on baking trays. Sprinkle lightly with the sea salt and bake for 40 minutes, or until the capsicum and sweet potato are tender and beginning to brown slightly on the edges. Leave the vegetables to cool, then arrange them on a serving platter.

4 Add the balsamic vinegar to the remaining oil mixture and drizzle over the salad. Serve sprinkled with the fresh oregano leaves.

Combine the oil, oregano or marjoram, and garlic in a small jug.

Cut the capsicums in half lengthways, and cut the sweet potato into long slices.

Brush the capsicum and sweet potato with the oil mixture and bake until tender.

BEAN SALAD

Preparation time: 30 minutes
Total cooking time: 5 minutes
Serves 8–10

250 g (8 oz) green beans, topped
   and tailed
400 g (12¾ oz) can chickpeas,
   drained and rinsed
425 g (13½ oz) can red kidney
   beans, drained and rinsed
400 g (12¾ oz) can cannellini
   beans, drained and rinsed
270 g (8¾ oz) can corn kernels,
   drained and rinsed
3 spring onions (scallions),
   sliced
1 red capsicum (pepper), finely
   chopped
3 celery sticks, chopped
4–6 gherkins, chopped (optional)
3 tablespoons chopped mint
3 tablespoons chopped flat-leaf
   (Italian) parsley

Mustard vinaigrette
125 ml (4 fl oz/½ cup) extra
   virgin olive oil
2 tablespoons white wine
   vinegar
1 teaspoon sugar
1 tablespoon Dijon mustard
1 clove garlic, crushed

1 Cut the green beans into short
lengths. Bring a small pan of water to
the boil, add the beans and cook for
2 minutes. Drain and rinse under cold
water then leave in a bowl of iced
water until cold. Drain well.
2 Place the beans, chickpeas, kidney
beans, cannellini beans, corn, spring
onion, capsicum, celery, gherkin, mint
and parsley in a large bowl. Season
with salt and freshly ground black
pepper and mix until well combined.
3 To make the mustard vinaigrette,
whisk together all the ingredients until
well combined. Drizzle over the salad
and toss gently to combine. Transfer
to a large serving bowl or platter.

*Cut the vegetables into small dice, trying to
make them all a similar size.*

*Add the beans to a pan of boiling water
and cook for 2 minutes.*

LEMON, FENNEL AND ROCKET SALAD

Preparation time: 25 minutes
Total cooking time: 5 minutes
Serves 4

2 lemons
2 oranges
1 large fennel bulb or 2 baby
    fennel
200 g (6½ oz) rocket (arugula)
100 g (3¼ oz) pecans, chopped
85 g (2¾ oz/½ cup) stuffed green
    olives, halved lengthwise

Toasted sesame dressing
1 tablespoon sesame oil
1 tablespoon sesame seeds
3 tablespoons olive oil
2 tablespoons white wine
    vinegar
1 teaspoon French mustard

1 Peel the lemons and oranges, removing all the white pith. Cut into thin slices and remove any seeds. Thinly slice the fennel. Wash and dry the rocket and tear into pieces. Chill while making the dressing.
2 To make the dressing, heat the oil in a small pan over moderate heat. Add the sesame seeds and fry, stirring constantly, until lightly golden. Remove from the heat and cool. Pour the mixture into a small jug, whisk in the remaining ingredients and season with salt and ground black pepper.
3 Combine the fruit, fennel, rocket, pecans and olives in a shallow serving bowl. Drizzle with the dressing.

COOK'S FILE

Note: Blood oranges have a lovely tart flavour and, when in season, are delicious in this recipe.

Cut the peeled lemons and oranges into thin slices and remove any seeds.

Using a large, sharp knife, thinly slice the fennel crossways.

Stir the sesame seeds in the sesame oil until they are lightly golden.

GADO GADO

Preparation time: 30 minutes
Total cooking time: 35 minutes
Serves 4

6 new potatoes
2 carrots, cut into thick strips
250 g (8 oz) snake (yard-long) beans, cut into 10 cm (4 inch) lengths
2 tablespoons peanut oil
250 g (8 oz) firm tofu, cubed
100 g (3¼ oz) baby English spinach leaves
2 Lebanese (short) cucumbers, cut into thick strips
1 large red capsicum (pepper), cut into thick strips
100 g (3¼ oz) bean sprouts
5 hard-boiled eggs

Peanut sauce
1 tablespoon peanut oil
1 onion, finely chopped
160 g (5¼ oz/⅔ cup) peanut butter
3 tablespoons kecap manis
2 tablespoons ground coriander
2 teaspoons chilli sauce
185 ml (6 fl oz/¾ cup) coconut cream
1 teaspoon grated palm sugar (jaggery)
1 tablespoon lemon juice

1 Cook the potatoes in boiling water until tender. Drain and cool slightly. Cut into quarters. Cook the carrots and beans separately in pans of boiling water until just tender. Plunge into iced water, then drain.
2 Heat the oil in a non-stick frying pan and cook the tofu in batches until crisp. Drain on paper towels.
3 To make the peanut sauce, heat the oil in a pan over low heat and cook the onion for 5 minutes, or until golden. Add the peanut butter, kecap manis, coriander, chilli sauce and coconut cream. Bring to the boil, reduce the heat and simmer for 5 minutes. Stir in the sugar and juice until dissolved.
4 Arrange the vegetables and tofu on a plate. Halve the eggs and place in the centre. Serve with the sauce.

Cut the cucumbers and capsicum into thick strips.

Cook the snake beans quickly in a pan of boiling water.

Heat the oil and cook the tofu in batches until crisp and golden brown.

Add the peanut butter, kecap manis, coriander, chilli sauce and coconut cream.

WARM WILD MUSHROOM SALAD

Preparation time: 15 minutes
Total cooking time: 15 minutes
Serves 4

100 g (3¼ oz) hazelnuts
1 mizuna lettuce
85 g (2¾ oz) baby curly endive
40 g (1¼ oz) baby English
  spinach leaves
2 tablespoons hazelnut oil
2 tablespoons light olive oil
500 g (1 lb) wild mushrooms
  (enoki, shimeji, Shiitake,
  oyster)
150 g (5 oz) strong blue cheese,
  crumbled

Tomato mustard vinaigrette
125 ml (4 fl oz/½ cup) light olive
  oil
2 tablespoons tarragon vinegar
1 teaspoon tomato mustard

1 Preheat the oven to moderate 180°C (350°F/Gas 4). Put the hazelnuts on a baking tray and cook for 10 minutes, shaking the tray occasionally. Remove from the oven, cool, and remove the skins by rubbing the nuts together in a tea towel. Coarsely chop the nuts.
2 Remove the tough lower stems from the mizuna and endive, and tear the larger leaves into bite-sized pieces. Wash the mizuna, endive and spinach under cold water, dry completely and refrigerate until well chilled.
3 To make the vinaigrette, whisk the ingredients together and season to taste with salt and freshly ground black pepper.
4 Heat the oils in a medium frying pan. Add the mushrooms and sauté for 3–4 minutes, or until they just begin to soften. Remove from the heat, allow to cool slightly, then stir in the vinaigrette. Arrange the salad greens on individual serving plates. Spoon the mushrooms over the top and sprinkle with the cheese, hazelnuts and freshly ground black pepper.

COOK'S FILE

Note: Chestnut mushrooms or chanterelles can also be used. Pink oyster mushrooms, if available, give a good colour contrast to this dish.

Rub the hazelnuts together in a tea towel to remove the skins.

Remove the tough lower stems from the baby curly endive.

Sauté the mushrooms until they just begin to soften.

137

Stir-fries

UDON NOODLE STIR-FRY

Preparation time: 15 minutes
Total cooking time: 10 minutes
Serves 4

500 g (1 lb 2 oz) fresh udon
  noodles
1 tablespoon oil
6 spring onions (scallions), cut
  into 5 cm (2 inch) lengths
3 cloves garlic, crushed
1 tablespoon grated fresh ginger
2 carrots, cut into 5 cm (2 inch)
  lengths

150 g (5½ oz) snow peas
  (mangetout), cut in half on
  the diagonal
100 g (3½ oz) bean sprouts
500 g (1 lb 2 oz) choy sum,
  cut into 5 cm (2 inch)
  lengths
2 tablespoons Japanese soy
  sauce
2 tablespoons mirin
2 tablespoons kecap manis
2 sheets roasted nori, cut into
  thin strips

1 Add the noodles to a pan of boiling
water and cook for 5 minutes, or until
tender. Rinse under hot water. Drain.

2 Heat the oil in a wok until hot, then
add the spring onion, garlic and
ginger. Stir-fry over high heat for
1–2 minutes, or until soft. Add the
carrot, snow peas and 1 tablespoon
water, toss well, cover and cook for
1–2 minutes, or until just tender.

3 Add the noodles, bean sprouts, choy
sum, soy sauce, mirin and kecap
manis, then toss until the choy sum is
wilted and coated with the sauce. Stir
in the nori just before serving.

Cut the roasted nori sheets into very thin strips.

Cook the udon noodles until they are tender and not clumped together.

Stir-fry the greens, noodles and sauces until well mixed.

VEGETABLE STIR-FRY

Preparation time: 15 minutes
Total cooking time: 5 minutes
Serves 4

2 spring onions (scallions)
250 g (9 oz) broccoli
1 red capsicum (pepper)
1 yellow capsicum (pepper)
150 g (5½ oz) button mushrooms
1 tablespoon oil
1 teaspoon sesame oil
1 garlic clove, crushed

2 teaspoons grated fresh ginger
3 tablespoons pitted black
   olives, halved
1 tablespoon soy sauce
1 tablespoon honey
1 tablespoon sweet chilli sauce
1 tablespoon sesame seeds

1 Finely slice the spring onions. Cut the broccoli in small florets. Cut capsicum in halves, remove seeds and membrane. Cut into thin strips. Cut mushrooms in half.

2 Heat oils in a wok or large frying pan. Add garlic, ginger and onions. Stir-fry over medium heat 1 minute. Add broccoli, capsicum, mushrooms and olives. Stir-fry for 2 minutes, or until vegetables are bright in colour and just tender.

3 Combine soy sauce, honey and chilli sauce. Place sesame seeds on an oven tray, toast under hot grill (broiler) until golden. Pour sauce over vegetables, toss lightly to combine. Sprinkle with sesame seeds and serve immediately.

COOK'S FILE

Storage time: Cook this dish just before serving.

TEMPEH STIR-FRY

Preparation time: 15 minutes
Total cooking time: 15 minutes
Serves 4

1 teaspoon sesame oil
1 tablespoon peanut oil
2 cloves garlic, crushed
1 tablespoon grated fresh ginger
1 red chilli, finely sliced
4 spring onions (scallions),
    sliced on the diagonal
300 g (10½ oz) tempeh, cut into

2 cm (¾ inch) cubes
500 g (1 lb 2 oz) baby bok
    choy (pak choi)
800 g (1 lb 12 oz) Chinese
    broccoli, chopped
125 ml (4 fl oz/½ cup)
    mushroom oyster sauce
2 tablespoons rice vinegar
2 tablespoons fresh coriander
    (cilantro) leaves
3 tablespoons toasted cashew
    nuts

1 Heat the oils in a wok over high heat, add the garlic, ginger, chilli and spring onion and cook for 1–2 minutes, or until the onion is soft. Add the tempeh cubes and cook for 5 minutes, or until golden. Remove and keep warm.
2 Add half the bok choy and Chinese broccoli and 1 tablespoon water to the wok and cook, covered, for 3–4 minutes, or until wilted. Remove and repeat with the remaining greens and more water.
3 Return the greens and tempeh to the wok, add the sauce and vinegar until warm. Top with coriander and nuts.

Stir-fry the garlic, ginger, chilli and spring onion for 1–2 minutes.

Add the tempeh and stir-fry for 5 minutes, or until golden.

Add the greens to the wok in two batches and cook until wilted.

TAMARI ROASTED ALMONDS WITH SPICY GREEN BEANS

Preparation time: 10 minutes
Total cooking time: 25 minutes
Serves 4–6

1 tablespoon sesame oil
500 g (1 lb 2 oz/2½ cups) jasmine rice
2 tablespoons sesame oil, extra
1 long red chilli, seeded and finely chopped
2 cm (¾ inch) piece ginger, peeled and grated
2 cloves garlic, crushed
375 g (13 oz) green beans, cut into 5 cm (2 inch) lengths
125 ml (4 fl oz/½ cup) hoisin sauce
1 tablespoon soft brown sugar
2 tablespoons mirin
250 g (9 oz) tamari roasted almonds, roughly chopped (see Note)

1 Preheat the oven to moderately hot 200°C (400°F/Gas 6). Heat the oil in a 1.5 litre (6 cup) ovenproof dish. Add the rice and stir until well coated. Stir in 1 litre (4 cups) boiling water. Cover and bake for 20 minutes, or until all the water is absorbed. Keep warm.

2 Meanwhile, heat the extra oil in a wok or large frying pan and cook the chilli, ginger and garlic for 1 minute, or until lightly browned. Add the beans, hoisin sauce and sugar and stir-fry for 2 minutes. Stir in the mirin and cook for 1 minute, or until the beans are tender but still crunchy.

3 Remove from the heat and stir in the almonds just before serving.

COOK'S FILE

Note: Tamari roasted almonds are available from health-food stores.

Wearing rubber gloves, remove the seeds from the chilli and finely chop.

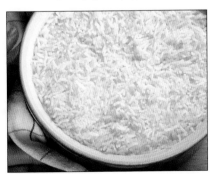

Cook the rice in the oven until all the water has been absorbed.

Stir-fry the beans for 2 minutes, coating them in the sauce.

143

PHAD THAI

Preparation time: 20 minutes
Total cooking time: 15 minutes
Serves 4

400 g (14 oz) flat rice-stick
  noodles
2 tablespoons peanut oil
2 eggs, lightly beaten
1 onion, cut into thin wedges
2 cloves garlic, crushed
1 small red capsicum (pepper),
  cut into thin strips
100 g (3½ oz) fried tofu, cut into
  5 mm (¼ inch) wide strips

6 spring onions (scallions),
  thinly sliced on the diagonal
25 g (1 oz/½ cup) chopped fresh
  coriander (cilantro) leaves
3 tablespoons soy sauce
2 tablespoons lime juice
1 tablespoon soft brown sugar
2 teaspoons sambal oelek
90 g (3¼ oz/1 cup) bean sprouts
3 tablespoons chopped roasted
  unsalted peanuts

1 Cook the noodles in a saucepan of boiling water for 5–10 minutes, or until tender. Drain and set aside.
2 Heat a wok over high heat and add enough peanut oil to coat the bottom and side. When smoking, add the egg and swirl to form a thin omelette. Cook for 30 seconds, or until just set. Roll up, remove and thinly slice.
3 Heat the remaining oil in the wok. Cook the onion, garlic and capsicum over high heat for 2–3 minutes, or until the onion softens. Add the noodles; toss well. Stir in the omelette, tofu, spring onion and half the coriander leaves.
4 Pour in the combined soy sauce, lime juice, sugar and sambal oelek, then toss to coat the noodles. Sprinkle with the bean shoots, peanuts and the remaining coriander. Serve at once.

Using a sharp knife, slice the fried tofu into 5 mm (¼ inch) wide strips.

Once the omelette is golden and set, carefully roll it up.

Stir in the omelette, tofu, spring onion and coriander.

SWEET AND SOUR NOODLES AND VEGETABLES

Preparation time: 12 minutes
Total cooking time: 15 minutes
Serves 4–6

200 g (7 oz) thin fresh egg
noodles
4 fresh baby corn
3 tablespoons oil
1 green capsicum (pepper),
sliced
1 red capsicum (pepper), sliced
2 stalks celery, sliced diagonally

1 carrot, sliced diagonally
250 g (9 oz) button mushrooms,
sliced
3 teaspoons cornflour
(cornstarch)
2 tablespoons brown vinegar
1 teaspoon chopped fresh
chilli
2 teaspoons tomato paste
(concentrated purée)
2 vegetable stock cubes,
crumbled
1 teaspoon sesame oil
450 g (1 lb) can chopped
pineapple pieces
3 spring onions (scallions),
sliced diagonally

1 Cook noodles in large pan boiling water for 3 minutes; drain well.

2 Slice corn diagonally. Heat oil in wok; add capsicum, celery, carrot and mushrooms. Stir over high heat for 5 minutes.

3 Add corn and noodles. Reduce heat to low; cook 2 minutes. Blend cornflour with vinegar in small mixing bowl until smooth. Add chilli, tomato paste, stock cubes, oil and undrained pineapple, stir to combine.

4 Pour pineapple mixture over ingredients in wok. Stir over medium heat 5 minutes, or until mixture boils and sauce thickens. Add spring onions; serve immediately.

Pasta & gnocchi

PUMPKIN AND HERB RAVIOLI

Preparation time: 40 minutes +
  30 minutes resting
Total cooking time: 1 hour 15 minutes
Serves 6

500 g (1 lb 2 oz) pumpkin, cut
  into chunks
215 g (7½ oz/1¾ cups) plain
  (all-purpose) flour
3 eggs, lightly beaten
¼ teaspoon ground nutmeg
15 sage leaves
15 fresh flat-leaf (Italian)
  parsley leaves
125 g (4½ oz) butter, melted
60 g (2¼ oz/½ cup) freshly
  grated Parmesan cheese
salt and pepper

1 Preheat oven to moderate 180°C
(350°F/Gas 4). Place pumpkin on a
baking tray and bake for 1 hour or
until tender; cool. Remove skin.

2 Place flour and eggs in a food
processor. Process for 30 seconds or
until mixture forms a dough. Transfer
to a lightly floured surface and knead
for 3 minutes, until dough is very
smooth and elastic. Cover with a clean
cloth and set aside for 30 minutes.

3 Place pumpkin in a bowl with
nutmeg and mash with a fork. Roll out
half the dough to a rectangle about
2 mm (⅛ inch) thick. Roll out
remaining half to a rectangle slightly
larger than the first.

4 On the first rectangle of dough,
place heaped teaspoonsful of pumpkin
mixture at intervals in straight rows
about 5 cm (2 inches) apart. Flatten
each pumpkin mound slightly; place
one whole sage or parsley leaf on top
of each spoonful of pumpkin mixture.

5 Brush lightly between mounds of
filling with water. Place second sheet
of dough on top, press down gently
between pumpkin mounds to seal. Cut
into squares with a knife or fluted
cutter. Bring a large pan of water to
the boil and drop in ravioli a few at a
time. Cook for 4 minutes, until just
tender. Drain well. Serve sprinkled
with salt and pepper and tossed with
melted butter and Parmesan cheese.

SPINACH FETTUCINE WITH RICH TOMATO SAUCE

Preparation time: 15 minutes
Total cooking time: 40 minutes
Serves 4

4 large ripe tomatoes
2 tablespoons olive oil
1 onion, finely chopped
2 garlic cloves, crushed
1 tablespoon red wine vinegar
3 tablespoons tomato paste
   (concentrated purée)
1 teaspoon sugar
1 teaspoon dried oregano
1 teaspoon dried basil leaves
500 g (1 lb 2 oz) spinach
   fettucine

1 Mark a small cross on the top of each tomato. Place tomatoes in boiling water for 1–2 minutes, then plunge into cold water. Peel skin down from cross. Roughly chop tomatoes.
2 Heat oil in a heavy-based pan. Cook the onion over a medium heat for 5 minutes, until lightly golden, stirring occasionally. Add garlic and cook for 1 minute. Add tomatoes and vinegar, bring to the boil. Reduce heat to medium-low and simmer, uncovered, for 25 minutes; stirring occasionally.
3 Add the tomato paste, sugar and herbs. Simmer for 15 minutes, stirring often. Cook fettucine in a large pan of boiling water until just tender; drain. Place on serving plates, top with tomato sauce and serve immediately.

COOK'S FILE

Storage time: Cook pasta just before serving. The tomato sauce can be frozen for up to six months.

VEGETABLE LASAGNE

Preparation time: 20 minutes
Total cooking time: 1 hour 15 minutes
Serves 6

3 large red capsicum (peppers)
2 large eggplants (aubergines)
2 tablespoons oil
1 large onion, finely chopped
3 garlic cloves, crushed
1 teaspoon dried mixed herbs
1 teaspoon dried oregano
500 g (1 lb 2 oz) mushrooms,
    sliced
440 g (15½ oz) can whole
    tomatoes, crushed
440 g (15½ oz) can red kidney
    beans, drained
1 tablespoon sweet chilli
    sauce
250 g (9 oz) packet instant
    lasagne sheets
1 bunch English spinach,
    chopped
50 g (1¾ oz/1 cup) fresh basil
    leaves
100 g (3½ oz/⅔ cup) sun-dried
    (sun-blushed) tomatoes,
    sliced
3 tablespoons grated Parmesan
    cheese
3 tablespoons grated Cheddar
    cheese

Cheese sauce
60 g (2¼ oz) butter
3 tablespoons plain (all-purpose)
    flour
500 ml (17 fl oz/2 cups) milk
600 g (1 lb 5 oz) ricotta cheese

1 Preheat oven to 180°C (350°F/Gas 4). Grease a 35 x 28 cm (14 x 11 inch) ovenproof casserole dish. Cut capsicum in quarters. Remove seeds and membrane. Place skin-side up on grill (broiler) tray. Brush with oil. Grill (broil) 10 minutes, or until skin is black. Cover with damp tea towel until cool. Peel off skin. Cut capsicum into long thin strips. Set aside. Slice eggplant into 1 cm (½ inch) rounds. Cook in pan of boiling water 1 minute, or until just tender, drain. Pat dry with paper towels. Set aside.

2 Heat oil in frying pan. Cook onion, garlic and herbs over medium heat for 5 minutes, or until onion is soft. Add mushrooms, cook 1 minute. Add tomatoes, beans and chilli sauce. Season. Bring to boil, reduce heat. Simmer, uncovered, 15 minutes, or until thick. Remove from heat. Dip lasagne sheets in hot water to soften slightly and arrange four sheets in the dish.

3 Arrange half of each of the eggplant, spinach, basil, capsicum, mushroom mixture and sun-dried tomatoes over pasta. Top with pasta; press gently. Repeat layers. Top with cheese sauce, sprinkle with combined cheeses. Bake for 45 minutes, or until pasta is soft.

4 To make cheese sauce, heat butter in pan, add flour. Stir over medium heat for 2 minutes, or until golden. Add milk gradually, stirring until mixture boils and thickens. Boil 1 minute. Add ricotta, stir until smooth.

SPINACH AND RICOTTA GNOCCHI

Preparation time: 45 minutes + 1 hour
   refrigeration
Total cooking time: 15 minutes
Serves 4–6

4 slices white bread, crusts
   removed
125 ml (4 fl oz/½ cup)
   milk
500 g (1 lb 2 oz) frozen spinach,
   thawed
250 g (9 oz/1 cup) ricotta
2 eggs

50 g (¾ oz/½ cup) grated
   Parmesan
3 tablespoons plain (all-purpose)
   flour
shaved Parmesan, to serve

Garlic butter sauce
100 g (3½ oz) butter
2 cloves garlic, crushed
3 tablespoons chopped fresh
   basil
1 ripe tomato, diced

1 Soak the bread in the milk for
10 minutes. Squeeze out any excess
milk from the bread. Squeeze out any
excess liquid from the spinach.

2 Combine the bread, spinach, ricotta,
eggs and Parmesan well. Chill,
covered, for 1 hour. Fold in the flour.
3 With floured hands, roll heaped
teaspoons of mixture into dumplings.
Lower batches of the gnocchi into a
large saucepan of boiling salted water.
Cook for 2 minutes, or until the
gnocchi rise to the surface. Transfer to
a serving plate and keep warm.
4 To make the sauce, combine all the
ingredients in a saucepan and cook
over medium heat for 3 minutes, or
until the butter is nutty brown. Drizzle
over the gnocchi and sprinkle with the
shaved Parmesan.

*Gently squeeze out any excess milk from
the bread.*

*With floured hands, roll teaspoons of the
mixture into dumplings.*

*Cook the gnocchi in batches until they rise
to the surface.*

151

FETTUCINE WITH CREAMY MUSHROOM AND BEAN SAUCE

Preparation time: 15 minutes
Total cooking time: 20 minutes
Serves 4

100 g (3½ oz/⅔ cup) pine nuts
375 g (13 oz) fettucine
250 g (9 oz) green beans
2 tablespoons oil
1 onion, chopped
2 garlic cloves, crushed
250 g (9 oz) mushrooms, sliced
125 ml (4 fl oz/½ cup) white wine
310 ml (10¾ fl oz/1¼ cups) cream

125 ml (4 fl oz/½ cup) vegetable stock
1 egg
3 tablespoons chopped fresh basil
3 tablespoons sun-dried (sun-blushed) tomatoes, cut into thin strips
50 g (1¾ oz) Parmesan cheese, shaved

1 Place pine nuts in small pan. Stir over medium heat until golden. Set aside. Cook fettucine in a large pot of boiling water with a little oil added until just tender. Drain and keep warm.

2 Trim tops and tails of beans and cut into long thin strips.

3 Heat oil in a large heavy-based frying pan. Cook onion and garlic over medium heat 3 minutes, or until softened. Add mushrooms, cook, stirring, for 1 minute. Add wine, cream and stock. Bring to boil, reduce heat, simmer for 10 minutes.

4 Lightly beat egg in a bowl. Stirring constantly, add a little cooking liquid to the egg. When combined, pour mixture slowly into pan, stirring constantly for 30 seconds. Add beans, basil, pine nuts and sun-dried tomatoes; stir until heated through. Season. Divide pasta among warmed serving plates and pour sauce over. Garnish with shaved Parmesan. Serve immediately.

PUMPKIN, BASIL AND RICOTTA LASAGNE

Preparation time: 20 minutes
Total cooking time: 1 hour 25 minutes
Serves 4

650 g (1 lb 7 oz) pumpkin
2 tablespoons olive oil
500 g (1 lb 2 oz) ricotta
4 tablespoons pine nuts, toasted
35 g (1¼ oz/¾ cup) firmly
    packed fresh basil
2 cloves garlic, crushed
4 tablespoons finely grated
    Parmesan

125 g (4½ oz) fresh lasagne
    sheets
185 g (6½ oz/1¼ cups) grated
    mozzarella

1 Preheat the oven to moderate 180°C (350°F/Gas 4). Lightly grease a baking tray. Cut the pumpkin into 1 cm (½ inch) slices and arrange in a single layer on the tray. Brush with oil and cook for 1 hour, or until softened, turning halfway through cooking.
2 Combine the ricotta, pine nuts, basil, garlic and Parmesan.
3 Brush a square 20 cm (8 inch) ovenproof dish with oil. Cook the pasta according to the packet instructions. Arrange one third of the pasta sheets over the base of the dish. Spread with the ricotta mixture. Top with half of the remaining lasagne.
4 Arrange the pumpkin evenly over the pasta with as few gaps as possible. Season and top with the final layer of pasta sheets. Sprinkle with mozzarella. Bake for 20–25 minutes, or until the cheese is golden. Leave for 10 minutes, then cut into squares.

COOK'S FILE

Note: If the pasta has no cooking instructions, blanch them one at a time in boiling water.

Mix together the ricotta, pine nuts, basil, garlic and Parmesan.

Cook the pasta according to the packet instructions until al dente.

Place the pumpkin on top of the lasagne sheet, leaving as few gaps as possible.

ROAST SWEET POTATO RAVIOLI

Preparation time: 45 minutes
Total cooking time: 1 hour 10 minutes
Serves 6

500 g (1 lb 2 oz) orange sweet
    potato, cut into large pieces
3 tablespoons olive oil
150 g (5½ oz) ricotta
1 tablespoon chopped fresh basil
1 clove garlic, crushed
2 tablespoons grated Parmesan
2 x 250 g (9 oz) packets egg won
    ton wrappers
50 g (1¾ oz) butter
4 spring onions (scallions),
    sliced on the diagonal
2 cloves garlic, crushed, extra
300 ml (10½ fl oz) cream
baby basil leaves, to serve

1 Preheat the oven to hot 220°C (425°F/Gas 7). Place the sweet potato on a baking tray and drizzle with oil. Bake for 40 minutes, or until tender.

2 Transfer the sweet potato to a bowl with the ricotta, basil, garlic and Parmesan and mash until smooth.

3 Cover the won ton wrappers with a damp tea towel. Place 2 level teaspoons of the sweet potato mixture into the centre of one wrapper and brush the edges with a little water. Top with another wrapper. Place onto a baking tray lined with baking paper and cover with a tea towel. Repeat with the remaining ingredients to make 60 ravioli, placing a sheet of baking paper between each layer.

4 Melt the butter in a frying pan. Add the spring onion and garlic and cook over medium heat for 1 minute. Add the cream, bring to the boil, then reduce the heat and simmer for 4–5 minutes, or until the cream has reduced and thickened. Keep warm.

5 Bring a large saucepan of water to the boil. Cook the ravioli in batches for 2–4 minutes, or until just tender. Drain, then divide among serving plates. Ladle the hot sauce over the top, garnish with basil leaves and serve immediately.

Drizzle the sweet potato with oil and bake until golden.

Cover the filling with a won ton wrapper, lining it up with the bottom won ton.

Simmer the cream mixture until it has reduced and thickened.

Cook the ravioli in batches until just tender.

WARM PESTO PASTA SALAD

Preparation time: 20 minutes
Total cooking time: 20 minutes
Serves 4

Pesto
2 cloves garlic, crushed
1 teaspoon sea salt
3 tablespoons pine nuts, toasted
60 g (2¼ oz/2 cups) fresh basil
50 g (1¾ oz/½ cup) grated
    Parmesan
4 tablespoons extra virgin
    olive oil

500 g (1 lb 2 oz) orecchiette
    or shell pasta
2 tablespoons olive oil
150 g (5½ oz) jar capers,
    drained and patted dry
2 tablespoons extra virgin olive
    oil
2 cloves garlic, chopped
3 tomatoes, seeded and diced
300 g (10½ oz) thin asparagus
    spears, halved and blanched
2 tablespoons balsamic vinegar

200 g (7 oz) rocket (arugula), cut
    into 3 cm (1¼ inch) lengths
shaved Parmesan, to garnish

1 To make the pesto, place the garlic, sea salt and pine nuts in a food processor or blender and process until combined. Add the basil and Parmesan and process until finely minced. With the motor running, add the oil in a thin steady stream and blend until smooth.
2 Cook the pasta in a large saucepan of boiling water until *al dente,* then drain well.
3 Meanwhile, heat the oil in a frying pan, add the capers and fry over high heat, stirring, for 4–5 minutes, or until

crisp. Remove from the pan and drain on paper towel.
4 In the same frying pan, heat the extra virgin olive oil over medium heat and add the garlic, tomato and asparagus. Cook for 1–2 minutes, or until warmed through, tossing continuously. Stir in the vinegar.
5 Drain the pasta and transfer to a large serving bowl. Add the pesto and toss, coating the pasta well. Cool slightly. Add the tomato mixture and rocket and season to taste with salt and cracked black pepper. Toss well and sprinkle with the capers and Parmesan. Serve warm.

Fry the capers over high heat, stirring occasionally, until crisp.

Add the pesto and toss thoroughly through the pasta.

155

PUMPKIN GNOCCHI WITH SAGE BUTTER

Preparation time: 30 minutes +
  5 minutes standing
Total cooking time: 1 hour 45 minutes
Serves 4

500 g (1 lb 2 oz) pumpkin
185 g (6½ oz/1½ cups) plain
  (all-purpose) flour
3 tablespoons freshly grated
  Parmesan cheese

Sage butter
100 g (3½ oz) butter
2 tablespoons fresh sage,
  chopped

3 tablespoons freshly grated
  Parmesan cheese, extra

1 Preheat oven to 180°C (350°F/Gas 4). Brush a baking tray with oil or melted butter. Cut pumpkin into large pieces and place on prepared tray. Bake for 1½ hours, until very tender. Cool slightly. Scrape flesh from skin, avoiding any tough or crispy parts. Place into a large mixing bowl. Sift flour into bowl, add Parmesan cheese and pepper. Mix until well combined. Turn onto a lightly floured surface, knead for 2 minutes, or until smooth.
2 Divide dough in half. Using floured hands, roll each half into a sausage 40 cm (16 inches) long then cut into 16 equal pieces. Form each piece into

an oval shape, indent with floured fork prongs.
3 Heat a large pan of water until boiling. Gently lower batches of gnocchi into water. Cook until gnocchi rise to the surface, and then 3 minutes more. Drain and keep warm.
4 To make sage butter, melt the butter in small pan, remove from heat and stir in sage. Set aside for 5 minutes to keep warm.
5 To serve, divide gnocchi among bowls, drizzle with sage butter and sprinkle with extra Parmesan cheese.

COOK'S FILE

Storage time: Gnocchi can be prepared up to four hours ahead. Cook just before serving.

1

2

3

CARROT PESTO SLICE

Preparation time: 45 minutes
Total cooking time: 50 minutes +
  30 minutes standing
Serves 4

50 g (1¾ oz) butter
60 g (2¼ oz/½ cup) plain (all-
  purpose) flour
750 ml (26 fl oz/3 cups) milk
160 g (5½ oz/⅔ cup) light sour
  cream
1 teaspoon cracked black pepper
100 g (3½ oz) Cheddar cheese,
  grated
4 eggs, lightly beaten
2 tablespoons bottled pesto

750 g (1 lb 10 oz) carrots,
  peeled and grated
250 g (9 oz) packet instant
  lasagne sheets
50 g (1¾ oz) Cheddar cheese,
  grated, extra

1 Grease a 30 x 20 cm (12 x 8 inch) ovenproof baking dish. Heat butter in large pan; add flour. Stir over low heat until mixture is lightly golden and bubbling. Add combined milk, sour cream and pepper gradually to pan, stirring until mixture is smooth. Stir constantly over medium heat for 5 minutes, or until it boils and thickens; boil 1 minute, remove from heat. Stir in cheese, cool slightly. Add eggs gradually, stirring constantly.

2 Pour one-third of the sauce into another bowl for topping; set aside. Add pesto and carrot to remaining sauce, stirring to combine.

3 Preheat oven to 150°C (300°F/Gas 2). Beginning with a layer of the carrot mixture, alternate layers of carrot with lasagne sheets in prepared dish. Use three layers of each, finishing with pasta. Spread reserved sauce evenly over the top. Sprinkle with extra cheese. Leave for 15 minutes before cooking (to allow pasta to soften). Bake for 40 minutes, or until the slice is set and firm to touch. Remove from the oven, cover and set aside for 15 minutes prior to serving (this will help it to slice cleanly).

Grains, pulses & tofu

Using a sharp knife, thinly slice 3 large French shallots.

Use a mortar and pestle to crush the Sichuan peppercorns.

Strain the mushrooms, reserving 125 ml (4 fl oz/½ cup) of the liquid.

ASIAN BARLEY PILAU

Preparation time: 10 minutes +
15 minutes standing
Total cooking time: 35 minutes
Serves 4

15 g (½ oz) dried sliced
    mushrooms
500 ml (17 fl oz/2 cups)
    vegetable stock
125 ml (4 fl oz/½ cup) dry
    sherry
1 tablespoon oil
3 large French shallots, thinly
    sliced
2 large cloves garlic, crushed
1 tablespoon grated fresh ginger
1 teaspoon Sichuan peppercorns,
    crushed (see Note)
330 g (11½ oz/1½ cups) pearl
    barley
500 g (1 lb 2 oz) choy sum, cut
    into 5 cm (2 inch) lengths

3 teaspoons kecap manis
1 teaspoon sesame oil

1 Place the mushrooms in a bowl and cover with boiling water, then leave for 15 minutes. Strain, reserving 125 ml (4 fl oz/½ cup) of the liquid.
2 Bring the stock and sherry to the boil in a saucepan, reduce the heat, cover and simmer until needed.
3 Heat the oil in a large saucepan and cook the shallotsover medium heat for 2–3 minutes, or until soft. Add the garlic, ginger and peppercorns and cook for 1 minute. Add the barley and mushrooms and mix well. Stir in the stock and mushroom liquid, then reduce the heat and simmer, covered, for 25 minutes, or until liquid evaporates.
4 Meanwhile, steam the choy sum until wilted. Add to the barley mixture. Stir in the kecap manis and sesame oil.

Simmer the pilau until all the liquid evaporates.

COOK'S FILE

Note: Buy Sichuan peppercorns at Asian food stores.

LENTIL AND CAULIFLOWER CURRY STACKS

Preparation time: 15 minutes
Total cooking time: 50 minutes
Serves 6

50 g (1¾ oz) ghee or butter
2 onions, thinly sliced
2 tablespoons Madras curry paste
2 cloves garlic, crushed
180 g (6 oz) button mushrooms, sliced
1 litre (4 cups) vegetable stock
300 g (10½ oz) brown or green lentils
400 g (14 oz) can chopped tomatoes
2 sticks cassia bark or cinnamon
300 g (10½ oz) cauliflower, cut into small florets
oil, for deep-frying
18 (8 cm/3 inch) pappadums
plain yoghurt, to serve
coriander (cilantro) sprigs, to garnish

1 Heat the ghee in a saucepan over medium heat and cook the onion for 2–3 minutes, or until soft. Add the curry paste, garlic and mushrooms and cook for 2 minutes, or until soft.
2 Add the stock, lentils, tomato and cassia bark and mix well. Bring to the boil and cook for 40 minutes, or until the lentils are tender. Add the cauliflower in the last 10 minutes and cover. If the curry is too wet, continue to cook, uncovered, until the excess liquid has evaporated. Season to taste. Remove the cassia bark.
3 Meanwhile, fill a deep heavy-based saucepan one third full of oil and heat until a cube of bread dropped into the oil browns in 15 seconds. Cook the pappadums in batches for 10 seconds, or until golden brown and puffed all over. Drain on crumpled paper towels and season with salt.
4 To assemble, place a pappadum on each serving plate and spoon on about 4 tablespoons of the curry. Place a second pappadum on top and spoon on some more curry. Cover with the remaining pappadum and top with a spoonful of yoghurt. Garnish with the coriander and serve immediately. (The pappadums will go soggy if left to stand for too long.)

If the curry is too wet, continue cooking to evaporate the excess liquid.

Drop the pappadums into the oil and cook until puffed and golden.

161

MUSHROOM RISOTTO

Preparation time: 15 minutes
Total cooking time: 40 minutes
Serves 4

1.5 litres (6 cups) vegetable
   stock
500 ml (17 fl oz/2 cups) white
   wine
2 tablespoons olive oil
60 g (2¼ oz) butter
2 leeks, thinly sliced
1 kg (2 lb 4 oz) flat mushrooms,
   sliced
500 g (1 lb 2 oz/2¼ cups)
   arborio rice

75 g (2½ oz/¾ cup) grated
   Parmesan
3 tablespoons chopped fresh
   flat-leaf (Italian) parsley
balsamic vinegar, to serve
shaved Parmesan, to garnish
fresh flat-leaf (Italian) parsley,
   to garnish

1 Place the stock and wine in a large saucepan, bring to the boil, then reduce the heat to low, cover and keep at a low simmer.

2 Heat the oil and butter in a large saucepan. Add the leek and cook over medium heat for 5 minutes, or until soft and golden. Add the mushrooms and cook for 5 minutes, or until tender.

Stir in the arborio rice for 1 minute, or until it is translucent.

3 Add 125 ml (4 fl oz/½ cup) stock, stirring constantly over medium heat until the liquid is absorbed. Continue adding stock, 125 ml (4 fl oz/½ cup) at a time, stirring constantly for 20–25 minutes, or until all the stock is absorbed and the rice is tender and creamy.

4 Stir in the Parmesan and chopped parsley for 1 minute, or until all the cheese is melted. Serve drizzled with vinegar and top with Parmesan shavings and parsley.

Cook the leek and mushrooms in a large saucepan until tender.

Stir the rice constantly until most of the liquid has been absorbed.

Stir the grated Parmesan and parsley into the risotto.

VEGETABLE PILAF

Preparation time: 20 minutes
Total cooking time: 35 minutes
Serves 4

3 tablespoons olive oil
1 medium onion, sliced
2 garlic cloves, crushed
2 teaspoons ground cumin
2 teaspoons paprika
½ teaspoon allspice
300 g (10½ oz/1½ cups) long-grain rice

375 ml (13 fl oz/1½ cups) vegetable stock
185 ml (6 fl oz/¾ cup) white wine
3 medium tomatoes, chopped
150 g (5½ oz) button mushrooms, sliced
2 zucchini (courgettes), sliced
150 g (5½ oz) broccoli, cut into florets

1 Heat oil in a heavy-based pan. Add the onion and cook for 10 minutes over medium heat until golden brown. Add the garlic and spices, cook 1 minute until aromatic.

2 Add rice to the pan, stir until well combined. Add vegetable stock, wine, tomatoes and mushrooms, bring to the boil. Reduce heat to low, cover pan with tight-fitting lid. Simmer for 15 minutes.

3 Add zucchini and broccoli to the pan, replace the lid and cook further 5–7 minutes, until vegetables are just tender. Serve immediately.

1

2

3

VEGETARIAN PAELLA

Preparation time: 20 minutes +
  overnight soaking
Total cooking time: 40 minutes
Serves 6

200 g (7 oz/1 cup) dried haricot
  beans
¼ teaspoon saffron threads
2 tablespoons olive oil
1 onion, diced
1 red capsicum (pepper), cut
  into 1 cm x 4 cm (½ inch x
  1½ inch) strips
5 cloves garlic, crushed
275 g (10 oz/1¼ cups) paella
  rice or arborio rice
1 tablespoon sweet paprika
½ teaspoon mixed spice
750 ml (26 fl oz/3 cups)
  vegetable stock
400 g (14 oz) can diced tomatoes
1½ tablespoons tomato paste
  (concentrated purée)
150 g (5½ oz/1 cup) fresh or
  frozen soya beans
100 g (3½ oz) silverbeet (Swiss
  chard) leaves (no stems),
  shredded
400 g (14 oz) can artichoke
  hearts, drained and quartered
4 tablespoons chopped coriander
  (cilantro) leaves

1 Cover the haricot beans in cold water and soak overnight. Drain and rinse well.
2 Place the saffron threads in a small frying pan over medium–low heat. Dry-fry, shaking for 1 minute, or until darkened. Remove from the heat and when cool, crumble into a small bowl. Pour in 125 ml (4 fl oz/½ cup) warm water and allow to steep.
3 Heat the oil in a large paella pan or frying pan. Add the onion and capsicum and cook over medium–high heat for 4–5 minutes, or until the onion softens. Stir in the garlic and cook for 1 minute. Reduce the heat and add the drained beans, rice, paprika, mixed spice and ½ teaspoon salt. Stir to coat. Add the saffron water, stock, tomatoes and tomato paste and bring to the boil. Cover, reduce the heat and simmer for 20 minutes.
4 Stir in the soy beans, silverbeet and artichoke hearts and cook, covered, for

8 minutes, or until all the liquid is absorbed and the rice and beans are tender. Turn off the heat and leave for

5 minutes. Stir in the coriander just before serving.

Allow the crumbled saffron threads to steep in warm water.

Add the haricot beans, rice, paprika, mixed spice and salt and stir to coat.

MEXICAN-STYLE VEGETABLES

Preparation time: 30 minutes +
  2 hours refrigeration
Total cooking time: 50 minutes
Serves 6

Polenta
330 ml (11¼ fl oz/1⅓ cups)
  vegetable stock
150 g (5½ oz/1 cup) polenta
  (cornmeal)
50 g (1¾ oz/½ cup) freshly
  grated Parmesan cheese
2 tablespoons olive oil

1 large green capsicum
  (pepper)
1 large red capsicum (pepper)
3 tomatoes
6 green button squash
1 fresh corn cob
1 tablespoon oil
1 onion, sliced
1 tablespoon ground cumin
½ teaspoon chilli powder
2 tablespoons chopped fresh
  coriander (cilantro)

1 To make the polenta, brush a 20 cm (8 inch) round springform tin with oil. Place stock and 250 ml (9 fl oz/1 cup) water in a medium pan and bring to the boil. Add the polenta and stir to combine; stir constantly for 10 minutes until very thick (see Note). Remove from heat and stir in Parmesan. Spread the mixture into the prepared tin and smooth the surface. Refrigerate for 2 hours. Turn out, then cut into six wedges. Brush one side with oil, cook under preheated grill (broiler) for 5 minutes, or until edges are browned. Repeat with other side.

2 Cut the capsicum into 2 cm (¾ inch) squares, chop tomatoes, cut squash into quarters and cut corn into 2 cm (¾ inch) slices, quartered.

3 Heat oil in large pan. Cook onion over medium heat 5 minutes, until soft. Stir in the cumin and chilli powder; cook 1 minute. Add vegetables. Bring to the boil, reduce heat. Simmer, covered, over low heat 30 minutes, or until vegetables are tender, stirring occasionally. Stir in the coriander and season with salt and pepper. Serve hot with wedges of polenta.

COOK'S FILE

Storage time: Vegetables can be cooked up to one day ahead. Polenta can be cooked one day ahead. Grill (broil) just before serving.
Note: Polenta must be stirred for the time given, otherwise it will be gritty.

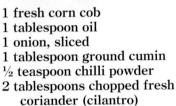

1

2

3

VEGETABLE AND TOFU KEBABS

Preparation time: 40 minutes +
30 minutes marinating
Total cooking time: 30 minutes
Serves 4

500 g (1 lb 2 oz) firm tofu, cut
into 2 cm (¾ inch) cubes
1 red capsicum (pepper), cut
into 2 cm (¾ inch) cubes
3 zucchini (courgettes), cut into
2 cm (¾ inch) lengths
4 small onions, cut into quarters
300 g (10½ oz) button
mushrooms, cut into quarters
125 ml (4 fl oz/½ cup) tamari
125 ml (4 fl oz/½ cup) sesame
oil
3 cm (1½ inch) piece ginger,
peeled and grated
175 g (6 oz/½ cup) honey
1 tablespoon sesame oil, extra
1 small onion, finely chopped
1 clove garlic, crushed
2 teaspoons chilli paste
250 g (9 oz/1 cup) smooth
peanut butter
250 ml (9 fl oz/1 cup) coconut
milk
1 tablespoon soft brown sugar
1 tablespoon tamari, extra
1 tablespoon lemon juice
3 tablespoons peanuts, roasted
and chopped
3 tablespoons sesame seeds,
toasted

1 Preheat the oven to hot 220°C
(425°F/Gas 7). Soak 12 bamboo
skewers in water for 2 hours. Thread
the tofu, capsicum, zucchini, onions
and mushrooms alternately onto the
skewers. Lay out in a large flat dish.

2 Combine the tamari, oil, ginger
and honey in a non-metallic bowl.
Pour over the kebabs. Leave for
30 minutes. Cook on a hot barbecue or
chargrill, basting and turning, for
10–15 minutes, or until just tender.
Keep warm.
3 Heat the extra oil in a frying pan
over medium heat and cook the onion,
garlic and chilli paste for 1–2 minutes,
or until the onion is soft. Reduce the
heat and stir in the peanut butter,
coconut milk, sugar, extra tamari and
lemon juice. Bring to the boil, then
reduce to a simmer for 10 minutes, or
until just thick. Stir in the peanuts. If
the sauce is too thick, add water.
4 Drizzle peanut sauce over the
kebabs and sprinkle with the toasted
sesame seeds.

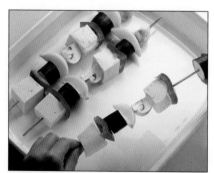

*Thread alternating pieces of tofu and
vegetables onto the skewers.*

*Cook the skewers, occasionally turning and
basting them.*

*Simmer the peanut sauce for 10 minutes,
or until just thickened.*

CHICKPEA PATTIES WITH CARAMELIZED ONION

Preparation time: 20 minutes
Total cooking time: 30 minutes
Serves 4

1 tablespoon olive oil
1 red onion, finely chopped
2 cloves garlic, crushed
1 tablespoon ground cumin
2 x 310 g (10½ oz) cans
 chickpeas, drained
3 tablespoons sunflower seeds
25 g (1 oz/½ cup) finely chopped
 fresh coriander (cilantro)
 leaves

2 eggs, lightly beaten
75 g (2½ oz/⅔ cup) besan
 (chickpea) flour
oil, for shallow-frying
40 g (1½ oz) butter
2 red onions, thinly sliced
3 teaspoons soft brown sugar
plain yoghurt, to serve
 (optional)

1 Heat the oil in a frying pan, add the onion and cook over medium heat for 3 minutes, or until soft. Add the garlic and cumin and cook for 1 minute. Remove from the heat and cool slightly.

2 Blend the chickpeas, sunflower seeds, coriander, egg and onion mixture in a food processor until smooth. Fold in the besan flour and season. Divide the mixture into eight portions and, using floured hands, form into patties. Heat 1 cm (½ inch) oil in a frying pan and cook the patties in two batches over medium heat for 2–3 minutes each side, or until firm. Drain. Keep warm.

3 Melt the butter in a frying pan over medium heat and cook the onion for 10 minutes, stirring occasionally. Add the sugar and cook for 1 minute, or until caramelized. Spoon over the patties with a dollop of yoghurt. Serve with a salad or use to make a burger.

Fold the besan flour into the chickpea purée.

Cook the chickpea patties in batches, until firm and golden on both sides.

Stir in the sugar and cook the onion until it is caramelized.

167

GREEN PILAU WITH CASHEWS

Preparation time: 15 minutes
Total cooking time: 1 hour 10 minutes
Serves 6

200 g (7 oz) baby English
    spinach leaves
100 g (3½ oz/⅔ cup) cashew
    nuts, chopped
2 tablespoons olive oil
6 spring onions (scallions),
    chopped
300 g (10½ oz/1½ cups) long-
    grain brown rice

2 cloves garlic, finely
    chopped
1 teaspoon fennel seeds
2 tablespoons lemon juice
625 ml (21½ fl oz/2½ cups)
    vegetable stock
3 tablespoons chopped fresh
    mint
3 tablespoons chopped fresh
    flat-leaf (Italian) parsley

1 Preheat the oven to moderate 180°C (350°F/Gas 4). Shred the spinach into 1 cm (½ inch) slices.
2 Place the cashew nuts on a baking tray and roast for 5–10 minutes, or until golden brown—watch carefully.

3 Heat the oil in a large frying pan and cook the spring onion over medium heat for 2 minutes, or until soft. Add the rice, garlic and fennel seeds and cook, stirring frequently, for 1–2 minutes, or until the rice is coated. Increase the heat to high, add the lemon juice, stock and 1 teaspoon salt and bring to the boil. Reduce to low, cover and cook covered for 45 minutes. Remove from the heat and sprinkle with the spinach and herbs. Stand, covered, for 8 minutes, then fork the spinach and herbs through the rice. Season. Serve sprinkled with the cashews.

Shred the baby English spinach leaves into 1 cm (½ inch) slices.

Stir the rice until it is evenly coated and starts to stick to the pan.

Fork the spinach and herbs through the rice mixture.

SPICY BEANS ON BAKED SWEET POTATO

Preparation time: 20 minutes
Total cooking time: 1 hour 30 minutes
Serves 6

3 (500 g/1 lb 2 oz in total) evenly
  shaped orange sweet potatoes
1 tablespoon olive oil
1 large onion, chopped
3 cloves garlic, crushed
2 teaspoons ground cumin
1 teaspoon ground
  coriander
½ teaspoon chilli powder
400 g (14 oz) can chopped
  tomatoes
250 ml (9 fl oz/1 cup) vegetable
  stock
1 large zucchini (courgette), cut
  into 1.5 cm (⅝ inch) cubes
1 green capsicum (pepper), cut
  into 1.5 cm (⅝ inch) cubes
310 g (10¾ oz) can corn
  kernels, drained
800 g (1 lb 12 oz) canned red
  kidney beans, rinsed and
  drained

3 tablespoons chopped fresh
  coriander (cilantro) leaves
sour cream, to serve
grated Cheddar, to serve

1 Preheat the oven to hot 210°C
(415°F/Gas 6–7). Rinse the sweet
potatoes, then pierce with a small
sharp knife. Bake on a baking tray for
1–1½ hours, or until soft when tested
with a skewer or sharp knife.
2 Heat the oil in a large saucepan and
cook the onion over medium heat for
5 minutes, stirring occasionally, until
very soft and golden. Add the garlic
and spices, stirring for 1 minute.

3 Add the tomato and stock, stir well,
then add the vegetables and beans.
Bring to the boil, then reduce the heat
and simmer, partially covered, for
20 minutes. Uncover, increase the heat
slightly, and cook for a further
10–15 minutes, or until the liquid has
reduced and thickened. Stir in the
coriander leaves just before serving.
4 To serve, cut the sweet potatoes in
half lengthways. Spoon the vegetable
mixture over the top, add a dollop of
sour cream and sprinkle with cheese.
Serve garnished with fresh coriander.

*Cook the spicy vegetable mixture until the
liquid has reduced.*

*Cut the cooked sweet potatoes in half
lengthways.*

169

LENTIL RISSOLES

Preparation time: 20 minutes +
40 minutes cooling
Total cooking time: 45 minutes
Serves 4

1 tablespoon oil
1 onion, finely chopped
2 large cloves garlic, crushed
2 teaspoons ground cumin
1 teaspoon ground coriander
1 small carrot, finely diced
250 g (9 oz/1 cup) red lentils
120 g (4¼ oz/1½ cups) fresh
    wholemeal (whole-wheat)
    breadcrumbs
65 g (2¼ oz/⅔ cup) walnuts,
    finely chopped
80 g (2¾ oz/½ cup) frozen peas
3 tablespoons chopped fresh
    flat-leaf (Italian) parsley
dry breadcrumbs, for coating
oil, for shallow-frying

1 Heat the oil in a large saucepan.
Cook the onion, garlic, cumin and
ground coriander over medium heat
for 2 minutes, or until the onion has
softened. Stir in the carrot, lentils and
500 ml (17 fl oz/2 cups) water. Slowly
bring to the boil, then reduce the heat
to low and simmer, covered, for
25–30 minutes, or until the lentils are
cooked and pulpy, stirring frequently
to stop the lentils sticking and burning
on the base. Remove the lid during the
last 10 minutes of cooking to
evaporate any remaining liquid.
2 Transfer to a bowl, cover with
plastic wrap and cool for 10 minutes.

*Simmer, covered, until the lentils are cooked
and pulpy.*

Stir in the fresh breadcrumbs, walnuts,
peas and parsley. Form into eight 7 cm
(2¾ inch) round rissoles. Cover and
refrigerate for 30 minutes, or until they
are firm.
3 Evenly coat the rissoles in dry
breadcrumbs, shaking off any excess.
Heat 1 cm (½ inch) oil in a deep frying
pan, add the rissoles and cook in two
batches for 3 minutes each side, or
until golden brown. Drain on crumpled
paper towels, season with salt and
serve with a salad.

*With clean hands, form the mixture into
eight round rissoles.*

FENNEL RISOTTO BALLS WITH CHEESY FILLING

Preparation time: 30 minutes + 1 hour refrigeration
Total cooking time: 50 minutes
Serves 4–6

1.5 litres (6 cups) vegetable stock
1 tablespoon oil
30 g (1 oz) butter
2 cloves garlic, crushed
1 onion, finely chopped
2 fennel bulbs, finely sliced
1 tablespoon balsamic vinegar
125 ml (4 fl oz/½ cup) white wine
660 g (1 lb 7 oz/3 cups) arborio rice
50 g (1¾ oz/½ cup) grated Parmesan
25 g (1 oz/½ cup) snipped fresh chives
1 egg, lightly beaten
150 g (5½ oz/1 cup) sun-dried (sun-blushed) tomatoes, chopped
100 g (3½ oz) mozzarella, diced
80 g (2¾ oz/½ cup) frozen peas, thawed
flour, for dusting
3 eggs, lightly beaten, extra
200 g (7 oz/2 cups) dry breadcrumbs
oil, for deep-frying

1 Heat the stock in a saucepan, cover and keep at a low simmer. Heat the oil and butter in a large saucepan and cook the garlic and onion over medium heat for 3 minutes, or until soft. Add the fennel and cook for 10 minutes, or until it starts to caramelise. Add the vinegar and wine, increase the heat and boil until the liquid evaporates. Add the rice and stir for 1 minute, or until translucent.

2 Add 125 ml (4 fl oz/½ cup) hot stock, stirring constantly over medium heat until the liquid is absorbed. Continue adding more stock, 125 ml (4 fl oz/½ cup) at a time, stirring for 20–25 minutes, or until all the stock is absorbed and the rice is tender and creamy. Stir in the Parmesan, chives, egg and tomato. Transfer to a bowl, cover and cool.

3 Place the mozzarella and peas in a bowl and mash together. Season.

4 With wet hands, shape the risotto into 14 even balls. Flatten each ball out, slightly indenting the centre. Place a heaped teaspoon of the pea mash into the indentation, then shape the rice around the filling to form a ball. Roll each ball in seasoned flour, then dip in the extra egg and roll in breadcrumbs. Place on a foil-covered tray and refrigerate for 30 minutes.

Stir the Parmesan, chives, egg and sun-dried tomato into the risotto.

5 Fill a deep heavy-based saucepan one third full of oil and heat until a cube of bread dropped into the oil browns in 15 seconds. Cook the risotto balls in batches for 5 minutes, or until golden and crisp and the cheese has melted inside. Drain on crumpled paper towels and season with salt. If the cheese has not melted, cook the balls on a tray in a moderate 180°C (350°F/Gas 4) oven for 5 minutes.

Place a heaped teaspoon of the cheesy pea mixture into the indentation.

ASIAN GREENS WITH TERIYAKI TOFU DRESSING

Preparation time: 15 minutes
Total cooking time: 20 minutes
Serves 6

650 g (1 lb 7 oz) baby bok choy
   (pak choi)
500 g (1 lb 2 oz) choy sum
440 g (15½ oz) snake
   (yard-long) beans, topped
   and tailed
3 tablespoons oil
1 onion, thinly sliced

4 tablespoons soft brown sugar
½ teaspoon ground chilli
2 tablespoons grated fresh
   ginger
250 ml (9 fl oz/1 cup) teriyaki
   sauce
1 tablespoon sesame oil
600 g (1 lb 5 oz) silken firm
   tofu, drained

1 Cut the baby bok choy and choy sum widthways into thirds. Cut the beans into 10 cm (4 inch) lengths.

2 Heat a wok over high heat, add 1 tablespoon of the oil and swirl to coat the side. Cook the onion in batches for 3–5 minutes, or until crisp.

Remove with a slotted spoon and drain on paper towels.

3 Heat 1 tablespoon of the oil in the wok, add half the greens and stir-fry for 2–3 minutes, or until wilted. Remove and keep warm. Repeat with the remaining oil and greens. Remove. Drain any liquid from the wok.

4 Add the combined sugar, chilli, ginger and teriyaki sauce to the wok and bring to the boil. Simmer for 1 minute. Add the sesame oil and tofu and simmer for 2 minutes, turning once—the tofu will break up. Divide among serving plates and top with the dressing. Sprinkle with fried onion.

Cut the baby bok choy and choy sum widthways into thirds.

Cook the combined greens in two batches until the leaves are wilted.

Turn the tofu with an egg-flip halfway through cooking.

SPICY VEGETABLE STEW WITH DHAL

Preparation time: 25 minutes +
  2 hours soaking
Total cooking time: 1 hour 35 minutes
Serves 4–6

Dhal
165 g (5¾ oz/¾ cup) yellow split
  peas
5 cm (2 inch) piece ginger,
  grated
2–3 cloves garlic, crushed
1 red chilli, seeded and chopped

3 tomatoes
2 tablespoons oil
1 teaspoon yellow mustard seeds
1 teaspoon cumin seeds
1 teaspoon ground cumin
½ teaspoon garam masala
1 red onion, cut into thin wedges
3 slender eggplants
  (aubergines), cut into 2 cm
  (¾ inch) slices
2 carrots, cut into 2 cm (¾ inch)
  slices
¼ cauliflower, cut into florets
375 ml (13 fl oz/1½ cups)
  vegetable stock
2 small zucchini (courgettes),
  cut into 3 cm (1¼ inch) slices
80 g (2¾ oz/½ cup) frozen peas
15 g (½ oz/½ cup) fresh
  coriander (cilantro) leaves

1 To make the dhal, place the split peas in a bowl, cover with water and soak for 2 hours. Drain. Place in a large saucepan with the ginger, garlic, chilli and 750 ml (26 fl oz/3 cups) water. Bring to the boil, then reduce the heat and simmer for 45 minutes, or until soft.

2 Score a cross in the base of the tomatoes, soak in boiling water for 2 minutes, then plunge into cold water and peel the skin away from the cross. Remove the seeds and roughly chop.

3 Heat the oil in a large saucepan. Cook the spices over medium heat for 30 seconds, or until fragrant. Add the onion and cook a further 2 minutes, or until soft. Stir in the tomato, eggplant, carrot and cauliflower.

4 Stir in the dhal purée and stock and simmer, covered, for 45 minutes, or until the vegetables are tender. Stir often. Add the zucchini and peas during the last 10 minutes of cooking. Stir in the coriander and serve hot.

Peel the skin away from the cross, then remove the seeds and chop.

Simmer the dhal mixture until the split peas are soft.

Simmer for 45 minutes, or until the vegetables are tender.

173

MUSHROOMS WITH BEAN PUREE, PUY LENTILS AND RED WINE SAUCE

Preparation time: 30 minutes
Total cooking time: 30 minutes
Serves 4

4 large (10 cm/4 inch) field
    mushrooms
1 tablespoon olive oil
1 red onion, cut into thin wedges
1 clove garlic, crushed
200 g (7 oz) puy lentils
185 ml (6 fl oz/¾ cup) red wine
440 ml (15½ fl oz/1¾ cups)
    vegetable stock
1 tablespoon finely chopped
    fresh flat-leaf (Italian)
    parsley
30 g (1 oz) butter
2 cloves garlic, crushed, extra

Bean purée
1 large potato, cut into chunks
2 tablespoons extra virgin olive
    oil
400 g (14 oz) can cannellini
    beans, drained and rinsed
2 large cloves garlic, crushed
1 tablespoon vegetable stock

Red wine sauce
170 ml (5½ fl oz/⅔ cup) red
    wine
2 tablespoons tomato paste
    (concentrated purée)
375 ml (13 fl oz/1½ cups)
    vegetable stock
1 tablespoon soft brown sugar

1 Remove the stalks from the mushrooms and chop. Heat the oil in a saucepan and cook the onion over medium heat for 2–3 minutes, or until soft. Add the garlic and mushroom stalks and cook for 1 minute. Stir in the lentils, wine and stock and bring to the boil. Reduce the heat and simmer, covered, for 20–25 minutes, stirring occasionally, or until reduced and the lentils are cooked through. If the mixture is too wet, remove the lid and boil until slightly thick. Stir in the parsley and keep warm.

2 To make the bean purée, bring a small saucepan of water to the boil over high heat and cook the potato for 4–5 minutes, or until tender. Drain and mash with a potato masher or fork until smooth. Stir in half the extra virgin olive oil. Combine the cannellini beans and garlic in a food processor bowl. Add the stock and the remaining oil and process until smooth. Transfer to a bowl and fold in the mashed potato. Keep warm.

3 Melt butter in a deep frying pan. Add the mushrooms and extra garlic and cook in batches over medium heat for 4 minutes each side, or until tender. Remove and keep warm.

4 To make the red wine sauce, add the red wine to the same frying pan, then scrape the bottom to remove any sediment. Add the combined tomato paste, stock and sugar and bring to the boil. Cook for about 10 minutes, or until reduced and thickened.

5 To assemble, place the mushrooms onto serving plates and top with the bean purée. Spoon on the lentil mixture and drizzle with the red wine sauce. Season and serve immediately.

COOK'S FILE

Note: The mushrooms will shrivel if kept warm in the oven—either turn the oven off or find another warm place for them.

Remove, then very finely chop the mushroom stalks.

Cook the lentils until they are cooked through and the liquid is reduced.

Fold the mashed potato into the cannellini bean purée.

Fry the mushrooms over medium heat until tender, turning once.

Scrape the bottom of the frying pan to remove any sediment stuck to the bottom.

Cook the red wine sauce until it is reduced and thickened.

ASPARAGUS AND PISTACHIO RISOTTO

Preparation time: 10 minutes
Total cooking time: 30 minutes
Serves 4–6

1 litre (4 cups) vegetable stock
250 ml (9 fl oz/1 cup) white wine
4 tablespoons extra virgin
    olive oil
1 red onion, finely chopped
440 g (15½ oz/ 2 cups)
    arborio rice
310 g (10¾ oz) asparagus
    spears, trimmed and cut into
3 cm (1¼ inch) pieces
125 ml (4 fl oz/½ cup) cream
100 g (3½ oz/1 cup) grated
    Parmesan
40 g (1½ oz/½ cup) shelled
    pistachio nuts, toasted and
    roughly chopped

1 Heat the stock and wine in a large saucepan, bring to the boil, then reduce the heat, cover and keep at a low simmer.
2 Heat the oil in another large saucepan. Add the onion and cook over medium heat for 3 minutes, or until soft. Add the rice and stir for 1 minute, until the rice is translucent.

3 Add 125 ml (4 fl oz/½ cup) hot stock, stirring constantly over medium heat until the liquid is absorbed. Continue adding more stock, 125 ml (4 fl oz/½ cup) at a time, stirring constantly for 20–25 minutes, or until all the stock is absorbed and the rice is tender and creamy in texture. Add the asparagus during the last 5 minutes of cooking. Remove from the heat.
4 Stand for 2 minutes, stir in the cream and Parmesan and season to taste with salt and black pepper. Serve sprinkled with pistachios.

Add the rice to the saucepan and stir until it is translucent.

Add a little more stock when most of the liquid has been absorbed.

Stir the cream and Parmesan through the risotto.

MISO TOFU STICKS WITH CUCUMBER AND WAKAME SALAD

Preparation time: 30 minutes +
20 minutes standing
Total cooking time: 15 minutes
Serves 4

3 Lebanese (short) cucumbers, thinly sliced into rounds
20 g (¾ oz) dried wakame
500 g (1 lb 2 oz) silken firm tofu, well drained
3 tablespoons shiro miso
1 tablespoon mirin
1 tablespoon sugar
1 tablespoon rice vinegar
1 egg yolk
100 g (3½ oz) bean sprouts, blanched
2 tablespoons sesame seeds, toasted

Dressing
3 tablespoons rice vinegar
¼ teaspoon soy sauce
1½ tablespoons sugar
1 tablespoon mirin

1 Sprinkle the cucumber generously with salt and leave for 20 minutes, or until very soft, then rinse and drain. To rehydrate the wakame, place it in a colander in the sink and leave it under cold running water for 10 minutes, then drain well.
2 Place the tofu in a colander, weigh down with a plate and leave to drain.
3 Stir the shiro miso, mirin, sugar, rice vinegar and 2 tablespoons water in a saucepan over low heat for 1 minute, or until the sugar dissolves. Remove from the heat and whisk in the egg yolk until glossy. Cool slightly.

4 Cut the tofu into thick sticks and place on a non-stick baking tray. Brush the miso mixture over the tofu and cook under a hot grill (broiler) for 6 minutes each side, or until light golden on both sides.
5 To make the dressing, place all the ingredients and ½ teaspoon salt in a bowl and whisk together well.

6 To assemble, place the cucumber in the centre of a plate, top with the sprouts and wakame, drizzle with the dressing, top with tofu and serve sprinkled with the sesame seeds.

Once the cucumber is very soft, rinse the salt off under running water.

Place the wakame in a colander and leave it under cold running water.

Brush the miso mixture over the tofu sticks and grill (broil) under golden.

177

THAI TEMPEH

Preparation time: 15 minutes +
  overnight marinating
Total cooking time: 20 minutes
Serves 4

2 stems lemon grass, finely
  chopped
2 makrut lime (kaffir) leaves,
  shredded, plus extra
2 small red chillies, seeded
  and finely chopped
3 cloves garlic, crushed
2 teaspoons sesame oil
125 ml (4 fl oz/½ cup) lime
  juice
2 teaspoons shaved palm
  (jaggery) sugar
125 ml (4 fl oz/½ cup) soy
  sauce
600 g (1 lb 5 oz) tofu tempeh,
  cut into twelve 5 mm (¼ inch)
  slices
3 tablespoons peanut oil
1 tablespoon shaved palm sugar,
  extra

100 g (3½ oz) snow pea
  (mangetout) sprouts or
  watercress

1 Place the lemon grass, lime leaves,
chilli, garlic, sesame oil, lime juice,
sugar and soy sauce in a non-metallic
bowl and mix. Add the tempeh and
stir. Cover and marinate overnight in
the fridge, turning occasionally.
2 Drain the tempeh, reserving the
marinade. Heat half the peanut oil in a
frying pan over high heat. Cook the
tempeh in batches, turning once, for

5 minutes, or until crispy, adding more
oil when needed. Drain on paper
towels. Heat the reserved marinade
with the extra palm sugar in a
saucepan until syrupy.
3 Divide one third of the tempeh
among four serving plates and top
with half the snow pea sprouts.
Continue with the remaining
ingredients to give three layers of
tempeh and two layers of sprouts,
finishing with the tempeh on top.
Drizzle with the reserved marinade
and sprinkle with extra lime leaves.

*Cook the tempeh in batches, turning once,
until crispy.*

*Heat the reserved marinade and extra
palm sugar in a saucepan until syrupy.*

RICE AND RED LENTIL PILAU

Preparation time: 15 minutes
Total cooking time: 25 minutes
Serves 4–6

1 tablespoon coriander seeds
1 tablespoon cardamom pods
1 tablespoon cumin seeds
1 teaspoon whole black
   peppercorns
1 teaspoon whole cloves
1 small cinnamon stick, crushed
3 tablespoons oil

1 onion, chopped
3 cloves garlic, chopped
200 g (7 oz/1 cup) basmati rice
250 g (9 oz/1 cup) red lentils
750 ml (26 fl oz/3 cups) hot
   vegetable stock
spring onions (scallions), sliced
   on the diagonal, to garnish

1 To make the garam masala, place all the spices in a dry frying pan and shake over medium heat for 1 minute, or until fragrant. Blend in a spice grinder or blender to a fine powder.

2 Heat the oil in a saucepan. Add the onion, garlic and 3 teaspoons garam masala. Cook over medium heat for 3 minutes, or until the onion is soft.

3 Stir in the rice and lentils and cook for 2 minutes. Add the stock and stir well. Slowly bring to the boil, then reduce the heat and simmer, covered, for 15–20 minutes, or until the rice is cooked and all the stock has been absorbed. Gently fluff the rice with a fork. Garnish with spring onion.

COOK'S FILE

Note: You can use ready-made garam masala instead of making it.

Finely chop all the spices in a spice grinder until they are a fine powder.

Stir the rice and lentils into the onion and garlic mixture.

Simmer, covered, until the rice is cooked and all the stock has been absorbed.

BROWN RICE AND CASHEW PATTIES WITH CORIANDER SAMBAL

Preparation time: 30 minutes +
overnight soaking + 30 minutes
refrigeration
Total cooking time: 2 hours 5 minutes
Serves 8

250 g (9 oz) dried chickpeas
660 g (1 lb 7 oz/3 cups) instant
    brown rice (see Note)
1 tablespoon oil
1 onion, finely chopped
125 g (4½ oz) roasted cashew
    paste
1 egg
3 tablespoons tahini
1 teaspoon ground cumin
1 teaspoon ground turmeric
2 tablespoons tamari
1 tablespoon lemon juice
1 vegetable stock cube
1 small carrot, grated
40 g (1½ oz/½ cup) fresh
    wholemeal (whole-wheat)
    breadcrumbs
oil, for shallow-frying
2 tablespoons oil, extra
310 g (10¾ oz) bok choy
    (pak choi), trimmed
    and washed
3 tablespoons tamari, extra

Coriander and coconut sambal
90 g (3¼ oz/3 cups) fresh
    coriander (cilantro) leaves
1 clove garlic, chopped
1 small fresh green chilli, seeded
    and finely chopped
1 teaspoon garam masala
2 tablespoons lime juice
3 tablespoons shredded coconut

1 Soak the chickpeas in cold water overnight. Drain. Place in a large saucepan and cover with water. Bring to the boil and cook for 1–1½ hours, or until cooked. Drain, reserving 2 tablespoons of the liquid.

2 Bring a saucepan of water to the boil and cook the rice over medium heat for 10–12 minutes, or until tender. Rinse well and drain. Keep warm.

3 Heat the oil in a frying pan and cook the onion for 2–3 minutes, or until golden. Set aside.

4 Mix the chickpeas, cashew paste, egg, tahini, cumin, turmeric, tamari, lemon juice, stock cube and reserved chickpea liquid in a food processor until smooth. Transfer to a large bowl and add the rice, onion, carrot and breadcrumbs and mix well. Divide the mixture into 16 even portions and form into patties 1.5 cm (⅝ inch) thick. Refrigerate for 30 minutes.

5 To make the sambal, finely chop all the ingredients in a food processor. Refrigerate until ready to use.

6 Heat the oil in a large deep frying pan over medium heat and cook the patties in batches for 3–4 minutes each side, or until golden and cooked through. Remove and keep warm. In the same pan, heat the extra oil and cook the bok choy, tossing, for 1–2 minutes, or until wilted. Pour on the extra tamari and toss through. Place the bok choy on eight serving plates and top with two patties. Spoon a dollop of chilled sambal on top and serve immediately.

COOK'S FILE

Note: The rice has been cooked, then dehydrated so it takes less time to cook than normal rice.

Cook the brown rice over medium heat until tender.

Mix the chickpeas and other ingredients in a food processor until smooth.

Using your hands, form the mixture into 16 even patties.

Finely chop all the sambal ingredients in a food processor.

Cook the patties in batches until golden brown and cooked through.

Cook the bok choy until wilted, then toss through the extra tamari.

181

TOFU BURGERS

Preparation time: 25 minutes +
　30 minutes refrigeration
Total cooking time: 30 minutes
Serves 6

1 tablespoon olive oil
1 red onion, finely chopped
200 g (7 oz) Swiss brown
　mushrooms, finely chopped
350 g (12 oz) hard tofu
2 large cloves garlic
3 tablespoons finely chopped
　fresh basil
200 g (7 oz/2 cups) dry
　wholemeal (whole-wheat)
　breadcrumbs
1 egg, lightly beaten
2 tablespoons balsamic vinegar
2 tablespoons sweet chilli
　sauce
150 g (5½ oz/1½ cups) dry
　wholemeal (whole-wheat)
　breadcrumbs, extra
olive oil, for shallow-frying
6 wholemeal (whole-wheat) or
　wholegrain bread rolls
125 g (4½ oz/½ cup) whole-egg
　mayonnaise
100 g (3½ oz) semi-dried (sun-
　blushed) tomatoes
60 g (2¼ oz) rocket (arugula)
sweet chilli sauce, to serve
　(optional)

1 Heat the oil in a frying pan and cook the onion over medium heat for 2–3 minutes, or until soft. Add the mushrooms and cook for a further 2 minutes. Cool slightly.
2 Blend 250 g (9 oz) of the tofu with the garlic and basil in a food processor until smooth. Transfer to a large bowl and stir in the mushroom mixture, breadcrumbs, egg, vinegar and sweet chilli sauce. Grate remaining tofu and fold through mixture, then refrigerate for 30 minutes. Form the mixture into six patties, pressing together well. Coat them in the extra breadcrumbs.
3 Heat 1 cm (½ inch) oil in a deep frying pan and cook the patties in two batches for 4–5 minutes each side, or until golden. Turn them over carefully to prevent them breaking up. Drain on crumpled paper towels and season.
4 Toast bread rolls under a hot grill (broiler). To assemble, spread the mayonnaise over both sides of each toasted bread roll. On bottom half of each roll, layer semi-dried tomatoes, a tofu patty and rocket leaves. Drizzle with sweet chilli sauce and top with the other half of the bread roll.

Blend the tofu, garlic and basil in a food processor until smooth.

Grate the remaining tofu and fold it into the mixture.

Carefully turn over the tofu patties with an egg flip.

VEGETABLE RISOTTO

Preparation time: 15 minutes
Total cooking time: 30 minutes
Serves 6

1.375 litres (5½ cups) vegetable
   stock
10 asparagus spears, cut into
   3 cm (1¼ inch) lengths
2 zucchini (courgettes), cut into
   2 cm (¾ inch) slices
100 g (3½ oz) snow peas
   (mangetout), cut into 2 cm
   (¾ inch) lengths
2 tablespoons olive oil
1 onion, finely chopped
330 g (11½ oz/1½ cups) short-
   grain rice
2 small tomatoes, chopped
50 g (1¾ oz/½ cup) grated
   Parmesan cheese

1 Place stock in a pan. Cover, bring to
the boil. Reduce heat and keep at a
simmer. Place asparagus, zucchini and
snow peas in a heatproof bowl, cover
with boiling water. Let stand
2 minutes; drain. Refresh with cold
water; drain.
2 Heat oil in a heavy-based pan. Add
onion, stir over medium heat until
golden; add rice. Reduce heat to
medium–low, stir rice for 3 minutes, or
until lightly golden. Add quarter of
stock to the pan, stirring constantly
for 7 minutes, or until all the stock
is absorbed.
3 Repeat the process until all but
125 ml (4 fl oz/½ cup) stock has been
used, and rice is almost tender. Add
vegetables, tomatoes and remaining
stock; stir for 5 minutes until liquid is
absorbed and vegetables are tender.
Stir in Parmesan. Serve at once.

COOK'S FILE

Storage time: Cook this dish just
before serving.

Pizzas, pies & pastries

SWEET POTATO AND LENTIL PASTRY POUCHES

Preparation time: 45 minutes
Total cooking time: 55 minutes
Makes 32

2 tablespoons olive oil
1 large leek, finely chopped
2 cloves garlic, crushed
125 g (4½ oz) button
    mushrooms, roughly chopped
2 teaspoons ground cumin
2 teaspoons ground coriander
95 g (3¼ oz/½ cup) brown or
    green lentils
125 g (4½ oz/½ cup) red lentils
500 ml (17 fl oz/2 cups)
    vegetable stock
300 g (10½ oz) sweet potato,
    diced
4 tablespoons finely chopped
    fresh coriander (cilantro)
    leaves
8 sheets ready-rolled puff
    pastry
1 egg, lightly beaten
½ leek, extra, cut into 5 mm
    (¼ inch) wide strips
200 g (7 oz) plain yoghurt
2 tablespoons grated Lebanese
    (short) cucumber
½ teaspoon soft brown sugar

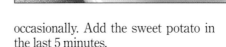

1 Preheat the oven to moderately hot 200°C (400°F/Gas 6). Heat the oil in a saucepan over medium heat and cook the leek for 2–3 minutes, or until soft. Add the garlic, mushrooms, cumin and ground coriander and cook for 1 minute, or until fragrant.

2 Add the combined lentils and stock and bring to the boil. Reduce the heat and simmer for 20–25 minutes, or until the lentils are cooked through, stirring occasionally. Add the sweet potato in the last 5 minutes.

3 Transfer to a bowl and stir in the coriander. Season to taste. Cool.

4 Cut the pastry sheets into four even squares. Place 1½ tablespoons of filling into the centre of each square and bring the edges together to form a pouch. Pinch together, then tie with string. Lightly brush the party with egg and place on lined baking trays. Bake for 20–25 minutes, or until the pastry is puffed and golden.

5 Soak the leek strips in boiling water for 30 seconds. Remove the string and re-tie with a piece of blanched leek. Mix the yoghurt, cucumber and sugar in a bowl. Serve with the pouches.

Transfer to a bowl and stir in the coriander leaves.

Put the filling in the centre of each square, form a pouch and tie with string

Blanch the long strips of leek by soaking them for 30 seconds in boiling water.

CARAMELIZED ONION AND SPINACH TART

Preparation time: 25 minutes +
10 minutes standing
Total cooking time: 2 hours
Serves 6

125 g (4½ oz/1 cup) plain
(all-purpose) flour
90 g (3¼ oz) butter, chopped
1 egg yolk

Filling
5 medium (1 kg/2 lb 4 oz) onions,
thinly sliced
3 tablespoons soft brown sugar
2 tablespoons brown vinegar
1 bay leaf
3 dried chillies

Topping
130 g (4½ oz/2 cups) finely
chopped English spinach
125 g (4½ oz/1 cup) grated
Cheddar cheese
3 tablespoons self-raising flour
1 teaspoon mustard powder
310 ml (10¾ fl oz/1¼ cups)
cream
2 eggs, lightly beaten

1 Preheat oven to 210°C (415°F/Gas 6–7). Grease a 20 cm (8 inch) round springform tin. Place flour and butter in food processor bowl. Using the pulse action, process for 15 seconds, or until the mixture is fine and crumbly. Add egg yolk and 1 tablespoon water and process for 20 seconds until smooth.

2 Press pastry evenly over base of prepared tin; refrigerate 10 minutes. Cut a sheet of greaseproof paper large enough to cover the pastry-lined tin. Spread a layer of rice evenly over paper. Bake 20 minutes; remove from oven and discard rice. Allow to cool. Combine onions, sugar, vinegar, bay leaf, chillies and 185 ml (6 fl oz/¾ cup) water in medium heavy-based pan. Stir over medium heat until sugar has dissolved and mixture is boiling. Reduce the heat and simmer, covered, 1 hour, stirring occasionally. Drain any excess liquid; discard bay leaf and chillies.

3 To make the topping, place all ingredients in large mixing bowl and mix well. Spread the cooled onion mixture evenly over the pastry base. Spoon the topping over the onion. Bake for 45 minutes, or until topping is golden. Serve warm or cool.

ROAST VEGETABLE TART

Preparation time: 30 minutes
Total cooking time: 1 hour 45 minutes
Serves 4–6

2 slender eggplants
    (aubergines), halved and cut
    into thick slices
350 g (12 oz) pumpkin, cut into
    large pieces
2 zucchini (courgettes), halved
    and cut into thick slices
1–2 tablespoons olive oil
1 large red capsicum (pepper),
    chopped
1 teaspoon olive oil, extra
1 red onion, cut into thin
    wedges
1 tablespoon Korma curry paste
plain yoghurt, to serve

Pastry
185 g (6½ oz/1½ cups) plain
    (all-purpose) flour
125 g (4½ oz) butter, chopped
100 g (3½ oz/⅔ cup) roasted
    cashews, finely chopped
1 teaspoon cumin seeds
2–3 tablespoons chilled water

1 Preheat the oven to moderately hot 200°C (400°F/Gas 6). Put the eggplant, pumpkin and zucchini on a lined oven tray, then brush with oil and bake for 30 minutes. Turn, add the capsicum and bake for 30 minutes. Cool.

2 Meanwhile, heat the extra oil in a frying pan and cook the onion for 2–3 minutes, or until soft. Add the curry paste and cook, stirring, for 1 minute, or until fragrant and well mixed. Cool. Reduce the oven to moderate 180°C (350°F/Gas 4).

3 To make the pastry, sift the flour into a bowl and add the butter. Rub the butter into the flour with your fingertips until it resembles fine breadcrumbs. Stir in the cashews and cumin seeds. Make a well in the centre and add the water. Mix with a flat-bladed knife, using a cutting action, until the mixture comes together in beads. Gather together and lift out onto baking paper. Flatten to a disc, then roll out to a 35 cm (14 inch) circle.

4 Lift onto an oven tray and spread the onion mixture over the pastry, leaving a 6 cm (2½ inch) border. Arrange the other vegetables over the onion, piling it slightly higher in the centre. Fold the edge of the pastry around in pleats over the vegetables. Bake for 45 minutes, or until the pastry is golden. Serve with yoghurt.

Spread the onion mixture over the pastry, leaving a 6 cm (2½ inch) border.

Fold the edge of the pastry over the vegetables in rough pleats.

FETA, TOMATO AND OLIVE PIZZA

Preparation time: 30 minutes +
  1 hour rising
Total cooking time: 50 minutes
Serves 4–6

Pizza base
7 g (⅛ oz) sachet dry yeast
90 g (3¼ oz/¾ cup) plain
  (all-purpose) flour
110 g (4 oz/¾ cup) wholemeal
  (whole-wheat) plain
  (all-purpose) flour
1 tablespoon olive oil
1 tablespoon oil
2 onions, sliced
2 teaspoons soft brown sugar
1–2 tablespoons olive paste
250 g (9 oz) cherry tomatoes,
  halved
200 g (9 oz) feta, crumbled
3 tablespoons loosely packed
  fresh basil, shredded

1 To make the dough, place the yeast and flours in a large bowl and mix well. Make a well in the centre and add the oil and 125 ml (4 fl oz/½ cup) warm water. Mix well, adding a little more water if it seems too dry, then gather together. Turn onto a lightly floured surface and knead for 5 minutes, then place into a lightly oiled bowl. Cover with plastic wrap and leave in a draught-free place for 1 hour.

2 Heat the oil in a frying pan and cook the onion over medium–low heat for 20 minutes, stirring often. Stir in the sugar and cook for 1–2 minutes, or until caramelized. Cool.

3 Preheat the oven to hot 220°C (425°F/Gas 7). Punch down the dough and knead for 1 minute. Roll out to a 30 cm (12 inch) round, then tuck 1 cm (½ inch) of the dough under to create a rim. Sprinkle an oven tray lightly with polenta or brush with oil, and place the dough on the tray.

4 Spread the paste over the dough, leaving a 1 cm (½ inch) border, then top with the onion. Arrange the tomato on the onion, and sprinkle with feta and basil. Bake for 25 minutes.

Pour the olive oil and 125 ml (4 fl oz/ ½ cup) warm water into the well.

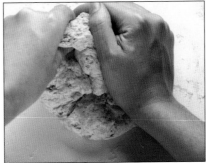

Turn the dough out onto a lightly floured surface and knead.

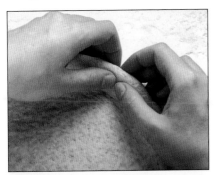

Fold the edges of the dough under to make a rim.

Sprinkle the feta over the onion and tomato.

TOMATO AND THYME QUICHE

Preparation time: 35 minutes +
  30 minutes refrigeration
Total cooking time: 50 minutes
Makes one 23 cm (9 inch) quiche

185 g (6½ oz/1½ cups) plain
  (all-purpose) flour
125 g (4½ oz) butter, chopped
1 egg yolk
2–3 tablespoons water
425 g (15 oz) can tomatoes
4 eggs
300 g (10½ oz) sour cream
3 tablespoons grated Parmesan
  cheese
2 spring onions (scallions),
  finely chopped

1–2 tablespoons chopped fresh
  thyme
ground black pepper

1 Preheat oven to moderately hot 210°C (425°F/Gas 6–7). Sift flour, rub in butter with fingertips for 2 minutes or until mixture is fine and crumbly. Add combined egg yolk and water, mix to a soft dough. Turn onto lightly floured surface, knead 10 seconds until smooth. Store, covered with plastic wrap, in refrigerator for 30 minutes. Roll pastry out to cover base and sides of shallow 23 cm (9 inch) flan tin. Cover with greaseproof paper. Spread a layer of dried beans or rice on top. Bake for 10 minutes. Remove from oven, discard paper and rice. Return pastry to oven for another 5 minutes or until lightly golden. Remove from

oven. Reduce heat to moderate 180°C (350°F/Gas 4).
2 Drain tomatoes, halve lengthways. Place cut-side down on paper towels to drain. Beat eggs and sour cream until combined; stir in cheese and onion.
3 Pour filling into pastry shell. Arrange tomatoes, cut-side down, over filling. Sprinkle with thyme and pepper. Bake for 30 minutes or until filling is set and lightly golden.

COOK'S FILE

Storage time: Pastry shell can be baked a day ahead and stored in an airtight container. Add filling and bake just before serving.

FILO VEGETABLE POUCHES

Preparation time: 45 minutes
Total cooking time: 35–40 minutes
Makes 12

8 sheets filo pastry
125 g (4½ oz) butter, melted
80 g (2¾ oz/½ cup) sesame
  seeds

Filling
465 g (1 lb/3 cups) grated carrot
2 large onions, finely chopped
1 tablespoon grated ginger
1 tablespoon finely chopped
  fresh coriander (cilantro)

230 g (8 oz) can water
  chestnuts, rinsed and sliced
1 tablespoon miso
3 tablespoons tahini paste

1 Preheat oven to 180°C (350°F/ Gas 4). Brush two oven trays with melted butter or oil. To make the filling, combine carrot, onions, ginger, coriander and 250 ml (9 fl oz/1 cup) water in large pan. Cover, cook over low heat 20 minutes. Uncover, cook a further 5 minutes, or until all liquid has evaporated. Remove from heat, cool slightly. Stir in water chestnuts, miso and tahini. Season with pepper.
2 Place one sheet of filo pastry on work surface. Brush lightly with butter. Top with another three pastry

sheets, brushing between each layer. Cut filo into six even squares. Repeat the process with the remaining pastry giving 12 squares in total.
3 Divide the filling evenly between each square, placing the filling in the centre. Bring the edges together and pinch to form a pouch. Brush the lower portion of each pouch with butter, then press in the sesame seeds. Place on prepared trays and bake for 10–12 minutes, or until golden brown and crisp. Serve hot with sweet chilli sauce, if liked.

COOK'S FILE

Hint: Miso is a salty soya bean paste, available from Asian food stores and supermarkets.

PUMPKIN TARTS

Preparation time: 20 minutes +
  30 minutes refrigeration
Total cooking time: 30 minutes
Serves 6

250 g (9 oz/2 cups) plain
  (all-purpose) flour
125 g (4½ oz) chilled butter, cut
  into cubes
125 ml (4 fl oz/½ cup) chilled
  water
1.2 kg (2 lb 12 oz) pumpkin, cut
  into 6 cm (2½ inch) pieces
125 g (4½ oz/½ cup) sour cream
  or cream cheese
sweet chilli sauce, to serve

1 Sift the flour and a pinch of salt into a large bowl and add the chopped butter. Rub the butter into the flour with your fingertips until it resembles fine breadcrumbs. Make a well in the centre, add the water and mix with a flat-bladed knife, using a cutting action, until the mixture comes together in beads. Gently gather the dough together and lift out onto a lightly floured work surface. Press together into a ball, flatten it slightly into a disc, wrap in plastic wrap and refrigerate for 30 minutes.

2 Preheat the oven to moderately hot 200°C (400°F/Gas 6). Divide the pastry into six balls and roll each one out to fit a 10 cm (4 inch) pie dish. Invert the pastry into the pie dishes. Trim the edges and prick the bases all over. Place on a baking tray and bake for 15 minutes, or until lightly golden, pressing down any pastry that puffs up. Cool, then remove the tart shelles from the tins.

3 To make the filling, steam the pumpkin pieces for about 15 minutes, or until tender.

4 Place a tablespoon of sour cream in the middle of each tart and pile the pumpkin pieces on top. Season with salt and cracked black pepper and drizzle with sweet chilli sauce to taste. Return to the oven for a couple of minutes to heat through. Serve immediately with a salad.

COOK'S FILE

Note: Try roasting the pumpkin with garlic, olive oil and fresh thyme to add a delicious flavour. For added texture, add cumin seeds to the pastry.

Fit the pastry into the 10 cm (4 inch) pie dishes, trim to fit, then prick the bases.

Pile the pumpkin pieces on top of the sour cream.

VEGETABLE SAMOSAS

Preparation time: 20 minutes
Total cooking time: 30 minutes
Makes 32

1 tablespoon ghee or oil
1 small onion, finely chopped
1 garlic clove, crushed
2 teaspoons grated fresh ginger
1 teaspoon mustard seeds
1 teaspoon ground cumin
½ teaspoon turmeric
¼ teaspoon chilli powder
300 g (10½ oz) potatoes
80 g (2¾ oz/½ cup) frozen peas
2 tablespoons chopped fresh
   coriander (cilantro)
4 sheets frozen shortcrust
   pastry
oil, for deep frying

Yoghurt dip
½ small cucumber
250 g (9 oz/1 cup) plain yoghurt
2 tablespoons finely chopped
   fresh mint

1 Heat ghee or oil in medium pan, add onion, garlic and ginger. Cook over low heat for 5 minutes, or until onion is soft. Add spices, cook for 1 minute.
2 Cut potatoes into 7 mm (¼ inch) cubes. Add to the pan and stir to combine. Add 185 ml (6 fl oz/¾ cup) water, cover and cook, stirring occasionally, for 5–10 minutes, or until potatoes are just tender. Drain.
3 Remove the pan from heat and stir in peas, coriander and salt; cool.
4 Cut sixteen 12 cm (5 inch) pastry circles and cut each in half. Fold each semicircle in half; pinch the straight sides together to form cones. Spoon 2 teaspoons of filling into each cone. Pinch edge to seal. Heat oil in a medium pan. Cook samosas in batches in moderately hot oil 2–3 minutes until crisp and golden. Drain on paper towels. Serve warm with yoghurt dip.
5 To make the yoghurt dip, peel cucumber, remove seeds and finely chop flesh. Combine with yoghurt and mint in a small bowl.

1

2

3

4

FRESH HERB QUICHE

Preparation time: 30 minutes +
  50 minutes refrigeration
Total cooking time: 1 hour
Serves 4–6

185 g (6 oz/1½ cups) plain
  (all-pupose) flour
3 tablespoons chopped parsley
125 g (4 oz) cold butter, chopped
1 egg yolk

Herb filling
30 g (1 oz) butter
1 small leek, thinly sliced
1–2 cloves garlic, crushed
4 spring onions (scallions),
  chopped
3 tablespoons chopped parsley
2 tablespoons chopped chives
2 tablespoons chopped dill
2 tablespoons oregano leaves
3 eggs
250 ml (8 fl oz/1 cup) cream
3 tablespoons milk
125 g (4½ oz/1 cup) grated
  Cheddar

1 Process the flour, parsley and butter until crumbly. Add the egg yolk and 1 tablespoon of water. Process in short bursts until the mixture comes together. Add a little extra water if needed. Turn out onto a floured surface and gather into a ball. Cover with plastic wrap and chill for 30 minutes.
2 Grease a loose-based flan tin measuring 24 cm (9½ inches) across the base. Roll out the pastry, line the prepared tin and trim off any excess. Chill the lined flan tin for 20 minutes. Preheat the oven to moderately hot 190°C (375°F/Gas 5). Cover the pastry

with baking paper and fill with baking beads. Bake for 15 minutes. Remove the paper and beads and bake for a further 10 minutes. Reduce the oven to moderate 180°C (350°F/Gas 4).
3 To make the filling, heat the butter in a heavy-based pan. Cook the leek, garlic and spring onion for 10 minutes,

stirring frequently until cooked. Add the herbs and cool.
4 Beat the eggs, cream and milk and season with pepper. Spread the leek and herb mixture over the base of the pastry. Pour over the egg mixture and sprinkle with the Cheddar. Bake for 25–30 minutes, or until golden.

When the mixture is crumbly, add the egg yolk and water.

When the leek is cooked, stir through the herbs.

Sprinkle the grated Cheddar over the top of the quiche.

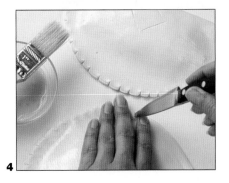

BRAISED CABBAGE TURNOVERS

Preparation time: 15 minutes
Total cooking time: 1 hour 5 minutes
Makes 6

60 g (2¼ oz) butter
2 onions, thinly sliced
1 stalk celery, thinly sliced
600 g (1 lb 5 oz) green cabbage,
    finely shredded
6 spring onions (scallions),
    finely chopped
3 tablespoons chopped fresh
    parsley
¼ teaspoon ground chilli powder
100 g (3½ oz) feta cheese,
    crumbled
6 sheets ready-rolled puff pastry
1 egg, lightly beaten

1 Preheat oven to 210°C (415°F/ Gas 6–7). Line two 32 x 28 cm (13 x 11 inch) oven trays with baking paper. Heat butter in medium pan; add onions and celery. Cook over low heat 15 minutes, stirring occasionally. Add cabbage and 3 tablespoons water. Stir over high heat 10 minutes, or until cabbage has wilted and almost all liquid has evaporated.

2 Add spring onions, parsley and chilli to pan; stir. Remove pan from heat; cool mixture slightly. Add cheese, mix well; season to taste, cool.

3 Brush each pastry sheet with egg. Divide cabbage mixture evenly into six portions. Place one portion of mixture at a time, slightly off-centre, on pastry square. Fold sheet in half, press to seal edges. Cut pastry into a half circle using an 18 cm (7 inch) saucepan lid as a guide; discard excess pastry. Repeat with remaining pastry and filling.

4 Brush tops of half circles with remaining egg. Using a sharp knife, cut a diamond pattern across top of pastry. (Do not cut through the pastry.) Use your finger and the back of knife to decorate the pastry edge. Arrange the pies on prepared trays. Bake for 40 minutes, or until puffed and browned. Serve warm or cool.

COOK'S FILE

Storage time: This dish can be made up to one day ahead.

SPINACH AND OLIVE BITES

Preparation time: 1 hour + 1 hour
refrigeration
Total cooking time: 15 minutes
Makes 30

250 g (9 oz/2 cups) plain
  (all-purpose) flour
200 g (7 oz) butter, cut into
  7 mm (¼ inch) cubes

Filling
60 g (2¼ oz) English spinach
  leaves
100 g (3½ oz) feta cheese
2 tablespoons chopped pitted
  black olives
2 teaspoons chopped fresh
  rosemary
1 garlic clove, crushed
2 tablespoons pistachios
1 egg, lightly beaten

1 Sift flour into a large mixing bowl; stir in the cubed butter until just combined. Make a well in the centre of the flour, add almost all 185 ml (6 fl oz/¾ cup) water. Mix to a slightly sticky dough with a knife, adding more water if necessary. Gather dough into a ball.

2 Turn onto a well-floured surface, and lightly press together until almost smooth. Do not overwork dough. Roll out to a neat 20 x 40 cm (8 x 16 inch) rectangle, trying to keep the corners fairly square. Fold the top third of the pastry down and fold the bottom third of the pastry up over it. Make a quarter turn to the right so that the edge of the top fold is on the right. Re-roll pastry to a 20 x 40 cm (8 x 16 inch) rectangle, and repeat folding step. Wrap pastry in plastic wrap and refrigerate for 30 minutes.

3 Repeat previous step, giving a roll, fold and turn twice more. Refrigerate for 30 minutes. Folding and rolling gives the pastry its flaky characteristics. Roll out pastry on a well-floured surface to a 3 mm (⅛ inch) thickness; cut out thirty 8 cm (3 inch) rounds.

4 Preheat oven to 180°C (350°F/Gas 4). Brush a large baking tray with melted butter or oil. Wash and dry spinach thoroughly, shred finely and place in mixing bowl. Crumble the feta on top, add olives, rosemary and garlic.

5 Spread pistachios on a baking tray and toast under a moderately hot grill (broiler) for 1–2 minutes. Cool and chop finely. Add to spinach mixture with egg, stir until well combined.

6 Place 2 teaspoonfuls of mixture in the centre of each round, fold in half and pinch edges to seal. Place on prepared tray, brush lightly with beaten egg and bake for 15 minutes, until golden and crisp. Serve hot.

COOK'S FILE

Storage time: Flaky pastry can be made up to one day in advance. Store in refrigerator. Assemble bites and cook just before serving.

Hints: Homemade flaky pastry is delicious and worth the effort if time permits. Have all the ingredients, equipment and room temperature as cool as possible—if it's too warm, the butter in the pastry will melt, making it difficult to work with.

Variation: Frozen puff pastry may be substituted in this recipe. Use ready-rolled sheets of butter puff pastry for best results.

Note: Feta cheese is available from delicatessens and supermarkets. It is a dry white cheese, cured in brine. The Bulgarian and Greek varieties are strongest in flavour. Originally made from goat's or ewe's milk, nowadays it is often made from cow's milk.

1

2

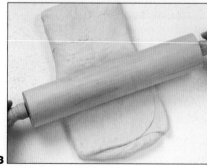

3

4

5

6

LEEK AND TURNIP PIE

Preparation time: 45 minutes
Total cooking time: 1 hour +
  12 minutes
Makes one 25 cm (10 inch) pie

250 g (9 oz/2 cups) plain
  (all-purpose) flour
125 g (4½ oz) butter, chopped
50 g (1¾ oz/½ cup) grated
  Parmesan cheese
1–2 tablespoons iced water

Filling
2 medium leeks
100 g (3½ oz) butter
750 g (1 lb 10 oz) white turnips,
  washed, peeled, thinly sliced
2 tablespoons caraway seeds
2 tablespoons soft brown sugar
2 tablespoons red wine vinegar
3 tablespoons chopped fresh
  basil
2 tablespoons plain (all-purpose)
  flour
125 g (4½ oz) Cheddar cheese,
  grated
3 tablespoons grated Parmesan
  cheese
1 egg, lightly beaten

1 Preheat oven to 180°C (350°F/
Gas 4). Brush a 25 cm (10 inch) pie
plate with melted butter or oil. Sift
flour into a large bowl and add butter.
Using fingertips, rub butter into flour
until mixture is fine and crumbly. Add
cheese and almost all the water; mix
to a firm dough, adding a little more
water if necessary. Turn onto a lightly
floured surface, knead 2 minutes, or
until smooth.

2 Divide dough in two. Roll out one
portion between two sheets of baking
paper, large enough to cover the base
and sides of pie plate. Trim edges. Cut
a sheet of greaseproof paper large
enough to cover pastry-lined tin.
Spread a layer of dried beans evenly
over paper. Bake 8 minutes. Remove
from oven; discard paper and beans.
Return pastry to oven for 5 minutes,
or until lightly golden. Cool.

3 Slice leeks finely. Heat butter in
large pan, add turnips and leeks. Cook
over medium heat for 4 minutes, or
until coated with butter. Cover and
cook for 10 minutes, shaking pan
occasionally to prevent sticking. Add
caraway seeds and brown sugar. Stir
until sugar melts. Add vinegar, cook
for 1 minute. Remove from heat, cool
slightly. Stir through basil and

1 tablespoon of the flour. Season.
4 Spoon one-third of turnip mixture
over pastry. Combine remaining flour
and cheeses. Sprinkle one-third over
turnip mixture. Continue layering,
finishing with cheese. Roll remaining
pastry into 4 cm (1½ inch) diameter
log, cut into 5 mm (¼ inch) slices.
Place overlapping pastry circles
around edge of pie. Brush between
each round with egg. Bake for
30–40 minutes, or until golden.

VEGETABLE TART

Preparation time: 30 minutes +
  20 minutes refrigeration
Total cooking time: 1 hour
Serves 6

155 g (5½ oz/1¼ cups) plain
  (all-purpose) flour
90 g (3¼ oz) butter, chopped
2–3 tablespoons iced water

Vegetable filling
1 small red capsicum (pepper)
1 small green capsicum
  (pepper)
200 g (7 oz) pumpkin
1 potato
150 g (5½ oz) broccoli
1 carrot
1 tablespoon oil
1 onion, finely sliced
50 g (1¾ oz) butter
3 tablespoons plain (all-purpose)
  flour
250 ml (9 fl oz/1 cup) milk
2 egg yolks
125 g (4½ oz/1 cup) grated
  Cheddar cheese

1 Preheat oven to 180°C (350°F/
Gas 4). Sift flour into large bowl; add
butter. Using fingertips, rub butter
into flour for 2 minutes until mixture
is fine and crumbly. Add almost all the
water, mix to firm dough, adding more
water if necessary. Turn onto lightly
floured surface, press together until
smooth. Roll out and line a deep 23 cm
(9 inch) fluted tin. Refrigerate for
20 minutes. Cut a sheet of greaseproof
paper large enough to cover pastry-
lined tin. Spread a layer of dried beans
evenly over paper. Bake 10 minutes,
remove from oven, discard paper and
beans. Return to oven for 10 minutes,
or until lightly golden. Cool.

2 To make vegetable filling, cut
capsicum, pumpkin and potato into
2 cm (¾ inch) squares. Cut broccoli
into florets. Cut carrots into 1.5 cm
(⅝ inch) slices.

3 Heat oil in a frying pan, add onion
and cook over medium heat 5 minutes,
until soft and golden. Add capsicum
and cook, stirring, 5 minutes until soft.
Transfer to a large mixing bowl to cool.
Steam or boil remaining vegetables for
3 minutes, until just tender. Drain well,
add to bowl and cool.

4 Heat butter in a small pan; add
flour. Stir over a low heat 2 minutes, or

until flour mixture is lightly golden.
Add milk gradually to pan, stirring
until mixture is smooth. Stir constantly
over medium heat until mixture boils
and thickens; boil 1 minute more,
remove from heat. Add yolks, beat
until smooth. Stir in half the cheese.
Pour the sauce over the cooked
vegetables, and stir to thoroughly
combine. Pour the mixture into the
pastry shell and sprinkle with the
remaining cheese. Bake for 25 minutes,
or until top is golden.

1

2

3

VEGETABLE STRUDEL

Preparation time: 30 minutes
Total cooking time: 35 minutes
Serves 4–6

12 English spinach leaves
2 tablespoons olive oil
1 medium onion, finely sliced
1 medium red capsicum
    (pepper), cut into strips
1 medium green capsicum
    (pepper), cut into strips
2 medium zucchini (courgettes),
    sliced
2 slender eggplant (aubergines),
    sliced
salt and pepper
6 sheets filo pastry
40 g butter (1½ oz), melted
4 tablespoons finely sliced fresh
    basil leaves
60 g (2¼ oz/½ cup) grated
    Cheddar cheese
2 tablespoons sesame seeds

1 Preheat oven to moderately hot 210°C (425°F/Gas 6–7). Brush an oven tray with melted butter or oil.

2 Wash spinach leaves thoroughly and steam or microwave until just softened. Squeeze out excess moisture and spread out to dry.

3 Heat oil in a frying pan, add onion and cook over medium heat for 3 minutes. Add capsicum, zucchini and eggplant; cook, stirring, for another 5 minutes or until vegetables have softened. Season with salt and pepper. Set aside to cool.

4 Brush 1 sheet of filo pastry with melted butter, top with a second sheet. Repeat with remaining pastry, brushing with butter between each layer. Place spinach, cooled vegetable mixture, basil and cheese along one long side of pastry, about 5 cm (2 inches) in from the edge. Fold sides over filling, fold short end over and roll up tightly.

5 Place strudel, seam-side-down, on prepared tray. Brush with remaining melted butter and sprinkle with sesame seeds. Bake for 25 minutes, or until golden brown and crisp.

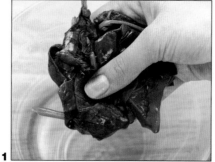

1

2

3

4

SPINACH PIE

Preparation time: 45 minutes + 1 hour
  refrigeration
Total cooking time: 55 minutes
Serves 6

Pastry
250 g (9 oz/2 cups) plain (all-
  purpose) flour
30 g (1 oz) chilled butter,
  chopped
3 tablespoons olive oil

Filling
500 g (1 lb 2 oz) English spinach
  leaves
2 teaspoons olive oil
1 onion, finely chopped
3 spring onions (scallions),
  finely chopped
200 g (7 oz) feta, crumbled
2 tablespoons chopped fresh
  flat-leaf (Italian) parsley
1 tablespoon chopped fresh dill
2 tablespoons grated kefalotyri
  cheese
3 tablespoons cooked white rice
3 tablespoons pine nuts, toasted
  and roughly chopped
¼ teaspoon ground nutmeg
½ teaspoon ground cumin
3 eggs, lightly beaten

1 Lightly grease a shallow 17 x 26 cm
(6¾ x 10½ inch) tin. To make the
pastry, sift the flour and ½ teaspoon
salt into a bowl. Add the butter and
rub in with your fingertips until the
mixture resembles fine breadcrumbs.
Make a well in the centre and add the
oil. Using your hands, mix together.
Add 125 ml (4 fl oz/½ cup) warm
water and mix with a flat-bladed knife,
using a cutting action until the mixture
comes together in beads. Gently gather
the dough together and lift out onto
a lightly floured surface. Press into a
ball and flatten into a disc. Wrap in
plastic wrap and refrigerate for 1 hour.
2 Trim and wash the spinach, then
coarsely chop. Wrap in a tea towel and
squeeze out excess moisture. Heat the
oil in a frying pan, add the onion and
spring onion and cook over low heat,
without browning, for 5 minutes, or
until softened. Place in a bowl with the
spinach and the remaining filling
ingredients and mix well. Season.

3 Preheat the oven to moderately hot
200°C (400°F/Gas 6). Roll out half the
pastry between two sheets of baking
paper, remove the top sheet and invert
the pastry into the tin, allowing any
excess to hang over the sides. Spoon
the filling into the tin. Roll out the
remaining pastry large enough to
cover the top. Place over the filling and
press the pastry edges firmly to seal.
Trim away any extra pastry. Brush

the top with a little oil, then score three
strips lengthways, then on the
diagonal to make a diamond pattern
on the surface. Make two slits in the
top to allow steam to escape.
4 Bake for 45–50 minutes, covering
with foil if the surface becomes too
brown. The pie is cooked when it
slides when the tin is gently shaken.
Turn out onto a rack for 10 minutes,
then cut into pieces and serve.

*Spoon the spinach filling into the pastry-
lined tin.*

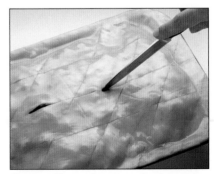

*Score a diamond pattern in the pastry,
then make two slits so steam can escape.*

VEGETABLE TART WITH SALSA VERDE

Preparation time: 30 minutes +
  30 minutes refrigeration
Total cooking time: 50 minutes
Serves 6

215 g (7½ oz/1¾ cups) plain
  (all-purpose) flour
120 g (4 oz) chilled butter,
  cubed
3 tablespoons cream
1–2 tablespoons chilled water
1 (250 g/9 oz) Desirée potato,
  cut into 2 cm (¾ inch) cubes
1 tablespoon olive oil
2 cloves garlic, crushed
1 red capsicum (pepper), cut
  into cubes
1 red onion, sliced into rings
2 zucchini (courgettes), sliced
2 tablespoons chopped fresh dill
1 tablespoon chopped fresh
  thyme
1 tablespoon drained baby
  capers
150 g (5½ oz) marinated
  quartered artichoke hearts,
  drained
30 g (1 oz/⅔ cup) baby English
  spinach leaves

Salsa verde
1 clove garlic
40 g (1½ oz/2 cups) fresh flat-
  leaf (Italian) parsley
4 tablespoons extra virgin olive
  oil
3 tablespoons chopped fresh
  dill
1½ tablespoons Dijon mustard
1 tablespoon red wine vinegar
1 tablespoon drained baby
  capers

1 Sift the flour and ½ teaspoon salt into a large bowl. Add the butter and rub into the flour with your fingertips until it resembles fine breadcrumbs. Add the cream and water and mix with a flat-bladed knife until the mixture comes together in beads. Gather together and lift onto a lightly floured work surface. Press into a ball, then flatten into a disc, wrap in plastic wrap and refrigerate for 30 minutes.

2 Preheat the oven to moderately hot 200°C (400°F/Gas 6). Grease a 27 cm (10¾ inch) loose-bottomed flan tin. Roll the dough out between 2 sheets of baking paper large enough to line the tin. Remove the paper and invert the pastry into the tin. Use a small pastry ball to press the pastry into the tin, allowing any excess to hang over the side. Roll a rolling pin over the tin, cutting off any excess. Cover the pastry with a piece of crumpled baking paper, then add baking beads. Place the tin on a baking tray and bake for 15–20 minutes. Remove the paper and beads, reduce the heat to moderate 180°C (350°F/Gas 4) and bake for 20 minutes, or until golden.

3 To make the salsa verde, combine all the ingredients in a food processor and process until almost smooth.

4 Boil the potato until just tender. Drain. Heat the oil in a frying pan and cook the garlic, capsicum and onion over medium heat for 3 minutes, stirring often. Add the zucchini, dill, thyme and capers, cook for 3 minutes. Reduce the heat to low; add the potato and artichokes until heated. Season.

5 To assemble, spread 3 tablespoons of the salsa over the pastry. Spoon the vegetable mixture into the case and drizzle with half the remaining salsa. Pile the spinach in the centre and drizzle with the remaining salsa.

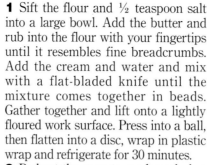

Mix with a flat-bladed knife until the mixture comes together in beads.

Remove the paper and use a rolling pin to invert the pastry into the tin.

Bake the pastry case until it is dry and golden brown.

Cook the vegetables until the potato and artichokes are heated through.

Spread a little of the salsa verde over the pastry base.

Lay the spinach leaves in the centre of the vegetable mixture.

HIGH-TOP VEGETABLE PIE

Preparation time: 25 minutes +
20 minutes refrigeration
Total cooking time: 1 hour 30 minutes
Serves 6

Pastry
125 g (4½ oz/1 cup) plain
(all-purpose) flour
60 g (2¼ oz) chilled butter,
chopped
1 egg yolk
2 teaspoons poppy seeds
1–2 tablespoons iced water

30 g (1 oz) butter
2 tablespoons oil
1 onion, cut into thin wedges
1 leek, sliced
3 potatoes, cut into large
chunks
300 g (10½ oz) orange sweet
potato, cut into large chunks
300 g (10½ oz) pumpkin, cut
into large chunks
200 g (7 oz) swede (rutabaga),
peeled and cut into large
chunks
250 ml (9 fl oz/1 cup) vegetable
stock
1 red capsicum (pepper), cut
into large pieces
200 g (7 oz) broccoli, cut into
large florets
2 zucchini (courgettes), cut into
large pieces
125 g (4½ oz/1 cup) grated
vintage peppercorn Cheddar

1 Preheat the oven to moderately hot 200°C (400°F/Gas 6). Sift the flour into a bowl, add the butter and rub in with your fingertips until it resembles fine breadcrumbs. Make a well in the centre and add the egg yolk, poppy seeds and water and mix with a flat-bladed knife, using a cutting action, until the mixture comes together in beads. Gently gather the dough together and lift out onto a lightly floured work surface. Press the dough together into a ball and flatten it slightly into a disc, wrap in plastic wrap and refrigerate for 20 minutes.
2 Roll the dough out between two sheets of baking paper, then remove the top sheet and invert the pastry

over a 23 cm (9 inch) pie plate. Use a small ball of pastry to help press the pastry into the plate, allowing any excess to hang over the sides. Use a sharp knife to trim any excess pastry. Prick the base with a fork and bake for 15–20 minutes, or until golden.
3 Heat the butter and oil in a large saucepan, cook the onion and leek over medium heat for 5 minutes, or until soft and golden. Add the potato, sweet potato, pumpkin and swede and cook, stirring occasionally, until the

vegetables start to soften. Add the stock and simmer for 30 minutes.
4 Add the remaining vegetables, reduce the heat and simmer for 20 minutes, or until the vegetables are soft and just mushy—some may break up slightly. Season. Cool a little.
5 Spoon the mixture into the shell, sprinkle with cheese and cook under a medium grill (broiler) for 5–10 minutes, or until the cheese is golden brown.

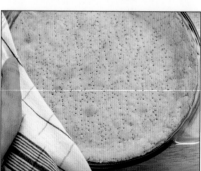

*Prick the base of the pastry all over with a
fork and bake until dry and golden.*

*Cook the vegetables until they are very soft
when tested with a knife.*

MINI PUMPKIN AND CURRY QUICHES

Preparation time: 30 minutes +
30 minutes refrigeration
Total cooking time: 35 minutes
Makes 8

Cream cheese pastry
185 g (6½ oz/1½ cups) plain
(all-purpose) flour
125 g (4½ oz) cream cheese,
chopped
125 g (4½ oz) butter, chopped

Filling
1 tablespoon oil
2 onions, finely chopped
3 cloves garlic, crushed
1 teaspoon curry powder
3 eggs
125 ml (4 fl oz/½ cup) thick
cream

250 g (9 oz/1 cup) mashed,
cooked pumpkin (about
350 g/12 oz raw)
2 teaspoons cumin seeds

1 Preheat oven to moderately hot
210°C (425°F/Gas 6–7). To make the
cream cheese pastry, sift flour into
large mixing bowl; add cream cheese
and butter. Using fingertips, rub
ingredients together for 2 minutes or
until mixture is smooth and comes
together in a ball.
Turn onto lightly floured surface,
knead 10 seconds or until smooth.
Store, covered with plastic wrap, in
refrigerator 30 minutes. Divide pastry
into 8 equal portions, roll out and line
8 deep, greased 10 cm (4 inch) flan
tins. Bake 15 minutes or until lightly
browned. Remove from oven. Reduce
heat to moderate 180°C (350°F/Gas 4).
2 To make filling, heat oil in small
pan, add onion and garlic, stir over

low heat 5 minutes or until soft. Add
curry powder, stir for 1 minute. Spread
over bases of pastry cases.
3 Combine eggs, cream and pumpkin
in large bowl, beat until combined.
Pour over onion mixture, sprinkle with
cumin seeds. Bake for 20 minutes or
until filling has set.

205

VEGETABLE AND POLENTA PIE

Preparation time: 20 minutes +
 15 minutes standing + refrigeration
Total cooking time: 50 minutes
Serves 6

2 eggplants (aubergines), thickly
 sliced
350 ml (12 fl oz/1⅓ cups)
 vegetable stock
150 g (5½ oz/1 cup) fine polenta
 (cornmeal)
50 g (1¾ oz/½ cup) finely grated
 Parmesan
1 tablespoon olive oil
1 large onion, chopped
2 cloves garlic, crushed
1 large red capsicum (pepper),
 cut into 1 cm (½ inch) cubes
2 zucchini (courgettes), thickly
 sliced
150 g (5½ oz) button
 mushrooms, quartered
400 g (14 oz) can chopped
 tomatoes
3 teaspoons balsamic vinegar
olive oil, for brushing

1 Spread the eggplant in a single layer on a board, and sprinkle with salt. Leave for 15 minutes, then rinse, pat dry and cut into cubes.
2 Line a 22 cm (8¾ inch) round cake tin with foil. Bring the stock and 350 ml (12 fl oz/1⅓ cups) water to the boil in a saucepan. Add the polenta in a thin stream and stir over low heat for 5 minutes, or until the liquid is absorbed and the mixture is thick and comes away from the side of the pan.
3 Remove from the heat and stir in the cheese until it melts. Spread into

the tin, smoothing surface as much as possible. Refrigerate until set.
4 Preheat the oven to moderately hot 200°C (400°F/Gas 6). Heat the oil in a saucepan, add onion and cook, stirring occasionally, over medium heat, for 3 minutes, or until soft. Add the garlic and cook for 1 minute. Add the eggplant, capsicum, zucchini, mushrooms and tomato. Bring to the boil, then reduce heat and simmer, covered, for 20 minutes, or until the

vegetables are tender—stir occasionally to prevent catching on base of pan. Stir in vinegar and season.
5 Transfer vegetable mixture to a 22 cm (8¾ inch) ovenproof pie dish, piling it up slightly in the centre.
6 Turn out polenta, peel off foil and cut into 12 wedges. Arrange in a single layer, over the vegetables. Brush with olive oil and bake for 20 minutes, or until lightly brown and crisp.

Cook the polenta, stirring, until all the liquid is absorbed and it is very thick.

Reduce the heat and simmer until the vegetables are tender.

Arrange the polenta wedges, smooth-side-down, over the vegetable mixture.

TOFU PASTRIES

Preparation time: 30 minutes +
  4 hours refrigeration
Total cooking time: 20 minutes
Serves 4

150 g (5½ oz) firm tofu
2 spring onions (scallions),
  chopped
3 teaspoons chopped fresh
  coriander (cilantro) leaves
½ teaspoon grated orange rind
2 teaspoons soy sauce
1 tablespoon sweet chilli sauce
2 teaspoons grated fresh
  ginger

1 teaspoon cornflour
  (cornstarch)
3 tablespoons sugar
125 ml (4 fl oz/½ cup) seasoned
  rice vinegar
1 small Lebanese (short)
  cucumber, finely diced
1 small red chilli, thinly sliced
1 spring onion (scallion), extra,
  thinly sliced on the diagonal
2 sheets ready-rolled puff pastry
1 egg, lightly beaten

1 Drain the tofu, then pat dry and cut into 1 cm (½ inch) cubes.
2 Put the spring onion, coriander, rind, soy and chilli sauces, ginger, cornflour and tofu in a bowl and gently mix. Cover, then refrigerate for 3–4 hours.
3 Place the sugar and vinegar in a small saucepan and stir over low heat until the sugar dissolves. Remove from the heat and add the cucumber, chilli and extra spring onion. Cool.
4 Preheat the oven to hot 220°C (425°F/Gas 7). Cut each pastry sheet into four squares. Drain the filling and divide into eight. Place one portion in the centre of each square and brush the edges with egg. Fold into a triangle and seal the edges with a fork.
5 Put the triangles on two lined baking trays, brush with egg and bake for 15 minutes. Serve with the sauce.

Gently mix the tofu and other ingredients together in a bowl.

Remove the saucepan from the heat and add the spring onion, cucumber and chilli.

Fold the pastry to enclose the filling, then seal the edges with a fork.

GOURMET VEGETABLE PIZZA

Preparation time: 30 minutes +
30 minutes standing
Total cooking time: 1 hour 10 minutes
Serves 6

Pizza dough
4 tablespoons fresh basil leaves,
 finely chopped
2 tablespoons polenta
 (cornmeal)
1 teaspoon dried yeast
1 teaspoon sugar
185 g (6½ oz/1½ cups) plain
 (all-purpose) flour
125 ml (4 fl oz/½ cup) warm
 water
1 teaspoon salt
1 tablespoon olive oil

Tomato sauce
1 tablespoon oil
1 small red onion, finely
 chopped
1 garlic clove, crushed
1 large tomato, finely
 chopped
1 tablespoon tomato paste
 (concentrated purée)
½ teaspoon dried oregano

Topping
60 g (2¼ oz) button mushrooms,
 finely sliced
100 g (3½ oz) fresh baby corn
225 g (8 oz/1½ cups) grated
 mozzarella cheese
50 g (1¾ oz) English spinach
 leaves, finely shredded
1 small red capsicum (pepper),
 cut into short thin strips
2 tablespoons pine nuts

1 Brush a 30 cm (12 inch) pizza tray
with oil and sprinkle with polenta.

2 To make pizza dough, combine
yeast, sugar and 2 tablespoons of the
flour in a small mixing bowl.
Gradually add the water; blend until
smooth. Stand, covered, with plastic
wrap, in a warm place for about
10 minutes, or until foamy.

3 Sift the remaining flour into a large
mixing bowl. Add salt and basil, and
make a well in the centre. Add the
yeast mixture and oil. Using a knife,
mix to a soft dough.

4 Turn dough onto a lightly floured
surface, knead for 5 minutes, or until
smooth. Shape dough into a ball, place
in a large, lightly oiled mixing bowl.
Leave, covered with plastic wrap, in a
warm place for 20 minutes, or until
well risen.

5 Meanwhile, to make the tomato
sauce, heat oil in a small pan, add
onion and garlic and cook over a
medium heat for 3 minutes, or until
soft. Add tomato and reduce heat;
simmer 10 minutes, stirring
occasionally. Stir in tomato paste and
oregano, cook for 3 minutes. Allow
sauce to cool before using.

6 Preheat oven to 210°C (415°F/
Gas 6–7). Turn dough out onto a
lightly floured surface and knead a
further 5 minutes until smooth. Roll
out to fit the prepared tray. Spread the
sauce onto the pizza base, arrange the
mushrooms and corn evenly on top.
Sprinkle over half the cheese, top with
the spinach, capsicum and remaining
cheese. Sprinkle with pine nuts. Bake
for 40 minutes, or until crust is golden.
Serve pizza immediately.

COOK'S FILE

Hint: Fresh baby corn can usually be
purchased from greengrocers. If it is
unavailable, use canned baby corn or
canned corn kernels.

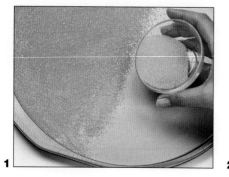
1

2

3

4

5

6

ROCKET, BASIL AND LEEK QUICHE

Preparation time: 30 minutes
Total cooking time: 1 hour
Makes one 23 cm (9 inch) quiche

150 g (5½ oz) rocket (arugula),
   stalks removed
185 g (6½ oz/1½ cups) plain
   (all-purpose) flour
125 g (4½ oz) butter, chopped
1–2 tablespoons water
1 tablespoon oil
1 large leek, white part only,
   thinly sliced
2 cloves garlic, crushed
2 eggs
125 ml (4 fl oz/½ cup) milk
125 ml (4 fl oz/½ cup) cream
10 g (¼ oz/½ cup) fresh basil
   leaves, shredded
50 g (1¾ oz/½ cup) shaved
   Parmesan cheese

1 Preheat oven to moderately hot 210°C (425°F/Gas 6–7). Wash rocket and shake off excess water; finely slice rocket leaves.

2 Sift flour into mixing bowl; add butter. Using fingertips, rub butter into flour for 2 minutes or until mixture is fine and crumbly. Add water, mix to a soft dough. Turn onto lightly floured surface, knead for 10 seconds or until smooth. Store, covered in plastic wrap, in refrigerator 30 minutes.

3 Roll pastry, between 2 sheets of plastic wrap, to cover base and sides of shallow 23 cm (9 inch) flan tin. Cut a sheet of greaseproof paper large enough to cover pastry-lined tin. Spread a layer of dried beans or rice over paper. Bake 10 minutes, remove from oven; discard beans. Return pastry to oven for 5 minutes or until lightly golden. Reduce the heat to moderate 180°C (350°F/Gas 4).

4 Heat oil in frying pan, add leek and garlic, stir over low heat for 5 minutes or until leek is soft. Add rocket, stir over heat for 1 minute. Remove from heat, cool. Spread over base of pastry shell. Combine eggs, milk and cream in a bowl, whisk until smooth. Pour into pastry shell. Bake in moderate oven for 50 minutes or until set and lightly golden. Serve topped with basil leaves and shaved Parmesan cheese.

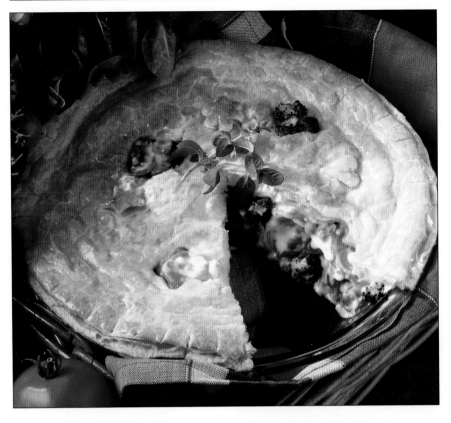

VEGETABLE PIE

Preparation time: 40 minutes +
  30 minutes standing
Total cooking time: 50 minutes
Serves 6

1 small eggplant (aubergine)
30 g (1 oz) butter
2 garlic cloves, crushed
2 spring onions (scallions),
  sliced
200 g (7 oz) orange sweet
  potato, cut into 1 cm (½ inch)
  cubes
1 carrot, thinly sliced
50 g (1¾ oz) button mushrooms,
  sliced
1 small red capsicum (pepper),
  finely sliced
150 g (5½ oz) broccoli, cut in
  small florets
40 g (1½ oz) butter, extra
2 tablespoons plain (all-purpose)
  flour
375 ml (13 fl oz/1½ cups) milk
125 g (4½ oz) feta cheese,
  crumbled
3 tablespoons grated Parmesan
  cheese
2 tablespoons pine nuts, toasted

1 teaspoon dried oregano
2 eggs, lightly beaten
2 sheets ready-rolled puff
  pastry
1 egg, extra, lightly beaten

1 Brush a 23 cm (9 inch) round pie
dish with melted butter or oil. Cut
eggplant into 2 cm (¾ inch) cubes.
Place in a colander, sprinkle with salt.
Leave for 30 minutes. Rinse; drain. Pat
dry with paper towels. Preheat oven to
180°C (350°F/Gas 4).
2 Heat butter in large pan. Cook
garlic and spring onion over medium
heat 1 minute. Add sweet potato,
carrot and mushrooms, stirring,
4 minutes, or until just tender. Add
capsicum and broccoli. Cook 3 minutes.
Add eggplant, cook 2 minutes. Remove
from heat.
3 Melt extra butter in medium pan.
Add flour, stir over medium heat
1 minute, or until mixture is lightly
golden and bubbling. Add milk
gradually to pan, stirring until mixture
is smooth. Stir constantly over medium
heat 4 minutes, or until it boils and
thickens. Add cheeses, pine nuts and
oregano. Combine vegetable mixture
and sauce in a bowl. Add eggs, stir
until combined. Spoon into dish.

4 Cut a long strip of pastry slightly
wider than rim of pie dish. Brush rim
of the dish with water and press down
strip. Brush the strip with water. Place
pastry sheet over the top, press edges
to seal. Trim and decorate edge. Cut
out shapes from pastry top to allow
steam to escape and use the cutouts to
decorate the pie top. Brush top with
beaten egg. Bake for 35–40 minutes,
or until the pastry is golden brown
and puffed.

Roast the sweet potato and garlic cloves until the sweet potato is soft and coloured.

Remove the skin, then roughly chop the roasted garlic flesh.

Spoon the filling into the centre of the prepared pastry.

ORANGE SWEET POTATO, PINE NUT AND FETA STRUDEL

Preparation time: 25 minutes
Total cooking time: 1 hour 5 minutes
Serves 6

250 g (9 oz) orange sweet potato, peeled and cut into 2 cm (¾ inch) cubes
2 tablespoons olive oil
3 cloves garlic, unpeeled
250 g (9 oz) English spinach, blanched, excess moisture squeezed out
3 tablespoons pine nuts, toasted
125 g (4½ oz) low-fat feta cheese, crumbled
3 spring onions (scallions), including green part, chopped
50 g (1¾ oz/½ cup) black olives, pitted and sliced
3 tablespoons chopped basil
1 tablespoon chopped rosemary
8 sheets filo pastry
2 tablespoons sesame seeds

1 Preheat the oven to 180°C (350°F/ Gas 4). Place the sweet potato on a roasting tray and brush lightly with 1 tablespoon of the oil, then add the garlic cloves. Roast for 30 minutes, or until the sweet potato has softened and is slightly coloured. Remove and cool slightly.

2 Place the sweet potato, roughly chopped spinach, pine nuts, feta, spring onion, olives, basil and rosemary in a bowl. Cut off the end of each garlic clove and peel off the skin. Roughly chop the flesh, then add to the sweet potato mixture. Season with salt and freshly ground black pepper. Combine well.

3 Cover the pastry sheets with a slightly damp tea towel to prevent the pastry from drying and cracking. Lay the pastry sheets out in front of you, stacked on top of each other, and brush every second layer with the remaining oil. Spread the filling in the centre of the pastry, covering an area of about 10 cm x 30 cm (4 inch x 12 inch). Fold in the shorter ends of the pastry. Fold the long side closest to you over the filling, then carefully roll up. Place the strudel on a greased baking tray, seam-side down. Brush with any remaining oil and sprinkle with the sesame seeds. Bake for 35 minutes, or until the pastry is crisp and golden. Serve warm.

RATATOUILLE TARTE TATIN

Preparation time: 45 minutes +
  20 minutes refrigeration
Total cooking time: 50 minutes
Serves 6

185 g (6½ oz/1½ cups) plain
  (all-purpose) flour
90 g (3¼ oz) butter, chopped
1 egg
1 tablespoon oil
20 g (¾ oz) butter, extra
2 zucchini (courgettes), halved
  lengthways and sliced
250 g (9 oz) eggplant
  (aubergines), cut into 2 cm
  (¾ inch) cubes
1 red capsicum (pepper), cut
  into 2 cm (¾ inch) cubes
1 green capsicum (pepper), cut
  into 2 cm (¾ inch) cubes
1 large red onion, cut into 2 cm
  (¾ inch) cubes
250 g (9 oz) cherry tomatoes,
  halved
2 tablespoons balsamic vinegar
60 g (2¼ oz/½ cup) grated
  Cheddar
300 g (10½ oz) sour cream
3 tablespoons good-quality
  pesto

1 Sift the flour into a bowl. Add the butter and rub into the flour with your fingertips until it resembles fine breadcrumbs. Make a well in the centre, add the egg (and 2 tablespoons water if it is too dry) and mix with a flat-bladed knife, using a cutting action, until it comes together in beads. Gather the dough together and lift onto a floured work surface. Press into a ball, flatten slightly into a disc, wrap in plastic wrap and chill the dough for 20 minutes.

2 Preheat the oven to moderately hot 200°C (400°F/Gas 6). Grease and line a 25 cm (10 inch) springform tin. Heat the oil and extra butter in a frying pan and cook the zucchini, eggplant, capsicums and onion over high heat for 8 minutes, or until just soft. Add the tomatoes and vinegar and cook for 3–4 minutes.

3 Place the tin on a baking tray and neatly lay the vegetables in the tin, then sprinkle with cheese. Roll the dough out between two sheets of baking paper to a 28 cm (11 inch) circle. Remove the paper and invert the pastry into the tin over the filling. Tuck the edges of the pastry down the side of the tin. Bake for 30–35 minutes (some liquid will leak out), then stand for 1–2 minutes. Invert onto a platter. Combine the sour cream and pesto. Serve with the tarte tatin.

Mix with a flat-bladed knife until the mixture comes together in beads.

Add the cherry tomatoes and balsamic vinegar and cook for 3–4 minutes.

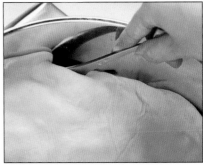

Use a spoon handle to tuck the edges of the pastry down the side of the tin.

Casseroles, curries & bakes

VEGETABLE CASSEROLE WITH HERB DUMPLINGS

Preparation time: 30 minutes
Total cooking time: 50 minutes
Serves 4

1 tablespoon olive oil
1 large onion, chopped
2 cloves garlic, crushed
2 teaspoons sweet paprika
1 large potato, chopped
1 large carrot, sliced
400 g (14 oz) can chopped
    tomatoes
375 ml (13 fl oz/1½ cups)
    vegetable stock
400 g (14 oz) orange sweet
    potato, cut into 1.5 cm
    (⅝ inch) cubes
150 g (5½ oz) broccoli, cut into
    florets
2 zucchini (courgettes), sliced
125 g (4½ oz/1 cup) self-raising
    flour
20 g (1 oz) chilled butter, cubed
2 teaspoons chopped fresh
    flat-leaf (Italian) parsley
1 teaspoon fresh thyme
1 teaspoon chopped fresh
    rosemary
4 tablespoons milk
2 tablespoons sour cream

1 Heat the oil in a saucepan and add the onion. Cook over low heat, stirring occasionally, for 5 minutes, or until soft. Stir in the garlic and paprika and cook, stirring, for 1 minute.
2 Add the potato, carrot, tomato and stock to the pan. Bring to the boil, then reduce the heat and simmer, covered, for 10 minutes. Add the sweet potato, broccoli and zucchini and simmer for 10 minutes, or until tender.

Preheat the oven to moderately hot 200°C (400°F/Gas 6).
3 Sift the flour and a pinch of salt into a bowl and add the butter. Rub the butter into the flour with your fingertips until it resembles fine breadcrumbs. Stir in the herbs and make a well in the centre. Add the milk, and mix with a flat-bladed knife, using a cutting action, until the

mixture comes together in beads. Gather up the dough and lift onto a lightly floured surface. Divide into eight portions, shaping each portion into a ball.
4 Add the sour cream to the casserole. Transfer to a 2 litre (8 cup) ovenproof dish and top with the dumplings. Bake for 20 minutes, or until golden and a skewer comes out clean.

Cook all the vegetables until they are tender.

Rub the butter into the flour until it resembles fine breadcrumbs.

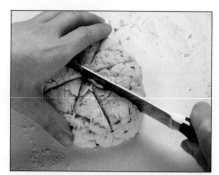

Divide the dough into eight equal portions.

CAULIFLOWER IN SPICY COCONUT SAUCE

Preparation time: 30 minutes
Total cooking time: 20 minutes
Serves 4–6

1 large onion
1 small red capsicum (pepper)
600 g (1 lb 5 oz) cauliflower
2 tablespoons peanut oil
20 g (¾ oz) butter
1 clove garlic, crushed
1 teaspoon ground turmeric
1 teaspoon ground cumin
½ teaspoon tandoori mix powder

1 teaspoon garam masala
1 teaspoon sambal oelek
1 teaspoon soft brown sugar
4 tablespoons prepared tomato
  pasta sauce
3 tablespoons vegetable stock
250 ml (9 fl oz/1 cup) coconut
  cream
2 tablespoons chopped coriander
  (cilantro) leaves

1 Peel and thinly slice onion. Cut the capsicum in half, remove the seeds and membrane and cut into thin strips. Cut cauliflower into small florets.

2 Heat the oil and butter in a large heavy-based pan. Add onion and cook, stirring, for 2 minutes. Add garlic, turmeric, cumin, tandoori powder, garam masala, sambal oelek and sugar. Cook over medium heat for 1 minute.

3 Add tomato pasta sauce, stock and coconut cream to pan, mix well. Stir in cauliflower florets and capsicum strips. Bring to boil, reduce heat and simmer, uncovered, for 10 minutes or until the cauliflower is tender. Stir in coriander leaves. Serve hot, garnished with fresh bay leaves, if desired.

COOK'S FILE

Hint: If the sauce is too thick, add a little extra stock.

SWEET SPICED GOLDEN NUGGETS

Preparation time: 35 minutes
Total cooking time: 1 hour
Serves 4

4 golden nugget pumpkins
1 tablespoon olive oil
210 g (7½ oz/1 cup) brown and
    wild rice blend
30 g (1 oz) butter
1 onion, finely chopped
300 g (10½ oz) orange sweet
    potato, cut in 1 cm (½ inch)
    cubes

65 g (2¼ oz/1 cup) chopped
    spring onions (scallions)
2 teaspoons ground cumin
½ teaspoon ground ginger
1 teaspoon ground coriander
1 teaspoon ground turmeric
1 teaspoon garam masala
2 tablespoons currants, soaked
    in hot water
4 tablespoons grated Cheddar
    cheese

1 Preheat oven to 180°C (350°F/
Gas 4). Slice the top third off each
pumpkin horizontally. Scoop out seeds,
leaving a deep cavity. Brush lightly
with oil. Stand pumpkins in baking
dish. Pour in enough water to come
halfway up the sides of the pumpkins.
Place lid on each. Bake 20 minutes.
Remove from water bath, allow to cool.
Cook rice in large pan of boiling water
until tender. Drain and cool.

2 Heat butter in frying pan. Add
onion and sweet potato. Cover and
cook over medium heat 5 minutes. Add
spring onion and cook, uncovered,
1 minute. Stir in spices, cook 2 minutes.
Remove from heat. Fold through rice
and drained currants.

3 Spoon filling into pumpkin cavities.
Sprinkle with cheese. Place lid on at
an angle, then cover with foil. Bake for
20 minutes. Serve hot with salad.

1

2

3

BAKED ROOT VEGETABLES WITH SWEET GINGER GLAZE

Preparation time: 25 minutes
Total cooking time: 1 hour 10 minutes
Serves 4–6

150 g (5½ oz) orange sweet
    potato
1 medium potato
1 medium carrot
1 medium parsnip
1 medium turnip
3 cm (1¼ inch) piece fresh
    ginger
2 tablespoons olive oil
60 g (2¼ oz) butter
2 tablespoons caster (superfine)
    sugar
3 tablespoons water

1 Preheat oven to moderately hot 210°C (425°F/Gas 6–7). Brush a large baking tray with oil. Peel sweet potato, potato, carrot, parsnip and turnip and cut into sticks about 5 cm (2 inches) long and 1 cm (¾ inch) thick. Peel and finely grate the ginger (you will need about 1 tablespoon).

2 Place vegetables in a single layer on prepared baking tray and brush all over with olive oil. Bake for 1 hour or until golden.

3 Melt butter in a small pan. Add the sugar and stir over low heat until sugar has dissolved. Add grated ginger and water and stir to combine. Bring to boil, reduce heat to low and simmer, uncovered, for 5 minutes, until mixture has reduced and thickened slightly.

4 Pour glaze over baked vegetables, toss to coat and return tray to the oven for 5 minutes. Serve immediately.

COOK'S FILE

Hint: These vegetables make an easy and delicious dish for vegetarians who love the baked vegetable part of a roast dinner.

Variation: Cut vegetables into even-sized chunks. Toss some chopped fresh thyme or parsley through the baked vegetables just before serving.

1

2

3

4

ROAST FENNEL WITH THYME

Preparation time: 20 minutes
Total cooking time: 1 hour
Serves 4

2 large fennel bulbs
1 medium leek, finely sliced
250 ml (9 fl oz/1 cup) good-
   quality white wine
2 tablespoons fresh thyme
   leaves

2 small tomatoes, cut into
   wedges
1 tablespoon fresh thyme leaves,
   extra

1 Preheat oven to moderately hot 210°C (425°F/Gas 6–7). Brush a baking dish with oil. Trim stalks from fennel and cut both fennel bulbs into quarters. Remove as much of the core as possible from each bulb, without separating layers.

2 Place leek slices over the base of oiled dish. Place fennel on top and pour in the white wine. Sprinkle with thyme. Cover, place in oven and bake for 30 minutes.

3 Add tomato to dish and spoon some of the liquid over. Bake, uncovered, for another 30 minutes. Serve sprinkled with fresh thyme leaves.

COOK'S FILE

Storage time: Vegetables may be prepared up to 1 hour before cooking.

MUSHROOM MOUSSAKA

Preparation time: 20 minutes
Total cooking time: 1 hour
Serves 4–6

1 (250 g/9 oz) eggplant
    (aubergine), cut into 1 cm
    (½ inch) slices
1 large potato, cut into 1 cm
    (½ inch) slices
30 g (1 oz) butter
1 onion, finely chopped
2 cloves garlic, finely chopped
500 g (1 lb 2 oz) flat
    mushrooms, sliced
400 g (14 oz) can chopped
    tomatoes
½ teaspoon sugar
40 g (1½ oz) butter, extra
4 tablespoons plain (all-purpose)
    flour
500 ml (17 fl oz/2 cups) milk
1 egg, lightly beaten
40 g (1½ oz) grated Parmesan

1 Preheat the oven to hot 220°C (425°F/Gas 7). Line a baking tray with foil and brush with oil. Arrange the eggplant and potato in a single layer and season. Bake for 20 minutes.

2 Melt the butter in a frying pan over medium heat. Cook the onion, stirring for 3–4 minutes, or until soft. Add the garlic and cook for 1 minute. Increase the heat to high, add the mushrooms, stirring for 2–3 minutes, or until soft. Add the tomato, reduce the heat and simmer rapidly for 8 minutes, or until reduced. Stir in the sugar.

3 Melt the extra butter in a saucepan over low heat. Add the flour and cook for 1 minute, or until pale and foaming. Remove from the heat and gradually stir in the milk. Return to the heat, stirring until it boils and thickens. Reduce the heat and simmer for 2 minutes. Remove from the heat and, when the bubbles subside, stir in the egg and Parmesan.

4 Reduce the oven to moderate 180°C (350°F/Gas 4). Grease a shallow 1.5 litre (6 cup) ovenproof dish. Spoon one third of the mushroom mixture into the dish. Cover with the potato, half the remaining mushrooms, then the eggplant. Finish with the remaining mushrooms, pour on the sauce and then smooth the top. Bake for 30–35 minutes, or until the edges bubble. Rest for 10 minutes and serve.

Stir the sugar into the thickened vegetable mixture.

Remove the saucepan from the heat and stir in the egg and Parmesan.

Cover the mushroom mixture with the potato slices.

LAYERED POTATO AND APPLE BAKE

Preparation time: 20 minutes
Total cooking time: 45 minutes
Serves 6

2 large potatoes
3 medium green apples
1 medium onion
60 g (2¼ oz/½ cup) finely grated
    Cheddar cheese
250 ml (9 fl oz/1 cup) cream
¼ teaspoon ground nutmeg

1

black pepper

1 Preheat oven to moderate 180°C (350°F/Gas 4). Brush a shallow 2-litre (8 cup) ovenproof dish with melted butter or oil. Peel potatoes and cut into 5 mm (¼ inch) slices. Peel, core and quarter apples. Cut into 5 mm (¼ inch) slices. Slice onion into very fine rings.
2 Layer potatoes, apple and onions into prepared dish, ending with a layer of potato. Sprinkle evenly with cheese. Pour cream over top, covering as evenly as possible.

2

3 Sprinkle with nutmeg and freshly ground black pepper to taste. Bake for 45 minutes, until golden brown. Remove from oven and set aside for 5 minutes before serving.

COOK'S FILE

Note: To prevent the sliced potato and apple browning before assembling dish, place in a bowl of cold water with a squeeze of lemon juice. Drain and pat them dry with paper towel before using.
Storage time: Can be made up to a day ahead.

3

SPICY CHICKPEA AND VEGETABLE CASSEROLE

Preparation time: 25 minutes +
    overnight soaking
Total cooking time: 1 hour 30 minutes
Serves 4

330 g (11½ oz/1½ cups) dried
    chickpeas
2 tablespoons oil
1 large onion, chopped
1 clove garlic, crushed
3 teaspoons ground cumin
½ teaspoon chilli powder
½ teaspoon allspice
425 g (15 oz) can peeled
    tomatoes, crushed

375 ml (13 fl oz/1½ cups)
    vegetable stock
300 g (10½ oz) pumpkin, cut
    into 2 cm (¾ inch) cubes
150 g (5½ oz) green beans, cut
    into 3 cm (1¼ inch) lengths
200 g (7 oz) button squash,
    quartered
2 tablespoons tomato paste
    (concentrated purée)
1 teaspoon dried oregano

1 Place chickpeas in a large bowl, cover with cold water and soak overnight; drain.
2 Heat oil in a large pan, add onion and garlic; stir-fry for 2 minutes or until tender. Add cumin, chilli and allspice and stir-fry 1 minute.
3 Add chickpeas, tomatoes and stock

to pan. Bring to boil, reduce heat and simmer, covered, for 1 hour, stirring occasionally.
4 Add pumpkin, beans, squash, tomato paste and oregano. Stir to combine. Simmer, covered, for a further 15 minutes. Remove lid from pan and simmer uncovered for a further 10 minutes to reduce and thicken sauce slightly.

COOK'S FILE

Hints: A quick way to soak chickpeas is to place them in a large saucepan and cover with cold water. Bring to the boil, remove from heat and soak for two hours. if you are in a hurry, substitute with canned chickpeas. Drain and rinse thoroughly before use.

1

2

3

Layered Potato and Apple (top) and Spicy Chickpea and Vegetable Casserole

COUSCOUS VEGETABLE LOAF

Preparation time: 20 minutes +
  cooling time + overnight
  refrigeration
Total cooking time: 10 minutes
Serves 6

1 litre (4 cups) vegetable stock
500 g (1 lb 2 oz) instant
  couscous
30 g (1 oz) butter
3 tablespoons olive oil
2 cloves garlic, crushed
1 onion, finely chopped
1 tablespoon ground coriander
1 teaspoon ground cinnamon
1 teaspoon garam masala
250 g (9 oz) cherry tomatoes,
  quartered
1 zucchini (courgette), diced
130 g (4½ oz) can corn kernels,
  drained
8 large fresh basil leaves
150 g (5½ oz) sun-dried
  (sun-blushed) capsicums
  (peppers) in oil
60 g (2¼ oz/1 cup) chopped
  fresh basil, extra
4 tablespoons orange juice
1 tablespoon lemon juice
3 tablespoons chopped fresh
  flat-leaf (Italian) parsley
1 teaspoon honey
1 teaspoon ground cumin

1 Bring the stock to the boil. Put the couscous and butter in a bowl, cover with the stock. Leave for 10 minutes.
2 Heat 1 tablespoon of the oil in a frying pan and cook the garlic and onion over low heat for 5 minutes, or until soft. Add the spices and cook for 1 minute. Remove from the pan.

3 Add the remaining oil to the pan and cook the tomatoes, zucchini and corn over high heat until soft.
4 Line a 3 litre (12 cup) loaf tin with plastic wrap, overhanging the sides. Form the basil into two flowers on the base. Drain the capsicums, reserving 2 tablespoons of the oil, then roughly chop. Add the onion mix, tomato mix,

capsicum and extra basil to the couscous and mix. Cool.
5 Press the mixture into the tin and cover with the plastic wrap. Weigh down with cans and chill overnight.
6 Place the remaining ingredients and reserved capsicum oil in a jar with a lid and shake. Turn out the loaf, slice and serve with the dressing.

Cook the tomatoes, zucchini and corn until softened.

Arrange the basil leaves in the shape of two flowers in the base of the loaf tin.

Mix together the onion mixture, vegetables, capsicum, basil and couscous.

BAKED RICOTTA AND RED CAPSICUM WITH PESTO

Preparation time: 10 minutes
Total cooking time: 45 minutes
Serves 6

1 large red capsicum (pepper),
    cut into quarters and seeded
750 g (1 lb 10 oz/3 cups) low-fat
    ricotta cheese
1 egg
6 slices wholegrain bread

Pesto
2 tablespoons pine nuts
100 g (3½ oz/2 cups) basil
2 cloves garlic
2 tablespoons good-quality olive
    oil
2 tablespoons finely grated fresh
    Parmesan cheese

1 Grill (broil) the capsicum, skin-side up, under a hot grill (broiler) for 5–6 minutes, or until the skin blackens and blisters. Place in a bowl and cover with plastic wrap until cool enough to handle. Peel off the skin and slice the flesh into 2 cm (¾ inch) wide strips.

2 To make the pesto, place the pine nuts, basil and garlic in a food processor and process for 15 seconds, or until finely chopped. While the processor is running add the oil in a continuous thin stream, then season with salt and freshly ground black pepper. Stir in the Parmesan.

3 Preheat the oven to 180°C (350°F/ Gas 4). Grease six large muffin holes.

4 Mix the ricotta and egg until well combined. Season with salt and freshly ground black pepper. Divide the capsicum strips among the muffin holes, top with 2 teaspoons pesto and spoon in the ricotta mixture.

5 Bake for 35–40 minutes, or until the ricotta is firm and golden. Cool, then unmould. Toast the bread slices and cut them into fingers. Serve with the baked ricotta and the remaining pesto on the side.

Grill (broil) the capsicum until blackened and blistered, then peel off the skin.

Top the capsicum strips with 2 teaspoons of the pesto mixture.

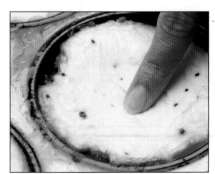

Bake the ricotta cakes until they are firm and golden.

CHILLI AND CORIANDER FRITTATA

Preparation time: 25 minutes
Total cooking time: 30 minutes
Serves 6

3 medium potatoes, peeled, cut
   into small cubes
2 medium banana chillies
2 tablespoons olive oil
1 medium onion, finely
   chopped
1 red chilli, finely chopped
1 tablespoon coriander (cilantro)
   leaves
5 eggs, lightly beaten

1 Cook potatoes in a large pan of boiling water until just tender, then drain well.

2 Slice banana chillies, remove seeds. Heat half the oil in a non-stick frying pan. Cook chillies over medium heat for 2 minutes or until softened. Remove from pan and set aside. Heat remaining oil in pan. Add onion and small chilli, cook over medium heat for 3 minutes or until soft.

3 Add potato, toss to combine. Remove from pan, set aside. Return half the banana chillies to pan, sprinkle with coriander leaves. Layer half the potato mixture, remaining banana chillies, and the remaining potato and chilli mixture.

4 Pour eggs into pan, swirling to distribute evenly. Cook over medium low heat for 8 minutes until eggs are almost cooked through, then place under hot grill (broiler) for 5 minutes to cook top.

5 Invert frittata onto plate, cut into wedges. Serve hot or cold.

COOK'S FILE

Storage time: Frittata is best eaten on the day it is made.

GREEN CURRY WITH SWEET POTATO AND EGGPLANT

Preparation time: 15 minutes
Total cooking time: 25 minutes
Serves 4–6

1 tablespoon oil
1 onion, chopped
1–2 tablespoons green curry
   paste (see Note)
1 eggplant (aubergine),
   quartered and sliced
375 ml (13 fl oz/1½ cups)
   coconut milk

250 ml (9 fl oz/1 cup) vegetable
   stock
6 makrut lime (kaffir) leaves
1 orange sweet potato, cut into
   cubes
2 teaspoons soft brown sugar
2 tablespoons lime juice
2 teaspoons lime rind

1 Heat the oil in a large wok or frying pan. Add the onion and curry paste and cook, stirring, over medium heat for 3 minutes. Add the eggplant and cook for a further 4–5 minutes, or until softened. Pour in the coconut milk and stock, bring to the boil, then reduce the heat and simmer for 5 minutes. Add

the lime leaves and sweet potato and cook, stirring occasionally, for 10 minutes, or until the vegetables are very tender.

2 Mix in the sugar, lime juice and lime rind until well combined with the vegetables. Season to taste with salt. Garnish with some fresh coriander leaves and extra lime leaves if desired, and serve with steamed rice.

COOK'S FILE

Note: Make sure you read the label and choose a green curry paste without shrimp paste.

Using a sharp knife, quarter and slice the eggplant.

Stir-fry the onion and curry paste over medium heat for 3 minutes.

Cook, stirring occasionally, until the vegetables are tender.

MUSHROOM NUT ROAST WITH TOMATO SAUCE

Preparation time: 25 minutes
Total cooking time: 50 minutes
Serves 6

2 tablespoons olive oil
1 large onion, diced
2 cloves garlic, crushed
300 g (10½ oz) cap mushrooms, finely chopped
200 g (7 oz/1¼ cups) cashew nuts
200 g (7 oz/1¼ cups) brazil nuts
125 g (4½ oz/1 cup) grated Cheddar

3 tablespoons grated Parmesan
1 egg, lightly beaten
2 tablespoons chopped fresh chives
80 g (2¾ oz/1 cup) wholemeal (whole-wheat) breadcrumbs
1½ tablespoons olive oil, extra
1 onion, finely chopped, extra
1 clove garlic, crushed, extra
400 g (14 oz) tin chopped tomatoes
1 tablespoon tomato paste (concentrated purée)
1 teaspoon caster (superfine) sugar

1 Preheat the oven to moderate 180°C (350°F/Gas 4). Grease a 14 x 21 cm (5½ x 8½ inch) tin and line with baking paper. Heat the oil in a frying pan and fry the onion, garlic and mushrooms over medium heat for 2–3 minutes, or until soft. Cool.
2 Finely chop the nuts in a food processor, but do not over-process.
3 Combine the nuts, mushroom mix, cheeses, egg, chives and breadcrumbs. Bake in the tin for 45 minutes, or until firm. Stand for 5 minutes, then turn out of the tin.
4 Heat the extra oil in a frying pan and add the extra onion and garlic. Cook over low heat for 5 minutes, or until soft. Add the tomato, paste, sugar and 4 tablespoons water. Simmer for 3–5 minutes, or until thick.

Finely chop the cashews and brazil nuts in a food processor.

Press the nutty mushroom mixture into the prepared tin.

Simmer the tomato mixture until thickened.

VEGETABLE TAGINE WITH COUSCOUS

Preparation time: 20 minutes
Total cooking time: 1 hour
Serves 4–6

2 tablespoons oil
2 onions, chopped
1 teaspoon ground ginger
2 teaspoons ground paprika
2 teaspoons ground cumin
1 cinnamon stick
pinch saffron threads
1.5 kg (3 lb 5 oz) vegetables, peeled and cut into large chunks (orange sweet potato, carrot, eggplant (aubergine), parsnip, potato, pumpkin)
½ preserved lemon, rinsed, pith and flesh removed, thinly sliced
400 g (14 oz) can peeled tomatoes
250 ml (9 fl oz/1 cup) vegetable stock
100 g (3½ oz) dried pears, halved
50 g (1¾ oz) pitted prunes
2 zucchini (courgettes), cut into large chunks
300 g (10½ oz) instant couscous
1 tablespoon olive oil
3 tablespoons chopped fresh flat-leaf (Italian) parsley
50 g (1¾ oz/⅓ cup) almonds

1 Preheat the oven to moderate 180°C (350°F/Gas 4). Heat the oil in a large saucepan or ovenproof dish, add the onion and cook over medium heat for 5 minutes, or until soft. Add the spices and cook for 3 minutes.
2 Add the vegetables, stir until coated with spices and they begin to soften.

Add the lemon, tomatoes, stock, pears and prunes. Cover, and bake for 30 minutes. Add the zucchini and bake for 15–20 minutes, or until tender.
3 Cover the couscous with the olive oil and 500 ml (17 fl oz/2 cups) boiling water and stand until the water has been absorbed. Flake with a fork.

4 Remove the cinnamon stick from the vegetables, then stir in the parsley. Serve the couscous on a platter formed into a ring and the tagine in the centre. Sprinkle with the almonds.

Cook the vegetables until they are coated in spices and the outside starts to soften.

Once all the water has been absorbed, flake the couscous with a fork.

Before serving, remove the cinnamon stick with a pair of tongs.

SOYA BEAN MOUSSAKA

Preparation time: 25 minutes
Total cooking time: 1 hour
Serves 4

2 eggplants (aubergines)
1 tablespoon oil
1 onion, finely chopped
2 cloves garlic, crushed
2 ripe tomatoes, peeled, seeded
    and chopped
2 teaspoons tomato paste
    (concentrated purée)
½ teaspoon dried oregano
125 ml (4 fl oz/½ cup) dry white
    wine
300 g (10½ oz) can soya beans,
    rinsed and drained
3 tablespoons chopped fresh
    flat-leaf (Italian) parsley
30 g (1 oz) butter
2 tablespoons plain (all-purpose)
    flour
pinch ground nutmeg
315 ml (10¾ fl oz/1¼ cups)
    milk
4 tablespoons grated
    Cheddar

1 Preheat the oven to moderate 180°C (350°F/Gas 4). Cut the eggplants in half lengthways. Spoon out the flesh, leaving a 1.5 cm (⅝ inch) border and place on a large baking tray, cut-side-up. Use crumpled foil around the sides of the eggplant to help support it.
2 Heat the oil in a frying pan. Cook the onion and garlic over medium heat for 3 minutes, or until soft. Add the tomato, paste, oregano and wine. Boil for 3 minutes, or until the liquid is reduced and the tomato is soft. Stir in the soya beans and parsley.
3 To make the sauce, melt the butter in a saucepan. Stir in the flour and

cook over medium heat for 1 minute, or until pale and foamy. Remove from the heat and gradually stir in the nutmeg and milk. Return to the heat and stir constantly until the sauce boils and thickens. Pour one third of the white sauce into the tomato mixture and stir well.
4 Spoon the mixture into the eggplant shells. Smooth the surface before spreading the remaining sauce evenly over the top and sprinkling with cheese. Bake for 50 minutes, or until cooked through. Serve hot. Serve with a fresh salad, if desired.

Scoop out the eggplant flesh, leaving a border all the way around.

Add the soya beans and parsley to the tomato mixture and stir well.

COCONUT CREPES WITH INDIAN CURRY

Preparation time: 25 minutes
Total cooking time: 45 minutes
Serves 4

60 g (2¼ oz/½ cup) plain
 (all-purpose) flour
1 egg
140 ml (4½ fl oz) coconut milk
25 g (1 oz) butter, melted
500 g (1 lb 2 oz/2 cups) coconut
 cream
30 g (1 oz) ghee or butter
1 onion, cut into thin wedges
2 cloves garlic, crushed
1 teaspoon garam masala
1 teaspoon ground cardamom
1 tablespoon Madras curry paste
125 ml (4 fl oz/½ cup) vegetable
 stock
125 ml (4 fl oz/½ cup) coconut
 milk, extra
4 sticks cassia bark
5 cardamom pods
400 g (14 oz) pumpkin, diced
2 small zucchini (courgettes),
 halved lengthways and sliced
 on the diagonal
1 potato, diced
80 g (2¾ oz/½ cup) frozen peas
2 teaspoons soft brown sugar
raita, to serve (see Note)

1 Sift the flour into a bowl and gradually whisk in the combined egg, coconut milk and butter until smooth.
2 Heat a 17 cm (6¾ inch) non-stick crêpe pan or frying pan and grease. Pour some batter into the pan, swirling to thinly coat, then pour off any excess. Cook for 30 seconds, or until the edges curl. Turn and brown the other side. Transfer to a plate and line with paper towels. Keep warm. Repeat, making seven more crêpes. (If the batter thickens, add water.)
3 To make the filling, add the coconut cream to a wok and bring to the boil over high heat. Boil for 10 minutes, stirring occasionally, or until it starts to separate.
4 Meanwhile, heat the ghee in a frying pan and cook the onion over high heat for 2–3 minutes, or until soft. Add the garlic and spices and cook for 1 minute, or until fragrant.
5 Add the curry paste to the coconut cream and stir for 3–4 minutes, or until fragrant. Add the stock, extra coconut milk, cassia bark and cardamom pods, bring to the boil and cook for 5 minutes. Stir in the onion mixture, pumpkin, zucchini, potato and peas and simmer for 15 minutes, or until the vegetables are tender and the curry is thick. Stir in the sugar. Remove the cassia bark and cardamom pods. To serve, place 3 tablespoons of filling in the centre of each crêpe and roll up. Keep warm. Serve topped with raita. Spoon on any remaining curry.

COOK'S FILE

Note: Raita is an Indian mixture of yoghurt and fruit and vegetables.

Cook the crêpes for 30 seconds, or until the edges curl, then turn over.

Cook the coconut cream on the boil for 10 minutes, or until it starts to crack.

Desserts

RED FRUIT SALAD WITH BERRIES

Preparation time: 5 minutes +
  30 minutes cooling + 1 hour
  30 minutes refrigeration
Total cooking time: 5 minutes
Serves 6

Syrup
3 tablespoons caster (superfine)
  sugar
125 ml (4 fl oz/½ cup) dry red
  wine
1 star anise
1 teaspoon finely chopped lemon
  zest

250 g (9 oz) strawberries, hulled
  and halved
150 g (5½ oz) blueberries
150 g (5½ oz) raspberries,
  mulberries or other red
  berries
250 g (9 oz) cherries
5 small red plums (about 250 g
  or 9 oz), stones removed and
  quartered
low-fat yoghurt, to serve

1 To make the syrup, place the sugar,
wine, star anise, lemon zest and
125 ml (4 fl oz/½ cup) water in a small
saucepan. Bring to the boil over
medium heat, stirring to dissolve the
sugar. Boil the syrup for 3 minutes,
then set aside to cool for 30 minutes.
When cool, strain the syrup.
2 Mix the fruit together in a large
bowl and pour on the red wine syrup.
Mix well to coat the fruit in the syrup
and refrigerate for 1 hour 30 minutes.
Serve the fruit dressed with a little
syrup and the yoghurt.

*Remove the stems, then cut the strawberries
in half.*

*Boil the sugar, wine, star anise, lemon zest
and water for 3 minutes.*

*Mix together the strawberries, blueberries,
raspberries, cherries and plums.*

MANDARIN ICE

Preparation time: 10 minutes +
freezing
Total cooking time: 10 minutes
Serves 4–6

10 mandarins
125 g (4½ oz/½ cup) caster
(superfine) sugar

1 Squeeze the mandarins to make 500 ml (17 fl oz/2 cups) juice and strain.
2 Place the sugar and 250 ml (9 fl oz/1 cup) water in a small saucepan. Stir over low heat until the sugar has dissolved and simmer for 5 minutes. Remove from the heat and leave to cool slightly.
3 Stir the mandarin juice into the sugar syrup, then pour into a shallow metal tray. Freeze for 2 hours, or until frozen. Transfer to a food processor and blend until slushy. Return to the freezer and repeat the process three more times.

Squeeze the mandarins (as you would other citrus fruits) to give 500 ml of juice.

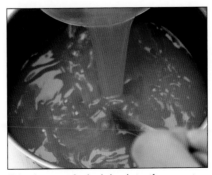

Stir the mandarin juice into the saucepan of sugar water.

Blend the frozen mixture in a food processor until slushy.

FRUIT EN PAPILOTTE WITH YOGHURT

Preparation time: 15 minutes
Total cooking time: 15 minutes
Serves 4

1 large ripe mango
4 passionfruit
100 ml (3½ fl oz) orange
  juice
4 tablespoons caster (superfine)
  sugar
4 bananas
1 tablespoon lemon juice
1 vanilla bean

1 Preheat the oven to 180°C (350°F/ Gas 4). Cut the mango down each side of the centre stone. Using a large metal spoon, remove the flesh from the skin. Remove the remaining flesh from the stone. Halve the passionfruit and remove the pulp. Pass the pulp through a sieve, pressing down well to loosen the pulp. Discard the seeds.

2 Blend the orange juice, sugar, passionfruit pulp and a quarter of the mango in a food processor or blender until smooth.

3 Fold four double layers of foil (about 30 cm or 12 inches long). Place a 25 cm (10 inch) square piece of baking paper on top of the foil. Cut the bananas in half lengthways and place 2 halves on each piece of foil. Divide the remaining mango pieces among the four portions then sprinkle with the lemon juice.

4 Cut the vanilla bean in half lengthways, then cut each piece in half. Scrape the seeds onto the fruit then place a piece of the empty pod on top. Spoon on the fruit syrup.

5 Leaving a 2 cm (¾ inch) gap

between the fruit and the foil, fold the foil neatly over to create a parcel. Place on a baking tray and bake for 12 minutes.

6 To serve, open the parcels carefully

and transfer the fruit to a serving bowl or place the opened parcel on a plate. Serve with low-fat yoghurt or ice cream on the side.

Remove the mango flesh from the skin using a large metal spoon.

Place a piece of the empty vanilla pod on top of the mango slices.

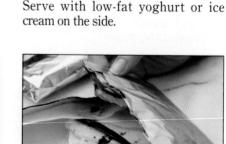

Neatly fold in the sides, then fold the paper and foil over the fruit to create a parcel.

APPLE SAGO PUDDING

Preparation time: 15 minutes
Total cooking time: 50 minutes
Serves 4

4 tablespoons caster (superfine)
   sugar
100 g (3½ oz/½ cup) sago
600 ml (21 fl oz) fat-reduced
   milk
4 tablespoons sultanas
1 teaspoon vanilla essence

pinch ground nutmeg
¼ teaspoon ground cinnamon
2 eggs, lightly beaten
250 g (9 oz; about 3 small) ripe
   apples, peeled, cored and
   very thinly sliced
1 tablespoon soft brown sugar

1 Preheat the oven to 180°C (350°F/
Gas 4). Grease a 1.5 litre (6 cup)
ceramic souffle dish. Place the sugar,
sago, milk, sultanas and ¼ teaspoon
salt in a saucepan. Heat the mixture,
stirring often. Bring to the boil, then

reduce the heat and simmer for
5 minutes.

2 Stir in the vanilla essence, nutmeg,
cinnamon, egg and the apple slices,
then pour into the prepared dish.
Sprinkle with the brown sugar and
bake for 45 minutes, or until set and
golden brown.

COOK'S FILE

Note: If you prefer, you can use skim
milk instead of fat-reduced milk.

*Bring the sugar, sago, milk, sultanas and
salt to the boil, stirring frequently.*

*Stir in the vanilla, ground spices, egg and
apple slices.*

*Sprinkle the surface of the pudding with
the brown sugar.*

237

BROWNIES

Preparation time: 15 minutes
Total cooking time: 40 minutes
Makes 18

60 g (2¼ oz/½ cup) self-raising
   flour
60 g (2¼ oz/½ cup) plain
   (all-purpose) flour
60 g (2¼ oz/½ cup) cocoa
   powder
½ teaspoon bicarbonate of soda
   (baking soda)
pinch of salt

230 g (8 oz/1¼ cups) soft brown
   sugar
2 eggs
250 ml (9 fl oz/1 cup)
   buttermilk
2 teaspoons vanilla essence
2 tablespoons oil
icing (confectioners') sugar,
   to dust

1 Preheat the oven to 180°C (350°F/
Gas 4). Lightly grease a 28 cm x 18 cm
(11 inch x 7 inch) shallow tin and line
the base with baking paper, extending
over the two long sides.
2 Sift the flours, cocoa powder,
bicarbonate of soda and salt into a
mixing bowl, then stir in the sugar.
Whisk the eggs, buttermilk, vanilla
and oil in a jug.
3 Gently stir the egg mixture into the
dry ingredients until combined—do
not overheat. Pour into the tin and
bake for 40 minutes, or until it springs
back to a light touch in the centre.
Leave in the tin for 5 minutes, then
turn out onto a wire rack to cool
completely.
4 To serve, cut into 18 squares and
dust with icing sugar. Store in an
airtight container for up to 3 days.

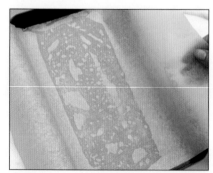

*Line the tin with baking paper, leaving it
hanging over the two long sides.*

*Gently stir the egg mixture into the dry
ingredients until combined.*

*The brownies are cooked if the centre
springs back when lightly touched.*

GRILLED FIGS WITH RICOTTA

Preparation time: 10 minutes
Total cooking time: 10 minutes
Serves 4

2 tablespoons honey
1 cinnamon stick
3 tablespoons flaked
   almonds
4 large (or 8 small) fresh figs
125 g (4½ oz/½ cup) low-fat
   ricotta cheese
½ teaspoon vanilla essence
2 tablespoons icing
   (confectioners') sugar, sifted
pinch ground cinnamon
½ teaspoon finely grated orange
   zest

1 Place the honey and cinnamon stick in a small saucepan with 4 tablespoons water. Bring to the boil, then reduce the heat and simmer gently for 6 minutes, or until thickened and reduced by half. Lift out the cinnamon stick with a pair of tongs, then stir in the flaked almonds.

2 Preheat the grill (broiler) to moderately hot and grease a shallow ovenproof dish large enough to fit all the figs side by side. Slice the figs into quarters from the top to within 1 cm (½ inch) of the bottom, keeping them attached at the base. Arrange in prepared dish.

3 Combine the ricotta, vanilla, icing sugar, ground cinnamon and orange zest in a small bowl. Divide the filling among the figs, spooning it into their cavities. Spoon the syrup over the top. Place under the grill and cook until the juices start to come out from the figs and the almonds are lightly toasted. Cool for 2–3 minutes. Spoon the juices and any fallen almonds from the bottom of the dish over the figs.

Cut each fig into quarters from the top, without cutting through the base.

Spoon the ricotta filling into the fig cavity, then spoon some syrup on top.

239

Beat the egg mixture, flour, lemon juice, zest and passionfruit pulp until combined.

Carefully mould a piece of filo pastry into each muffin hole.

Pour the lemon and passionfruit mixture into the pastry cases.

INDIVIDUAL LEMON AND PASSIONFRUIT TARTS WITH RASPBERRIES

Preparation time: 15 minutes
Total cooking time: 25 minutes
Makes 6

60 g (2½ oz) low-fat margarine
4 tablespoons caster (superfine) sugar
2 eggs

2 tablespoons self-raising flour, sifted
3 tablespoons lemon juice
1 teaspoon grated lemon zest
1 passionfruit, pulp removed
3 sheets filo pastry
125 g (4½ oz) fresh raspberries

1 Preheat the oven to 180°C (350°F/ Gas 4). Beat the margarine and sugar until light and creamy. Add the eggs one at a time, beating well after each addition.

2 Add the flour, lemon juice, zest and passionfruit pulp and beat until well combined.

3 Fold each sheet of filo pastry in half from the short end up. Fold again and cut in half. Carefully line six 125 ml (4 fl oz/½ cup) muffin holes with a piece of pastry. Pour in the lemon mixture and bake for 20–25 minutes, or until set. Serve topped with the raspberries and, if desired, whipped light cream.

Beat the ricotta, fromage frais, sugar and vanilla until smooth.

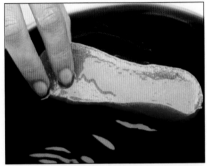

Dip the sponge finger biscuits in the coffee and Marsala mixture.

Arrange half the coffee-soaked biscuits in a single layer over the base of the dish.

Spread half the ricotta mixture over the biscuits with a spatula.

TIRAMISU

Preparation time: 20 minutes +
overnight refrigeration
Total cooking time: Nil
Serves 6

500 g (1 lb 2 oz) low-fat ricotta
cheese
2 x 200 g (7 oz) tubs low-fat
French vanilla fromage frais
1½ tablespoons caster
(superfine) sugar
1 teaspoon vanilla essence
185 ml (6 fl oz/¾ cup) strongly
brewed coffee, cooled
185 ml (6 fl oz/¾ cup) Marsala
250 g (9 oz) thin sponge finger
biscuits

1 tablespoon unsweetened Dutch
cocoa powder

1 Beat the ricotta, fromage frais,
sugar and vanilla essence with electric
beaters in a bowl until smooth.
Combine the coffee and Marsala in a
large shallow dish.
2 Dip half the biscuits, a few at a
time, into the coffee mixture for a few
seconds until both sides become moist
but not soggy. Arrange the biscuits in
a single layer over the base of a 2 litre
(8 cup) serving dish. Spread half the
ricotta mixture over the biscuits, then
repeat another layer.
3 Cover and refrigerate for 6 hours or
overnight. Dust with the cocoa powder
before serving.

COEUR A LA CREME WITH BERRIES

Preparation time: 20 minutes +
overnight refrigeration
Total cooking time: Nil
Serves 4

100 g (3½ oz) low-fat ricotta
cheese
3 tablespoons fat-reduced cream
cheese
3 tablespoons light sour cream
2 tablespoons icing
(confectioners') sugar

1 egg white
170 g (6 oz) mixed berries
(strawberries, blueberries,
raspberries)
icing (confectioners') sugar,
extra, to dust

1 Beat the ricotta, cream cheese and sour cream with 1 tablespoon icing sugar until mixed. Beat the egg white in a separate clean bowl until stiff peaks form, then carefully fold into cheese mixture with a metal spoon.
2 Line four ceramic heart-shaped moulds with a square of dampened muslin. Fill with the cheese mixture.

Bring the remaining muslin up over the top to cover and lightly press. Put the moulds on a tray and refrigerate for 6 hours, or preferably overnight.
3 Blend half the berries and the remaining sugar in a food processor until combined. Strain.
4 To serve, unmould the crèmes onto a plate and place a pile of berries to the side. Drizzle with the purée and dust with icing sugar.

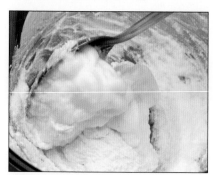

Gently fold the stiffly beaten egg white into the cheese mixture.

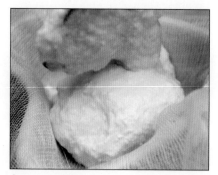

Spoon the cheese mixture into the heart-shaped moulds.

Blend the berries and sugar in a food processor until combined.

APPLE, BLUEBERRY AND RHUBARB CRUMBLE

Preparation time: 20 minutes
Total cooking time: 40 minutes
Serves 6

5 Granny Smith apples (1 kg or 2lb 4 oz), peeled and diced
250 g (9 oz/2 cups) diced rhubarb
1 tablespoon lemon juice
125 g (4½ oz/½ cup) sugar
2 tablespoons cornflour (cornstarch)
125 ml (4 fl oz/½ cup) apple juice

1 teaspoon grated orange zest
150 g (5½ oz/1 cup) blueberries, fresh or frozen

Crumble
65 g (2¼ oz/⅔ cup) rolled oats
100 g (3½ oz/⅔ cup) plain wholemeal (whole-wheat) flour
4 tablespoons soft brown sugar
½ teaspoon ground cinnamon
4 tablespoons chopped macadamia nuts
80 g (2¾ oz) butter, melted

1 Preheat the oven to 180°C (350°F/ Gas 4). Grease a 2 litre (8 cup) rectangular 20 x 30 cm (8 x 12 inch) ovenproof dish. Combine the apple and rhubarb in a bowl, drizzle with lemon juice and sprinkle with half the sugar. Leave for 5 minutes.

2 Combine the cornflour with the apple juice until smooth, then add to the rhubarb and apple mixture with the orange zest and remaining sugar. Toss the blueberries through until combined, then spoon the fruit mixture into the prepared dish.

3 To make the crumble, place the oats, flour, brown sugar, cinnamon and nuts in a bowl. Add the butter and rub it in with your fingertips, mixing thoroughly. Sprinkle the crumble over the fruit and bake for 40 minutes, or until crisp and golden.

Sprinkle half the sugar over the combined pieces of apple and rhubarb.

Stir the blueberries through the apple, rhubarb, sugar and orange zest.

Rub the butter through the crumble mixture with your fingertips.

243

BAKED LEMON CHEESECAKE

Preparation time: 10 minutes +
  5 hours 30 minutes refrigeration
Total cooking time: 45 minutes
Serves 8

100 g (3½ oz) plain sweet
  biscuits, crushed
75 g (2½ oz) low-fat canola
  margarine, melted
300 g (10½ oz) low-fat ricotta
  cheese
200 g (7 oz) low-fat cream
  cheese
125 g (4½ oz/½ cup) caster
  (superfine) sugar
4 tablespoons lemon juice
2 tablespoons grated lemon zest
1 egg
1 egg white

1 Preheat the oven to 160°C (315°F/ Gas 2–3). Lightly grease an 18 cm (7 inch) springform tin and line the base with baking paper. Combine the crushed biscuits and margarine and press into the base of the tin. Refrigerate for 30 minutes.

2 Beat the ricotta, cream cheese, sugar, lemon juice and 3 teaspoons of lemon zest with electric beaters until smooth. Beat in the egg and egg white.

3 Pour the mixture into the tin, then sprinkle the surface with remaining lemon zest. Bake for 45 minutes—the centre will still be a little wobbly. Leave to cool, then refrigerate for at least 5 hours before serving.

Press the crushed biscuit mixture into the base of the prepared tin.

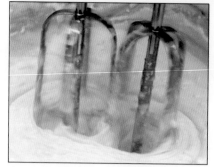

Beat the ricotta, cream cheese, sugar, lemon juice and zest until smooth.

Pour the filling mixture into the tin, scraping the bowl with a spatula.

PLUM COBBLER

Preparation time: 20 minutes
Total cooking time: 40 minutes
Serves 4

825 g (1 lb 13 oz) can pitted
   dark plums
1 tablespoon honey
2 ripe pears, peeled, cored and
   cut into eighths

Topping
250 g (9 oz/1 cup) self-raising
   flour
1 tablespoon caster (superfine)
   sugar
¼ teaspoon ground
   cardamom
40 g (1½ oz) chopped chilled
   butter
3 tablespoons low-fat milk
extra milk, for brushing
1 tablespoon caster (superfine)
   sugar, extra
¼ teaspoon ground cardamom,
   extra

1 Preheat the oven to moderately hot 200°C (400°F/Gas 6). Grease an 18 cm (7 inch) round (1.5 litre 6 cup) ovenproof dish. Drain the plums, reserving 185 ml (6 fl oz/¾ cup) of the syrup. Place the syrup, honey and pear in a large wide saucepan and bring to the boil. Reduce the heat and simmer for 8 minutes, or until the pear is tender. Add the plums.
2 To make the topping, sift the flour, sugar, cardamom and a pinch of salt into a large bowl. Rub in the butter with your fingers until it resembles fine breadcrumbs. Stir in the milk using a flat-bladed knife, mixing lightly to form a soft dough—add a little more milk if necessary. Turn onto a lightly floured surface and form into a smooth ball. Roll out to a 1 cm (½ inch) thickness and cut into rounds with a 4 cm (1½ inch) cutter. Spoon the hot fruit into the prepared dish, then arrange the circles of dough in an overlapping pattern over the fruit, on the inside edge of the dish only—leave the fruit in the centre exposed. Brush the dough lightly with the extra milk. Combine the extra sugar and cardamom and sprinkle over the dough. Place the dish on a

baking tray and bake for 30 minutes, or until the topping is golden brown and cooked.

Cook the pears in the plum syrup until tender—test with the tip of a sharp knife.

Overlap the circles of dough around the inside edge of the dish.

APRICOT BREAD AND BUTTER PUDDING

Preparation time: 10 minutes
Total cooking time: 1 hour 25 minutes
Serves 6–8

4 thick slices multigrain
    bread
1 tablespoon margarine
2 tablespoons apricot jam
3 tablespoons sultanas
425 g (15 oz) can apricot halves,
    drained
625 ml (21½ fl oz/2½ cups)
    skim milk

½ vanilla bean
2 eggs
2 tablespoons caster (superfine)
    sugar
freshly grated nutmeg, to
    sprinkle

1 Preheat the oven to 160°C (315°F/ Gas 2–3). Spread one side of bread with the margarine and jam, keeping the crusts intact. Sprinkle half the sultanas on the base of a 2 litre (8 cup) rectangular ceramic baking dish. Cut the slices of bread in half and arrange, jam-side up, over the sultanas. Cover with the apricot halves and the remaining sultanas.

2 Place the milk in a saucepan. Split the vanilla bean horizontally and scrape the seeds into the milk, then add the pod. Heat the milk until just below boiling point. Beat the eggs and sugar in a bowl until thick and pale. Gradually add hot milk, stirring constantly. Strain the mixture and gently pour over the bread. Sprinkle lightly with grated nutmeg. Place in a deep baking tray and pour in enough boiling water to come halfway up the sides of the dish. Bake for 1¼ hours, or until the custard is set.

Sprinkle the remaining sultanas on top of the bread slices.

Strain the hot milk mixture through a fine sieve to remove the vanilla bean.

Place the dish in a baking tray and pour in boiling water to come halfway up the sides.

APPLE AND PEAR SORBET

Preparation time: 10 minutes
  + freezing
Total cooking time: 10 minutes
Serves 4–6

4 large green apples, peeled,
  cored and chopped
4 pears, peeled, cored and
  chopped
1 piece of lemon zest (1.5 cm x
  4 cm or ⅝ inch x 1½ inch)
1 cinnamon stick
3 tablespoons lemon juice
4 tablespoons caster (superfine)
  sugar
2 tablespoons Calvados or poire
  William liqueur (optional)

1 Place the apple and pear in a large deep saucepan with the lemon zest, cinnamon stick and enough water to just cover the fruit. Cover and poach the fruit gently over medium–low heat for 6–8 minutes, or until tender. Remove the lemon zest and cinnamon stick. Place the fruit in a food processor and blend with the lemon juice until smooth.

2 Place the sugar in a saucepan with 4 tablespoons water; bring to the boil. Simmer for 1 minute. Add the fruit puree and liqueur and mix well.
Pour into a shallow metal tray and freeze for 2 hours, or until the mixture is frozen around the edges. Transfer to a food processor or bowl and blend or beat until smooth. Pour back into the tray and return to the freezer. Repeat this process three times. For the final freezing, place in an airtight container—cover the surface with a piece of greaseproof paper and cover with a lid. Serve in small glasses or bowls.

COOK'S FILE

Notes: The length of cooking time to poach the apple and pear will depend on the ripeness of the fruit.
Pour an extra nip of Calvados over the sorbet to serve, if desired.

Check if the fruit is tender by using the tip of a sharp knife.

Blend the partially frozen mixture in a food processor until smooth.

Fold in the flours alternately with the date mixture in two batches.

Pour the pudding mixture into the prepared cake tin.

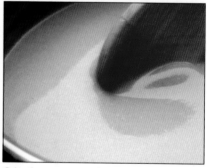

Stir the sauce continually with a wooden spoon until it thickens slightly.

STICKY DATE PUDDING

Preparation time: 15 minutes
Total cooking time: 1 hour
Serves 8

280 g (10 oz/1½ cups) chopped
    dates
1 teaspoon vanilla essence
2 teaspoons bicarbonate of soda
    (baking soda)
90 g (3½ oz) low-fat margarine
95 g (3¼ oz/½ cup) soft brown
    sugar
2 eggs
150 g (5½ oz) wholemeal
    (whole-wheat) self-raising
    flour, sifted
60 g (2¼ oz/½ cup) self-raising
    flour, sifted

Sauce
1 tablespoon margarine

185 ml (6 fl oz/¾ cup) low-fat
    evaporated milk
95 g (3¼ oz/½ cup) soft brown
    sugar
1 teaspoon custard
    powder

1 Preheat the oven to moderate 180°C
(350°F/Gas 4). Lightly grease and line
the base and side of a 20 cm (8 inch)
round cake tin.
2 Place dates and 375 ml (13 fl oz/
1½ cups) water in a saucepan. Bring
to the boil then reduce the heat and
simmer for 5 minutes, or until soft. Stir
in the vanilla essence and bicarbonate
of soda and set aside to cool to room
temperature.
Beat the margarine and sugar with
electric beaters until pale and creamy.
Gradually add the eggs, beating well
after each addition—the mixture may
look curdled at this stage, but a
spoonful of flour will bring it back

together. Fold in the flours and the
date mixture in two batches, using a
metal spoon.
3 Pour the mixture into the prepared
tin. Bake for 50 minutes, or until a
skewer comes out clean when inserted
into the centre of the pudding. Cool in
the tin for 10–15 minutes.
4 To make the sauce, heat the
margarine evaporated milk and
brown sugar in a saucepan until
almost boiling. Combine the custard
powder and 1 teaspoon water until
smooth, then gradually add to the
sauce, stirring continually over
medium heat until it thickens slightly.
Serve warm with the pudding.

CHOCOLATE AND ORANGE SELF-SAUCING PUDDINGS

Preparation time: 15 minutes
Total cooking time: 35 minutes
Serves 4

2 tablespoons cocoa powder
125 g (4½ oz/1 cup) self-raising
    flour
3 tablespoons low-fat cream
    cheese
1 teaspoon finely grated orange
    zest
125 g (4½ oz/½ cup) caster
    (superfine) sugar
125 ml (4 fl oz/½ cup) skim milk
4 tablespoons freshly squeezed
    orange juice
95 g (3¼ oz/½ cup) soft brown
    sugar
1 tablespoon cocoa powder,
    extra
icing (confectioners') sugar,
    to dust

1 Preheat the oven to 180°C (350°F/ Gas 4). Sift the cocoa powder with the flour, at least twice. Using a wooden spoon, blend the cream cheese, orange zest and caster sugar until smooth.

2 Fold the flour mixture and milk alternately into the cream cheese mixture and stir in the orange juice. Pour the mixture into four greased 310 ml (10¾ fl oz/1¼ cup) ramekins.

3 Combine the brown sugar and extra cocoa and sprinkle evenly over the surface of the puddings. Carefully pour 4 tablespoons boiling water over the back of a spoon onto each pudding. Place on a baking tray and bake for 35 minutes, or until firm. Dust with icing sugar and serve.

Blend the cream cheese, orange zest and sugar until smooth.

Evenly pour the pudding mixture into the ramekins, scraping the bowl with a spatula.

Gently pour the boiling water over the back of a spoon onto each pudding.

Index

Published in 2011 by Murdoch Books Pty Limited.

Murdoch Books Australia
Pier 8/9, 23 Hickson Road, Millers Point NSW 2000
Phone: +61 (0)2 8220 2000 Fax: +61 (0)2 8220 2558
www.murdochbooks.com.au

Murdoch Books UK Limited
Erico House, 6th Floor North, 93–99 Upper Richmond Road
Putney, London SW15 2TG
Phone: + 44 (0) 20 8785 5995 Fax: + 44 (0) 20 8785 5985
www.murdochbooks.co.uk

Chief Executive: Juliet Rogers
Publishing Director: Chris Rennie

Publisher: Lynn Lewis
Senior Designer: Heather Menzies
Designer: Kylie Mulquin
Editor: Justine Harding
Editorial Coordinator: Liz Malcolm

National Library of Australia Cataloguing-in-Publication Data

Title: Vegetarian
ISBN: 978-1-74266-264-0 (pbk.)
Series: Step-by-step
Notes: Includes index
Subjects: Vegetarian cooking. Cooking (Vegetables)
641.5636

Printed by 1010 Printing International Limited. PRINTED IN CHINA.